SOUTHWOLD

An Earthly Paradise

SOUTHWOLD

An Earthly Paradise

GEOFFREY C. MUNN FSA

ANTIQUE COLLECTORS' CLUB

ISBN 10: 1-85149-518-5
ISBN 13: 978-1-85149-518-4

British Library Cataloguing-in-Publication Data
A catalogue record for this book is available from the British Library

Dancers by Philip Wilson Steer. Pencil on paper. c.1884.
This lyrical drawing was made at Walberswick. Carefree youth and summer sunshine have inspired three girls to join hands to dance on the sand. In this small drawing Wilson Steer has managed to capture the nostalgia of childhood holidays by the sea.   Victoria & Albert Museum

Frontispiece: Girls on a Pierhead, Walberswick by Philip Wilson Steer (1860-1942). Oil on canvas. 1887.
When Philip Wilson Steer went to Paris in 1882 he saw the work of James Whistler and this, together with a posthumous exhibition of works by Eduard Manet, left a lasting impression on the young painter. Soon afterwards, in Walberswick, the sea and landscapes he saw there resulted in an explosion of colour. This lyrical painting is an example of Steer's greatest gift. Alan Gwynne Jones called it "A clean decisive and exquisite sense of tone expressed in high key in singing colour."   Private collection, USA

Title page: Arrival of the Ferry Boat at Southwold Harbour by Frederick Baldwin (1899-1984). Pencil and watercolour on paper. 1961. (See p.173)

Endpapers: Baiting the line. Platinum print. c.1886. This atmospheric photograph of the beach below The Sailors' Reading Room was taken 120 years ago. It goes a long way to raising the ghosts of Southwold's people and its fast-fading past.   George Eastman House, New York

Printed in China
for the Antique Collectors' Club Ltd., Woodbridge, Suffolk, England

CONTENTS

Southwold Groyne and Pier *by Wladyslaw Mirecki (b.1956). Watercolour on paper. 2002.*
Coastal erosion has been a constant menace to the town. Here the sea defences of wood and iron are seen
against the new pier built in 2001.   © Wladyslaw Mirecki

MIRECKI 2002

Suwold, Suwolda,
Southwalda, Sudholda,
Sothold, Soule, Soulde,
Southolt, Sowtholl, Swole,
Swoul, Sole, Stokes,
Southwaud, Southwood,

Southwold

ACKNOWLEDGEMENTS

Charlotte Gere has followed almost every step in the preparation of this book with the interest and enthusiasm of someone who loves art and knows Southwold well. I am indebted to her in more ways than it is possible to describe here.

This book would not have been possible without the generosity of Richard Scott author of *Artists at Walberswick – East Anglian Interludes 1880-2000*. I am deeply grateful to him not only for supplying me with the foundations for my research, but also for his patience in answering a seemingly endless stream of enquiries. Richard has seen more paintings of Walberswick and Southwold than anybody else. As a result he has a unique knowledge of local topography and has kindly shared it with me.

Above:
Southwold Harbour *by Charles Keene (1823-1870). Ink (?) on paper. c.1870.*
This is a view of the wooden pier on the Walberswick side of the river Blyth. In the foreground the detachable spokes of a capstan contrast with the parallel boards of the pier. Beyond is a wooden block for tying up and the black sheds of the lookout men. (See illustration Glasses round *on p.150).*   The Fine Art Society

Opposite:
A Tale of the Sea *by Walter Osborne. Oil on canvas. 1884.*
Beyond the capstans and the wooden bridge a small cluster of houses and sheds can be seen. They were built to service the fishing trade on which Walberswick and Southwold had depended for centuries. In the bright summer sunshine the younger boys have been playing with a toy sailing boat, but those with the straw hats are already at work. After the capstans have been used to haul the fishing boats alongside, they will be expected to fill their baskets with herrings. Seagulls anticipate the arrival of the catch.
Richard Green Fine Paintings

Donato Esposito not only gave me exhaustive details of the paintings of Southwold in the British Museum, but it was he who suggested I widen my search to include the British Library. It was there that Peter Barber drew my attention to the remarkable collection of drawings by Henry Davy some of which feature in the chapter on Henry Davy (pp.106-115).

Rupert Maas has not only allowed me access to the library of the Maas Gallery in London, but has repeatedly given me the benefit of his vast knowledge of British painting.

Susan Morris is the librarian at Richard Green where, thanks to the generosity of the directors, I have been allowed virtually a free run. Susan has, on many an occasion, given up her valuable time to help me with my research and I am deeply in her debt.

Stephen Wildman, curator of the Ruskin Library at Lancaster University, knows Southwold well and is a fount of knowledge about its artistic past. He has suggested numerous avenues of research and directed me to some remarkable paintings in both public and private collections.

My colleagues at Wartski must be thanked for their support and especially for their forbearance when my research trespassed on the firm's time.

My heartfelt thanks is also due to the artists, collectors, dealers, auctioneers, historians and librarians who have helped in ways too various to outline here.

They include: John Abbott of Abbott and Holder; Jane Abdy; Douglas Annan of the Annan Galleries; Ian and Julia Ball; Janet Barnes; Wendy Baron; Rosie Bass at Tate Britain; the Duke of Beaufort; Sir Richard Beckett; Paul Bennett; Heather Birchall and Juliet Cooke at the Print Room at Tate Britain; Elizabeth Blackadder; Kenneth Blackwell; John Blatchly; Gill Booth; Nicholas Bowlby; Silvie Brame of the Catalogue de L'oeuvre de Fantin-Latour; David Brangwyn; Sue Breakell at the Tate Gallery archives; George Breeze; Judith Bronkhurst; Natalie Brooke; Julian Brooks of the Ashmolean Museum; Lindsay Brooks of The Lowry; George Brown; Helen Brown of Cheltenham Art Gallery and Museum; Peter Brown of Christie's; Ian Campbell of the Carlyle Society; Wendy Cawthorne, the assistant librarian at The Geological Society; Margaret Chadd; Tom Chapman, the bursar at St. Felix's School in Southwold; Nicholas Clark of the Britten-Pears Library; Lizzy Collins of Christie's South Kensington; Peter Cormack at the William Morris Gallery; Simon Cotton; the descendants of Ellen Terry, John and Tom Craig; Paul Crane; John Craxton; Keith Cunliffe, Paul Davis, the Registrar of the Natural History Museum; Michael Day of Burlington Paintings; Michael Dickens; Sally Dummer of Ipswich Museum; Bernard Dunstan; Judy Egerton; Betty Elzea; Philip Errington of the John Masefield Society; Kate Euston of the National Portrait Gallery; William Feaver; Lucy Franklin of Sotheby's; Jill Freud; Lucian Freud; Andre Gailani of the *Punch* cartoon archive; Jane Greenham; Miss Grenhall at the Society for the Protection of Ancient Buildings; David Greysmith; Colin Harrison; Alan Hart, the Collections Leader of the Natural History Museum; Janice Helland; Annie Heron at Historic Royal Palaces; Charles Hind, Keeper of Drawings at the RIBA; Damien Hirst; Alan Hobart of The Pyms Gallery; Lenn Hodds; Mimi Hodgkin; Merlin Holland; Christine Hopper of Bradford Museum; Libby Horner; Simon Houfe; Hilary Huckstep; Rose M. Hughes; Howard Hull, the director at Brantwood; Richard Hurley of the

Stanley Spencer Gallery; Marigold Hutton, wife of the glass engraver the late John Hutton; John Illston of the *Lord Nelson*; Joachim Jacobs; Miss A. Jenkins; Jay Joplin at White Cube; Andrew Karsh; Susan Kent of Sotheby's; Charles Kidd of Debretts; Lord Killanin and Sheila, Lady Killanin; Elizabeth King and Mary Anne Stevens at the Royal Academy of Arts; Christopher Kingzett, Susan Sloman and Andrew Wild of Agnews; Lyn Knights of Denny's in Southwold; Simon Knott; David de Kretser; Lionel Lambourne; Bruce Laughton; David Lee; Sir Thomas Lighton at Waddington Galleries; Penny Lindley; Gabriel Lineham at Lambeth Palace Library; Fiona Lings of Hazlitt, Gooden and Fox; Pamela Lister; Dominique Lobstein of the Musée d'Orsay; Simon Loftus; Alice Magnay at *Country Life*; Penny Marks and Victoria Law at Richard Green; Margaret Mellis; Michael Meredith, the College Librarian at Eton; David Messum; Michael Millgate; Wladyslaw Mirecki; Jennie Moloney of the National Gallery of Victoria; Rosemarie Morgan; Mr and Mrs Richard Morphet; Geoffrey Nunn; Bernard Nurse, Librarian of the Society of Antiquaries; Richard Ormond; Victoria Osborne at Birmingham City Museum and Art Gallery; Jonathan Ouvry; Kirsty Overman of F. Starr Associates; Geoffrey Parton at Marlborough Fine Art; Nancie Pelling, the archivist at St. Felix School; Janet Pennington; Matthew Percival of the Witt Library at the Courtauld Institute of Art; Father Andrew Phillips of the Russian Orthodox Church in Exile; Michael Phipps, Librarian of the Henry Moore Foundation; Joachim Pissarro; Steven Plunkett; Kenneth Pople; Roger Quarm and Liza Verity at the National Maritime Museum; Simon Reynolds; Ann Ridler of the Borrow Society; Pamela Robertson of the The Hunterian Museum and Art Gallery; Andrew Rodgers; Cees van Romburgh of the Netherlands Maritime Museum; Patrick Roper; Douglas Schoenherr; David Scrase of the Fitzwilliam Museum Cambridge; Peyton Skipwith, Max Donnelly and Simon Edsor of the Fine Art Society; Eyke Shannon; Ian Shapiro of Argyll Etkin; Allison Sharpe of the York Art Gallery; Richard Shone; Frances Spalding; Carl Spandoni; Christopher Sprayne; Phyllis Stanley; Virginia Surtees; Sian Thomas; Pamela Thompson of the Royal College of Music; Ann Thornton; Anne Thorold; John Tooke; Mary Trumpess; Judith Tydeman at the Britten-Pears Library; Virginia Verran; Peter Warner; Norma Watt of Norwich Castle Museum; the Duke of Westminster; Timothy Wilcox; Dorothy, Richard and Stephen Wildman; Dinah Winch at Oldham Art Gallery; Julie Winyard; Caroline Worthington at York Art Gallery; Clara Young of the McManus Gallery in Dundee.

I am grateful to the art historian and writer Ian Collins, author of *A Broad Canvas*. It is a book that was the inspiration for this, my own, and continues to be a joy to all those who are interested in East Anglian art. Its eagerly awaited sequel *Making Waves – Painters at Southwold* was published in 2005.

Keith Davey at Prudence Cumming Associates has taken the majority of the photographs for this book and once again I am grateful to him for his great patience and expertise.

Diana Steel and her colleagues at The Antique Collectors' Club have published a number of my books; I am grateful to them for the free hand they have given me in all of them, including this one. Special thanks are due to my editor Susannah Hecht and designer Lynn Taylor.

INTRODUCTION

This book is not a comprehensive history of Southwold, rather a series of essays that are the result of a personal voyage of discovery that began in 1982. That same year John Gere, Keeper of Prints and Drawings at the British Museum, and his wife, the art historian and painter, Charlotte, were the latest in a succession of antiquaries and artists to have visited the town since the early eighteenth century. They had invited me to a house they had in Stradbroke Road, almost opposite the lighthouse. It was September and the Suffolk sky seemed enormous to someone who had just arrived from London by coach. Once I had settled in, Charlotte and John quickly introduced me to some of the famous delights of the town: a numbing swim in the North Sea, the glint of wet carnelians in the late summer sunlight, a jug of the mood-enhancing local beer, and the towering beauty of the ancient church. Evidently, this was a very old place, but at the time I never imagined the full drama and complexity of its past or that it might be possible for me to elaborate on its history.

By the time my wife Caroline, our two sons, Alexander and Edward, and I had made Southwold our own with the acquisition of one of the famous beach huts, we had become addicted to the place. From the beginning, the fascination of Southwold had me in its grip, but then we started to venture further afield. Sometimes we searched for ancestral tombstones in Halesworth and other times we went to Dunwich. It seemed inconceivable to us that this small collection of buildings was once a great city that had struck "*terror and feare*" into the heart of its enemies; by the time we had arrived it had sunk, like Atlantis, into the sea. The grim reality of this tragic story was soon brought to bear on us the first time we walked as a family on Dunwich beach. The night before, a storm had undermined the last corner of All Saints churchyard and a skeleton, complete with gaping skull, confronted us at the foot of the cliff. Surprisingly, our small sons were unperturbed by this gruesome sight and tested their knowledge of human biology on the pitiful remains, now pitched out of their final resting place. On another occasion we crossed over the river Blyth by way of the ancient ferry and discovered that next to nothing remained of the thriving mediaeval hamlet of Walberswick. The church, dedicated to St. Andrew, a Galilean fisherman of Bethsaida (see illustration on p.28), had once been a richly decorated Gothic edifice and was now a romantic ruin. However, the breathtakingly beautiful and sumptuous church of Holy Trinity at Blythburgh, known locally as the "*Cathedral of the Marshes*" was the greatest testimony to a prosperous past. Throughout the day and

---

Opposite:
Sam May's Hut, Southwold *by Joseph Southall. Tempera on linen. 1923.*
Sam May was a lifeboat man of great bravery who died the year this painting was made. The herring basket and winch in the foreground indicate that this shed, situated just below Gun Hill, belongs to a fisherman with a boat of his own. Wearing a straw hat and distinctive leather thigh boots, he partially obscures a bathing machine. The artist has cleverly incorporated both sources of Southwold's prosperity: fishing and sea bathing. The reading room on Gun Hill, known as the 'Casino', is seen to the left of the composition.
Private Collection

Blythburgh *by Joseph Southall. Tempera. 1927. The frame for the picture was gilded by Mrs Southall.*

Painted from the high ground above Wenhaston Lane the composition centres on the fifteenth century church of Holy Trinity, known locally as the "Cathedral of the Marshes". It is late summer and Rose Bay Willow Herb is in flower. The church towers above what remains of a mediaeval town and the ruins of its priory. An almost surreal stillness highlights the famous beauty of the church, a beauty compared by the Rector, Barry Naylor, to Jacob's first sight of Bethel:

"How awesome is this place! This is none other than the house of God: it is the very gate of heaven"

   (Genesis 28:17)

Albert Dawson Collection

14

floodlit night it towers above a small cluster of relatively modern buildings and is the last reminder of an ancient abbey and a large congregation. Sadly no churches remain to bear testimony to the thriving community of Easton. Situated immediately north of Southwold, it was, as its name suggests, once the most easterly point of the United Kingdom. However, the same storms that destroyed almost all of Dunwich finally undermined Easton completely. The river harbour was the first to go, followed by the town's *"well-peopled streets, her goodly and numerous residences...her fertile pastures and corn fields – extensive deer parks and thickly planted forests."* [1] With them went the church dedicated to St. Nicholas, patron saint of fishermen and the pilgrim chapel of St. Margaret. In the end all the townspeople were pitched out their houses and even their graves as, little by little, every vestige succumbed to the swirling waves below. By 1754 Easton had been reduced to two dwelling houses and about ten souls. Today, an abundance of wild fennel is the only reminder of an ancient community and the brisk fishing trade that supported it.

The religious standardisation required by King Charles I resulted in the cleaving away of a part of Southwold's identity. In 1637 the Rev. John Youngs (1598-1671) "gathered his flock and founded the town of Southold, Long Island".[2] When this small band of Puritans left

16

Southwold Pier *by Katherine Hamilton. Oil on canvas. 2002.*
The new pier built in 2001 replaces that which was washed away in the storm of 1953. It is a perfect scale for Southwold and more than 500,000 visitors a year walk out over the sea to look back on the town. The beach in high summer is a place that is difficult to leave. This painting brilliantly evokes all the pleasures of the seaside, but lengthening shadows anticipate the end of a perfect day.
Author's collection. Photograph: Messum Gallery © Katherine Hamilton 2002

Southwold and set sail from Yarmouth for America, it aspired to a society where religious freedom was paramount. In that regard these early emigrants had jumped from the frying pan into the fire: by 1658 Southold had become a place where Quakers were vigorously suppressed with fines, the whip and the branding iron. There, tolerance had given way to superstition, and fear of witchcraft was rife. The remote origins of these pious men was securely commemorated in Southold's name. Back in Southwold, Suffolk the memory of its puritan kinsmen is kept alive on California Sands, Long Island and New York Cliffs.

The German Ocean (North Sea) was the silent witness to the bloody fight, known as the Battle of Sole Bay, which took place off the coast of Southwold in 1672. It is the want of evidence that makes the battle's terrible story all the more compelling and Henry James

articulated just that when he said: "*There is a presence in what is missing — there is history in being so little*".

For these and a thousand other reasons my curiosity was kindled and a growing pile of books rapidly fuelled a fire that had started as a slow burn. In them I discovered Southwold's past as it had been set down by three very different historians. The antiquary Thomas Gardner, in 1754, wrote *An Historical Account of Dunwich, Blithburgh and Southwold*, which was illustrated with copper plate engravings. A rare book, my copy, which has been meticulously — even pedantically — annotated by several different hands over more than 250 years, has an elegantly gold-tooled leather spine. In 1839, Robert Wake produced *Southwold and its Vicinity*. James Maggs's *Southwold Diaries* are certainly the most vivid account and take the form of an annotated scrapbook compiled between 1818 and 1876. All three are archival, but a number of creative writers have also found inspiration in Southwold and the surrounding area.

One of them was the poet George Crabbe (1754-1832); it was he who asked the profound question "*who is brave enough to paint the sea?*"; and the answer is: very few. In fact, next to none of the droves of artists who came to the Blyth Valley accepted the enormity of the challenge, and even fewer were able to meet it. Nonetheless, a vivid pictorial record of Southwold matches the written accounts described above. It begins in the sixteenth century and continues in the present day. Certainly the greatest artist to have visited the town was J.M.W. Turner. He arrived in Southwold in 1824 on the way from Aldeburgh. The drawings he made on the long hike to Lowestoft are kept at Tate Britain; preserved in the same leather-bound sketchbooks that he carried in his pocket as he walked along the

---

Ralph Vaughan Williams *by Edmund Kapp (1890-1928). Pencil on paper. 1915.*

It was probably at the suggestion of William Gooding that the composers Ralph Vaughan Williams (1872-1958) and George Butterworth (1885-1916) visited Southwold in 1910 and they may have stayed with him at his house at 49 High Street. On 24 and 25 October they visited the fishermen William and Robert Hurr and, in the tradition of Robert Burns, they noted down eleven traditional seafaring songs in order to preserve them for posterity. The same year that Vaughan Williams was in Southwold his Sea Symphony, *written to words by Walt Whitman, was performed at the choral festival in Leeds.*

The Barber Institute of Fine Arts, University of Birmingham

Southwold by Robert Greenham (1906-1976). Oil on canvas. c.1920.
Family-sized canvas windbreaks divide the beach with blocks of pastel colour and a beach hut to the left of
the composition offers shade, showing that it is late afternoon. Greenham studied art at the Byam Shaw
School of Art and at the Royal Academy and stayed at Cleveland Cottage, near the Bell Inn *in Walberswick.*
Bonham's

coastline. The privilege of handling them was almost nothing compared to the excitement of recognising several of the delicate drawings as views of Southwold and Walberswick.

Though Turner left only very faint footprints in Southwold's art-historical sand, Henry Davy (1793-1865) followed in them. His beautiful watercolour drawings are distinguished by the detail and icy clarity of his technique, but they are also the most evocative visual record that we have of Southwold's lively past. Henry Davy recognised and captured the moment of transition when Southwold turned from being a thriving fishing port into a fashionable watering place.

The name of Southwold not only evokes the sight but also the sound of the waves and it is well known that musicians always gravitate towards the sea. It was the composer and local resident George Butterworth (1885-1916) who introduced his intimate and distinguished friend Ralph Vaughan Williams (1872-1958) to the town in 1910. He was followed there, from time to time, by the composer Benjamin Britten (1913-1976) and his companion, the singer Peter Pears.

Today Southwold is remembered by the majority as a happy, carefree place where the sun always shines and childhood memories continue to be made – and in that regard it is has proved an earthly paradise for some.

My purpose in writing this book is not to sully these memories, but to balance them with the truth about Southwold's turbulent past; to try to describe the essence of the place, and explore why its hold over us all continues to be powerful and hypnotic.

HOLY EDMUND PRAY FOR US

In the autumn of 869 a young Anglo-Saxon king of East Anglia called Edmund was martyred by the Danes; he was named as a saint within living memory of his violent end. Despite the complexity of his cult and the many accounts of his life and death, most are agreed as to the manner of St. Edmund's martyrdom: he was bound, scourged, tied to a tree, pierced with arrows and, finally, decapitated.

Although in life he was unable to repel the Danish marauders, in death Edmund became one of the most powerful symbols of resistance in English history. His story, bound up with that of Southwold, reveals more than is generally known about the town and particularly its vulnerability to attack from land and sea.

The oldest source of the saint's life story is the *Anglo-Saxon Chronicle*, compiled a little before 890. The chronicler says:

"A great heathen army came to England and took up winter quarters in East Anglia; there they were supplied with horses and the East Angles made peace with them."

Leaving East Anglia victorious, the Danes were then involved in an indecisive campaign in Mercia before returning to York; in 869 they were back:

"In this year the raiding army rode across Mercia into East Anglia, and took up winter quarters at Thetford. And that winter King Edmund fought against them; and the Danes had the victory and killed the king and conquered all the land."[1]

Little else is known for certain about Edmund from contemporary accounts, though he did issue coins in sufficient number to suggest that he reigned for several years. Besides those issued by Edmund himself, there are also some coins made in his honour that date from the last decade of the ninth century.[2] From these we know that he was recognised as a saint even whilst Danish kings ruled East Anglia.

Later accounts are more specific about his life and terrible end. Abbo of Fleury was a continental scholar who spent some time at Ramsey Abbey and wrote *Passio Sancti Eadmundi* in 985. Abbo says that the Dane Hinguar was responsible for the martyrdom of Edmund.

Opposite:

The wolf with the head of St. Edmund *by Doris Zinkeisen (1898-1991). Oil on canvas.*

After St. Edmund's decollation, the Danes deliberately separated the head from the rest of his remains in the hope of denying him a safe passage into the afterlife. His subjects were understandably keen to reunite them and their search was rewarded when they found the head guarded by a benign wolf.

Doris Zinkeisen was a painter, as well as a costume and theatre designer. She made several portraits of actors including that of Dame Anna Neagle. She was responsible for Laurence Olivier's makeup in the role of Richard III. Towards the end of her life Doris Zinkeisen lived at Badingham, where she died in 1991.

St Edmundsbury Borough Council

The Martyrdom of St. Edmund. *Paintings on vellum from* The Life of St. Edmund *by the monk and prolific versifier John Lydgate.*

This is the moment after St. Edmund has been cut down from the tree and Hinguar, the Dane, is preparing to smite off his head with a magical sword, sharp enough to draw blood from the wind. Edmund is crying out for Jesus to receive his soul.

Unto Tirantis ys nat victoryous
Thouh they thy servantis slen off fals hatrede;
For thylke conquest is more glorious
Wher that the soule hath of deth no dreede.
Now, blissid Jhesu, for myn eternal meede,
Only of mercy, medlyd with thy ryht,
Receyue the speryt of me that am thy knyht!

The British Library

The folkys dide ther bysy dilligence
[T]his holy tresour, this relik sovereyne
[T]o take it uppe with dew reverence,
And bar it forth, tyl they dide atteyne
Unto the body, and of thylke tweyne
Togidre set, god by myracle anoon
Enjoyned hem, that they were maad bothe oon.

The Abbot of Bury gave The Life of St. Edmund *to the young Henry VI when the king stayed with him in 1433. In the extended narrative, the saint's head is retrieved from the wolf and is reunited with his body by monks. There were no rabbits in England in 869, but by the time the painting was made they were bred all around Bury, in warrens. St. Edmund and King Charles I remain the only English monarchs to have died for their faith.*
The British Library

St. Edmund, Virgin King and Martyr. *Detail from an engraved glass window by John Hutton. 1969. This is the face of the martyr, tied to the tree, moments before he is shot full of arrows. His crown and halo are powerful emblems of his rank. The glass was presented to the church by Sir Charles Tennyson who lived in Middle House, Park Lane in memory of his wife Ivy and his sons Penrose and Julian. Hutton was inspired by Romanesque and mediaeval sculpture and it is from this that his work derives its monumentality. His best known work is the great west screen of Coventry Cathedral.*   The Hon. Marigold Hutton

Hinguar had arrived in Northumbria with his brother Hubba and overrun it. Hubba remained there but Hinguar embarked from the north to the east coast with a fleet and attacked a city, which they burnt to the ground. Hinguar questioned the local people as to the whereabouts of Edmund and finding him at the village of Haegelisdun [now Hellesdon in Norfolk], sent a messenger demanding that Edmund reign under him, and divide his treasures with him. Hinguar was much feared, not only on his own account, but also because he was said to have in his possession a magical sword (see illustration opposite) sharp enough to draw blood from the wind. The bishops advised Edmund to flee; however, wanting to preserve his honour, Edmund said that nothing would separate him from the love of Christ and that he would only submit if the pagan Hinguar were to be christened. Soon Edmund was captured and martyred in a way strangely reminiscent of the agony of the Roman saint, Sebastian. At the start of the humiliation and torture the King's teeth were knocked out with a cudgel. The Danes then took him to some nearby woods, stripped him of every mark of royalty and tied him, almost naked, to an oak tree. There he was flogged. During this awful process Edmund repeatedly called out the name of Christ.

Enraged, the Danes fired arrows at him "*thick as winter rain*". Finally, Edmund's cries to God were silenced when Hinguar took him down from the tree and, with his magical sword, cut off the King's head. By tossing it into a nearby hedge the Danes hoped to deny Edmund a decent burial and, therefore, his passage into the afterlife. The Virgin King Edmund, who is believed to have reigned for 15 years, was just 29 when he died.

As soon as it was safe to do so his followers went to retrieve his corpse; the head was found, guarded by a benign wolf. Eventually Edmund's head and body were stitched back together and buried in a simple chapel near where he had died. Some years later the corpse was taken to Bedricesworth (now Bury) and it was here that his tomb became associated with a number of miracles. Eventually the relics found their way to the Basilica of Saint Sernin in Toulous. In 1901 they were given to be lodged under the high altar of the newly constructed Westminster Cathedral. Various antiquaries and writers, including M.R. James, expressed doubts about their authenticity and, as a result, the translation of the relics to the Cathedral never took place. The relics remained, instead, in their temporary resting place with the Duke of Norfolk at Arundel Castle until, in 1985, the 17th Duke gave permission for them to be examined. In 1991, an analysis began: it was discovered that the bones came from a total of twelve different skeletons including those of women.[3]

The accumulation of these dubious relics is evidence that the power of Edmund's cult had increased with time. More than a century after his death, the Danish king Swein – known as Fork Beard – came to Bury extorting tribute with threats of violence and the destruction of the saint's shrine. On 2 February 1014 a shining apparition of St. Edmund wielding a sword appeared to Swein in the night and actually frightened him to death; his corpse was sent back to Denmark, preserved in salt.

About thirty years after Swein had been vanquished by Edmund's death bolts the Bishop of East Anglia gave the manor of Southwold to the monks of Bury; there Edmund's relics were enshrined. It was from that moment that the magical association of saint and settlement began.

Late in the eleventh century Southwold was in trouble from another kind of marauder. The Norman knight Robert de Curzun persuaded the Sheriff of Norfolk, Roger Bigot, to let him take possession of St. Edmund's manor of Southwold, which he claimed was at the centre of his domain. He arrived in 1087, prepared for violence, but he was seemingly unaware of the danger of tampering with the saint's endowment. During his first advance on the manor he was repelled not by the poor inhabitants but by a supernatural tempest. Two of his followers, Turolf the Steward and a knight called Gyrenew de Mouneyn, were misguided enough to continue the siege, but a mysterious force drove them into a frenzy and they remained "*permanently demented*".

Improbable as it seems the de Curzun family failed to learn their lesson over Southwold. Nearly a century later, in 1186, William de Curzun, a successor to Robert, renewed the family claim to the manor. Via the archdeacon of Poictiers he applied to Henry II, who issued a mandate for its surrender. The Abbot of Bury appealed but William

Soulde – its fortress. *Watercolour and ink on vellum. 1588.*
This is probably a record of the defences mounted against the threat of a Spanish invasion. A battery of guns surmounts the fortified cliff. A triangular fort, known as Fort Sussex, with a moat fed with water from Buss Creek, is situated towards the north; and from it comes a foot soldier, carrying a pike. The only entrance to Southwold was over Mights Bridge, spanning the "marshes and low groundes" encircling the town. A bull, horse and sheep graze nearby. The architecture of the church and town has been conventionalised and ships steer a hazardous course between a roaring sea monster and a leviathan.

The National Archives

de Curzun won the judgement and immediately left London ready to seize Southwold. Apparently St. Edmund was determined that the de Curzuns should get the message once and for all: William was inexplicably struck down at Chelmsford. From there he was taken to Colchester Abbey where the monks received him as a raving maniac. He was bound and bandaged for his own safety and kept under restraint only with the greatest difficulty. De Curzun's wife was so horrified by the change in her husband that she deserted him forever. Hearing the news of William's fate, the Abbot of Bury knew there was only one way of placating his patron saint. He sent a messenger to de Curzun suggesting that he withdraw his claim to Southwold. William was still raving and in no fit

St. Edmund's Church, Southwold *by Frederick Baldwin. Watercolour on paper. 7 September 1935.*
The advantage of the church tower as a lookout post is obvious and even today it dominates its surroundings. During the Second World War the mayor, Edgar Pipe, announced that the bells of the church would be used to warn of daylight air raids. If they were "jangled" for a short time it was a warning for the public to clear the streets. The tolling of a single bell signalled the "all clear" and, on a number of occasions, it was the death knell for some of townspeople. A number of houses and commercial buildings represented in the picture were bombed and others have been taken down to make room for modern developments. This unusual view was evidently from the top of the lighthouse.

Birmingham City Museum and Art Gallery

state to make this important judgement himself. Richard, one of his attendants, offered himself as hostage if only the saint would take pity on his master. That same night William's madness subsided. De Curzun saw that he was beaten and finally renounced his claim to Southwold, remaining a devout servant of St. Edmund for the rest of his life.[4]

By the middle of the twelfth century St. Edmund's cult was at its height, and a chronicler called Geoffrey of Wells dedicated his *De Infantia Sancti Eamundi* to Abbot Ording of Bury. In it he said that Edmund was the adopted son of King Offa of East Anglia; this, like so much else in the saga is a fiction. However, less than 50 years later, in 1202, a chapel was erected in Southwold on the instigation of Bishop Samson of Bury by the command of Pope Innocent III in Rome.

The devout of Southwold must have truly believed in the power of St. Edmund's patronage. However, it was the drawbridge that once spanned Buss Creek, the ancient fortification on Eye Cliff (later Gun Hill) and the succession of batteries positioned there that were the real deterrent to invaders. The threat of the enemy was ever present and there are some notable examples of when the town was considered to be at particular risk: from the Spanish in the late 1580s; when the Dutch threatened to invade during the Battle of Sole Bay in 1672; when the Germans bombarded the cliffs from the sea in 1917; and when St. Edmund's Church was miraculously spared destruction by German bombers in the Second World War.

More than 1100 years since his martyrdom there are still numerous references to Edmund to be found in Southwold. The vantage point on the cliff that is called St. Edmund's Hill is the most significant because it was from here, in times of danger, that a beacon signalled the first sight of the enemy. Because an arsenal of guns and munitions was stored above the porch of St. Edmund's Church it was possible, as a last resort to defend it against the enemy.[5] Even in times of peace Edmund's presence was a permanent reassurance and was signalled in many ways. His crown and arrows are the central elements of the corporation seal, on the links of the Mayor's chain of office, and are repeated all over town: they define Southwold's boundaries on the railings of Might's Bridge, appear on the pump in Market Place and on a badge on a pew end dated 1849, and even on small portable souvenirs and beer mats. However, the greatest tribute of all to Southwold's guardian saint is his church. With its massive profile it is visible from every aspect and has dominated the town for centuries. Each year, exactly at noon on 20 November, the anniversary of the church's dedication, the shadows cast by the north and south sides of the building align with one another. Some believe that even the relative position of St. Edmund's Church to the sun is another, covert, tribute to its patron saint.[6]

Ancient liturgical tradition has it that an image of a patron saint should be hung at the north side of the high altar. It is, therefore, more than likely that a painting of St. Edmund was amongst the 130 "*superstitious pictures*" that were broken down when Cromwell's agent William Dowsing (1596?- 1679?) visited Southwold's church on 8 April 1644. In spite of the wholesale destruction, miraculously Edmund's crowned head and attributes survived on the church door; their modern successors are the great East window made by Sir Ninian Comper in 1954, the north window engraved by John Hutton in 1969 and the stone effigy over the porch that was carved by Andrew Swinley in 1989. The exterior of the church is decorated with monograms and lettering laid out in a type of decoration known as Suffolk flush work. This is made up of carefully napped flints contrasting with a white limestone from Lincolnshire and Caen in Normandy. It is an ideal medium in which to set out holy monograms and lettering. Over the West porch appears a supplication that was crucial to Southwold's protection in the past and possibly its well-being in the future:

ST EDMUNDE PRO NOBIS
Holy Edmund Pray for us

PARADISE ON EARTH

The imposing scale of Southwold's second church reflected not only the settlement's new prosperity but also the power of the sacraments taking place within. Today it remains a holy place. The passage of time has robbed the builder of his identity, though I believe that there is enough circumstantial evidence to name him.

In Walberswick, in 1426, a contract was drawn up with one Richard Russell, a stonemason from Dunwich, requiring him and his partner, Adam Powle, to build a new tower for St. Andrew's Church.[1] Russell probably had a powerful sense of his own identity[2] – records indicate that in 1427 he was a Member of Parliament for Dunwich – and he asserted it at Walberswick when he signed his finished work on St. Andrew's with his initials in the flint flushwork (see illustration on p.30). It is notable that the fabric and decoration of Russell's tower at Walberswick are strikingly similar to St. Edmund's, Southwold. However, there is further compelling evidence that Russell was responsible for both: at the feet of each of the columns that support the tower arch in St. Edmund's there is another signature (see illustration on p.30), again in the form of a pair of 'Rs'. It is my belief that they too stand for Richard Russell and that it was he who built the best part of Southwold's magnificent church.[3]

The wealthy benefactors who paid for Russell's richly decorated masterpiece in Southwold required it to be a fitting house for God. They wanted it to dominate the surrounding buildings in the same way that He dominated the lives of their inhabitants. The congregation was called to prayer from the darkness of their wattle and daub hovels and houses by the peals of massive bronze bells, which were thought loud enough to quell storms and drive away demons. Inside, the floor was strewn with yew and rosemary, and shafts of light, suffused with cobalt blue, red and yellow played on the dun, green and dirty-white clothes of the people. From behind richly painted walls and screens decorated with silver and gold, could be heard the Latin incantations of the priests and the plain song of the choir. It was in this secret inner sanctum that the altar stood, draped with richly worked silk, centred with a cross flanked by candlesticks and other devotional objects of silver and silver gilt. There the most sacred moments of the

The Old Chancel, Walberswick *by Richard Scott. Oil. 2002.*
St. Andrew's was the second church in Walberswick. The 90ft tower was constructed by Richard Russell and Adam Powle after 1426. The church was 124ft long and 60ft wide. It fell into disrepair in the late 17th century when the inhabitants could no long afford its upkeep. The romantic ruins have been a powerful inspiration to a number of artists including J.M.W. Turner.
© Richard Scott. Photograph: Douglas Atfield

The porch of St. Edmund's
Church, Southwold
by E.S. Lowther.
Watercolour on paper. c.1900.
The church porch was added
after the main body of the
church had been built and is
both imposing and, with its
benches on either side,
inviting. The original market
place was in front and the
porch must have played an
important role in the religious
and secular life of the parish.
Under its shelter, meetings
were held, notices posted and
lessons taught to children. It
is decorated with chequer
work in contrasting limestone
and napped flints. On the
lower course of the porch
there are numerous mono-
grams of 'M' and 'R', but they
also contain every letter of
Maria; because of this, it has
been suggested that the niche
above the door once contained
an image of Our Lady. Today
the position is filled with an
effigy of St. Edmund.
Tullie House Museum and
Art Gallery, Carslisle

services were signalled with teeming censers, candles, scented oils and the sound of silver bells; this was a place where priests, coped in bright silk velvet and cloth of gold, read the secret word of God from illuminated vellums and turned wine into His sacred blood.

Even today very few of us could remain unaffected by an assault of this magnitude on every one of our senses; in an age without synthetic paints and dyes, without the distraction of the internet, television and the cinema, these arrangements were numinous, vision-inducing, a short cut to an inner consciousness and to Paradise itself.

Regrettably this richness and beauty was short lived. Hardly more than a century after Southwold's church had been completed a programme of destruction began in the name of the Reformation and continued during the Commonwealth. Very little of the splendid interior was left intact.

The monumental rood, or crucifix, which hung against a painted loft and dominated the nave, has been torn down, though, quite unaccountably, the rood screen survived and is certainly Southwold's greatest treasure. Much remains of the original gesso,[4] raised and painted in shades of green, white and red and heightened with gold (see illustration on p.117). The panels of the prophets on the south aisle are fine, but the central group is the best and, despite defacement, still conveys a feeling of profound

Opposite:
St. Edmund's Church, Southwold *by Richard Scott. Oil on board. 2002. The morning light is falling on the side of the distinctive tower of Richard Russell's masterpiece, the Church of St. Edmund, King and Martyr. The same raking light accentuates the gravestones of those who once worshipped within. On the roof of the chancel is the distinctive flèche that accommodated a single bell. It was used to signal the holiest moments of the Eucharist, the Sanctus, the Elevation and the Communion. The elaborate decoration of the church was finished in the 1460s, since when it has been the centre of community life.*
Richard Scott is a painter and art historian, who has lived and worked in Walberswick for a number of years. His style is highly individual and is characterised by unusual effects in light and shade.

Author's Collection © Richard Scott

Left:
A flint flushwork panel from St. Andrew's Church in Walberswick. Above and below the Saint's emblem of a cross appear the initials of Richard Russell who built the tower in 1426. Photograph: Caroline Munn

spirituality. These paintings of the saints Philip, Matthew, James, Thomas, Andrew and Peter have an almost three-dimensional quality, suggesting they were intended to be clearly identifiable to the throngs of worshippers in the nave. Those on the north aisle are otherworldly and represent a shimmering Order of Angels, some with golden feathers and others crowned and wrapped in valuable furs.

These, however, are just some of the dozens of painted images that once decorated the church and included the Annunciation of the Virgin Mary, Saint Gabriel the Archangel, the Holy Trinity, Saint Saviour, St. John, the Lady of Pity, and St. Nicholas. A number of these were favourite objects of veneration and bequests were made to the church for their upkeep. In 1522 Mary Joye left £4 to cover the expenses of gilding the tabernacle of St. Saviour, the residue to be used for the purchase of two embroidered banners, one in the form of the Trinity and another decorated with the Lady of Pity. Although these were probably on permanent display they may well have headed the procession of priest and choir on the relevant saint's day. The following decade ushered in the Reformation with its trail of appalling destruction. Worse was to follow and, just over a century later, almost everything that could possibly be removed had been stripped out of St. Edmund's Church.

An impressive treasure made up of silver or silver-gilt was sold by the churchwardens in 1547, the first year of the reign of Edward VI. Thomas Godbold and Robert Dey had the consent of the whole town to sell a pair of chalices for 40 shillings to help pay for the expenses of 7 horse soldiers and for some of the upkeep of the town hall. In November of that year another destructive sale made fatal inroads into Southwold's riches: Thomas Jentylman and William Wright sold two crosses of silver and silver-gilt, three pairs of chalices in silver and parcel gilt, a pyx in silver gilt, a chrismatory in silver and silver gilt, two paxes in silver gilt, and a little silver bell. They were sold by weight and were undoubtedly destined for the melting pot. The churchwardens were paid 4s 4d an ounce for

Detail of The Rood Screen at St Edmund's, Southwold *by George E. Fox. Watercolour on paper. September 1885.*

The winged angel, who is a personification of 'Principalities', wears a red and gold mantle and an ermine cape. Against his halo is a rich gothic crown made up of trefoil fleurons and this, together with the gold mace, is an emblem of high rank. At his feet, at the edge of the sea, is a fortified town with lookout towers and tiled houses centring on a gilded pavilion. A romantic legend suggests that this fortification represents that which Henry III permitted the Earl of Gloucester to build in Southwold in the thirteenth century. The Society of Antiquaries, London

the silver and it is a measure of its importance that the total proceeds amounted to a substantial £110.[5]

Exactly when and where these devotional objects were made is uncertain but, considering Southwold's economic history, they are likely to have been contemporary with the present church and to have been amongst the best expressions of a mediaeval goldsmith's work (see illustration on p.120). Perhaps Thomas Jentylman knew this and, afterwards, his conscience troubled him a little, since he attempted to justify the destruction by declaring that the proceeds of the second sale were to be spent on maintenance of the harbour, and on gunpowder and shot for the defence of the town. There may, indeed, have been a genuine need for the money, but it was the return to Protestantism under the boy king Edward VI that gave official sanction to what seems now to have been a short-sighted act of philistinism.

At the same time that the wardens were selling the church's silver they also disposed of copes and vestments; sadly there is no record of their appearance. That they were sold for the substantial sum of £5 suggests that they were made of rich materials, almost certainly finely worked with silver and gold. An inventory made at St. Andrew's, Walberswick in 1492 gives a very good idea of the textiles that were in use in Southwold church.[6] There were two velvet copes, one in red and one in black, and several others made of white silk damask, white fustian and black worsted. A number of vestments were also itemised in the St. Andrew's inventory: one of green and blue worsted and another decorated with moons. There were also silk cloths for the pyx, painted cloths for the altar and several silk cushions.

All this splendour finally came to an end under Cromwell: at Southwold, in particular, when the iconoclast William Dowsing, born and buried in Laxfield, visited the town on 8 April 1644 and broke down 130 "*superstitious pictures*", one of which was of St. Andrew. The sheer number of these images suggests a proportion of them were of stained glass and that the ancient beauty of the church was

Detail of The Rood Screen at St Edmund's, Southwold *by George E. Fox. Watercolour on paper. September 1885.*
The winged angel, who is a personification of 'Virtues', wears a gold crown and carries another together with a pot of purifying flames. The smaller gold circlet is emblematic of the crowning of the cardinal virtues of prudence, temperance, fortitude and justice. The screen was restored by the painter George Richmond "for love" in 1874. He admitted that the repainted face of St. Jude, with its red beard and somewhat foxy look, was a caricature of the Rector of Southwold.
The Society of Antiquaries, London

hugely compromised. It seems even the pew ends were attacked. Gardner believed that they had been decorated with birds, animals and "*satyrs*" and certainly some similar beasts survive on the misericordes and choir stalls.

Standing just to the west end of the church is the stone font. Once it would have been decorated with relief carvings of the seven sacraments of baptism, confirmation, mass, penance, extreme unction, ordination and matrimony, each in a gothic arch surmounted by pinnacles. Now totally obliterated, only their frames and their empty silhouettes give the faintest reminder of the stonemason's skill; with them has gone the original painting and gilding. In the process of its virtual destruction, the nature of the font has changed: miraculously becoming a robust work of art of quite a different sort. Above it hangs a modern, brightly-painted cover. The original would have been richly carved and painted, probably in the manner of the rood screen and decorated with saints or angels; we shall never know. It was certainly elaborate enough to attract the attention of Dowsing, who tore it down that day in April 1644.

Far above, in an unassailable position behind the rood screen, supported on hammer beams in the form of crowned angels, is a painted ceiling made up of separate frames ornamented with chevrons and barley twists in green and white and red. From them a host of singing angels looks down from the blue firmament of heaven, blazing with gold stars (see illustration opposite).

Opposite:
Canopy of Honour, from the ceiling of the south side of the chancel of St. Edmund's church*, by George E. Fox. Watercolour. 1878.*
The ceiling consists of sixteen compartments, each carrying its own painted angel bearing (left to right) a crown of thorns, a scroll reading "nobis in", a scroll reading "domo David", a baton with a three-tongued scourge, St. Peter's sword with Malchus's ear on its edge, and a scroll reading "pueri sui" [And hath raised up the horn of salvation for us in the house of David His servant]. Beneath the angels run the inscriptions taken from the Te Deum. *Fox's minutely observed watercolours of the decoration of St. Edmund's church enable us to see it in far greater detail than might otherwise be possible. Through his painstaking observation, Fox anticipated the modern technique of computer enhancement. However, these paintings are not simply meticulous records, but beautiful works of art in their own right.*

The Society of Antiquaries, London

Detail of The Rood Screen in St. Edmund's Church *by George Wardle. (Obt. 1910). Watercolour on paper.*
This carefully observed drawing shows the mantle of St. Paul, decorated with lions, pomegranates, a swan and a dog. The lion is a symbol with many attributions including Christ's power and might. In the Middle Ages it stood for the Resurrection because, according to bestiaries, the cubs, when born, lay dead for three days until their father brought them to life by breathing in their faces. The pomegranate also stands for the Resurrection through its classical association with Proserpine who returned every spring to regenerate the earth. The swan stands for purity, grace and the Virgin Mary, and the dog with a bell on its collar may be an emblem of faith in Christ.

The Society of Antiquaries, London

Paintings on Bay of Roof over Rood Screen. — Southwold Church. Suffolk. — George E. Fox. 1878.

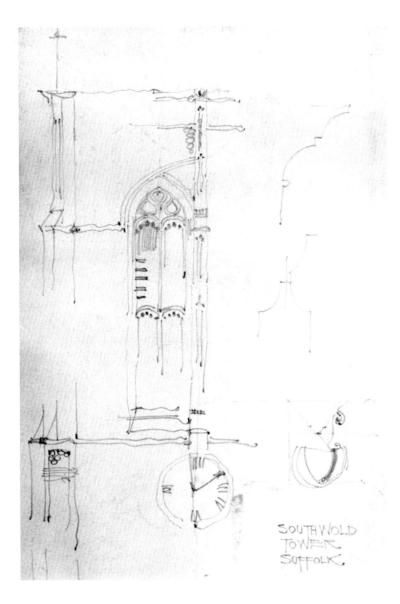

Four drawings of St. Edmund's, Southwold by Charles Rennie Mackintosh. Pencil on paper. 1897.
Like J.M.W. Turner before him, Mackintosh was fascinated by the architectural detail of the church and the rich decoration within. The artist has cleverly translated the scrolling gothic ornament of the church into the linear idiom of the Art Nouveau movement.

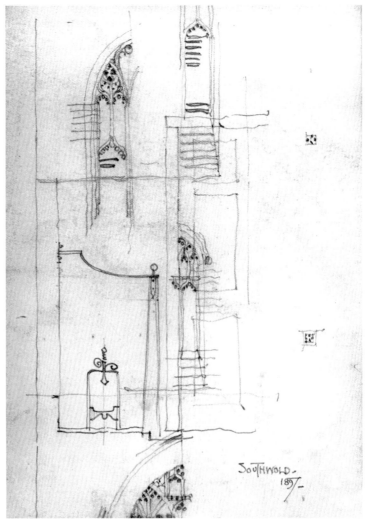

Southwold Tower, Suffolk.
The twinned windows of the tower and the eaves through which the sound of the bells escapes. The dial is that of the clock, which was presented by the Debney family in 1892. It shows that Mackintosh made this drawing at 11:10 in the morning.

Southwold 1897.
An interior view of the church and a box pew (later removed), complete with iron boot scraper.

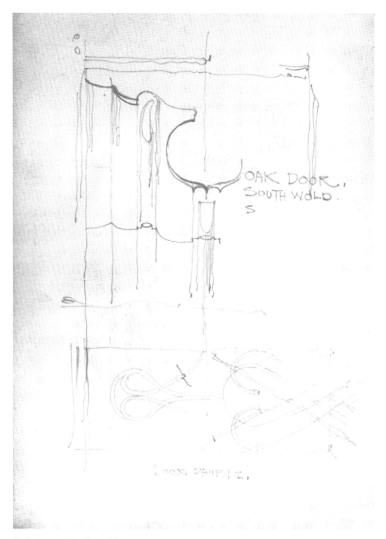

Southwold. Rood Screen Lower Panels Richly Decorated.
Mackintosh was attracted to the carved and gilded gothic arches that frame the painted panels of the screen.

Oak Door. Southwold.
A romantic legend suggests that the oak doors of the church were made for the first chapel built in Southwold in 1202. Iron nails remain from the time when parish notices were pinned to them. Evidently Mackintosh admired the original linenfold carving and found that it anticipated the curvilinear ornament of the Art Nouveau movement.

Certainly this ceiling added enormously to the overwhelming richness of the church's interior, as did the floor, which shone with finely engraved brass memorials. On 12 June 1644 a deputy of Dowsing's called Thomas Jessop visited a church in Lowestoft and tore up all the monumental brasses, engraved with prayers for the dead, that had survived the Reformation. The brasses from the floor and tombs in St. Edmund's, Southwold were to suffer the same fanatical spoliation. How many were destroyed is unknown, but some empty outlines remain to this day. The loss not only did immeasurable damage to the decoration of the church, but it also deprived historians of another way of understanding Southwold's social history.

Apparently there was nothing in the decoration of the pulpit that offended Puritan sensibilities and it, together with the secular figure of a soldier in full armour known as 'Southwold Jack', survived both destructive purges of the church. 'Jack', an armour-clad

The interior of St. Edmund's church, Southwold *by John Piper (1903-1992). Watercolour on paper. 1965.*
Piper visited the Aldeburgh Festival in 1958 and it was then that he painted Three Suffolk Towers, *now in the Tate Britain. At Blythburgh he made a drawing of the wrought-iron churchyard gate and, in Southwold, Piper managed to capture the mediaeval splendour of Southwold church in this near abstract painting of jewel-like intensity.* Prudential PLC.

figure, is made of painted wood that is contemporary with the church and retains its original paintwork. Once connected to the mechanics of the clock he struck the hours on an adjoining bell with a war hammer. Now the bell is used as a signal to the organist that the priest is robed and ready for worship. References to similar 'Jacks' in Shakespeare's *Richard II* and *Richard III* suggest that these now very rare and fascinating automata were once common.

Although the 'Jack' has come through the years virtually unscathed, the pulpit's ancient structure and original beauty have been obscured by disastrous alterations and restorations. In 1825 the sounding board above the pulpit was removed and for some while stored in the church tower until the decision was made to sell it to a certain Henry Garrod. He converted the board into a sign for a beer house on Gun Hill known as 'Tom and Jerry'.[7] To compensate for its loss to the acoustics of the church, the pulpit was raised by 9 inches (22.86cm) and, in 1853, it was "*renovated*", gilded and supplied with a new reading board by one Thomas Rounce. It was probably then that its original character was lost and subsequent restorations have completely destroyed the original patina; now it stands dressed in colours, raw and modern.

Although defaced, the rood screen has escaped damaging 'improvements'. The only attempt to restore it was made by George Richmond in 1874. He believed that the faces of the saints had "*got very faint partly from … the objectionable habit of certain parishioners who sat in the front pews of the nave and were wont to prop their umbrellas against their faces*". As Richmond worked on the screen during week days he was watched by the local pork butcher 'Porky' Naunton, a verger in the church, who wore a red wig that let the air in at the sides causing it to balloon. Richmond remembered an amusing story told to him by Naunton during the course of their long friendship:

"*There was an elderly maiden lady who attended church throughout the hot weather, and Porky, with an eye to a tip, every Sunday morning brought into church and put under his seat a bottle of water with a glass in readiness for any collapse among members of the congregation. Now a good many girls in the hot weather were apt to feel faint and leave the church, but they were no good for it, and on this elderly lady centred all the hopes of Porky. 'Oh, Sir' he said tragically, 'I **did** think I should get her!' But the old girl's as hard as nails, and I've had all my work for nothing.*"[8]

In an age in which religious faith is frequently called into doubt, some look to the past in their search for spirituality. This has led to a heightened sense of loss over the beautiful things that have been stripped out of our churches and destroyed. Sir John Betjeman summed these feelings up when he wrote:

"*And now it is all gone — like an insubstantial pageant faded; and between us and the old English there lies a gulf of mystery which the prose of the historian will never adequately bridge.*"

Ironically, it is our spiritual rather than our temporal legacy that has proved more enduring, and church is a place where religious mysteries continue to take place. Apparently one of them is unique to Southwold. As soon as the first chapel had been replaced by the present church, the yard that surrounded it was found to be inadequate and so, in April 1458, the priors of St. Peter's, Wangford and St. Mary, Thetford were persuaded to grant the people of Southwold a larger share of the surrounding land to the south and west. All the monks required in return was that an offering be made on the high altar on the anniversary of the feast day of St. John the Baptist. It was to be no more, or less, than a single rose (see illustration below).

The Dunwich Rose *by Charlotte Gere. Watercolour on paper. 2005.*
In 1839 Robert Wake observed that the Dunwich Rose, with its heart-shaped petals and tiny fretted leaves, grew all over Southwold, Reydon and Covehithe. It still survives on the north side of Southwold's churchyard where it has grown since the fifteenth century. The rose varies in colour from white to pale pink and yellow and has been immortalised by the Suffolk poet James Bird:

> There smiles the Dunwich rose with spotless blossom,
> White, pure, and soft as the cygnet's bosom.

A romantic tradition has it that this little rose was brought down from the north of England by the monks and planted in Dunwich. Its fragile beauty has caught the imagination of a number of writers including Edward Fitzgerald and Henry James.

IN THE SHADOW OF THE CITY

The Saxon city of Dunwich lies three miles south of Southwold, and most of it is under the sea. Bede (673-735), in the early eighth century, is said to have called it 'Dummoc', which, ironically, means deep water. It is difficult to believe that a low cliff is now all that remains of the thriving city that throughout the thirteenth century was Suffolk's chief port. In those days the river Blyth came from Blythburgh through Southwold and, turning south, met the little river Dunwich before finding the sea just north of the city. The evolution of this fine harbour and its eventual decay became a seesaw of fate with Southwold. The sad sequence of events is neatly summed up in the title of Thomas Gardner's book of 1754 *An Historical Account of Dunwich, antiently a City, now a Borough, Blithburgh, Formally a Town of Note, now a Village, Southwold, once a Village now a Town-corporate.*

The foundation of Dunwich is very ancient, and it may even have Roman origins. Described as a "*cultivated place*" in the seventh century, it was here that St. Felix based his East Anglian See; but the succession of bishops of Dunwich came to an end with the death of St. Edmund at the hands of the Danes in the ninth century. The *Domesday Book* tells us that Dunwich had one church; by 1086 two further churches had been added and the population had increased to 3,000. Even then the sea had begun to devour the agricultural land, nonetheless, the town's prosperity gradually increased and, by the beginning of the reign of Henry II, it was described as a "*rich, moated town defended with palisades*". In 1296 Dunwich returned two members of Parliament and continued to do so until the rotten borough was disfranchised in 1832.

During the twelfth century population growth and building development resulted in the establishment of eight parishes: St. Leonard, St. John the Baptist, St. Martin, St. Nicholas, St. Peter, St. Michael, St. Bartholomew, and All Saints. These and their stone churches were a statement of faith in Dunwich's future that was sadly misplaced; following the storm of 1286, the sea, which had provided everything, was eventually to take it all away again.

Opposite:

Dunwich Church *by Michael (Angelo) Rooker (1743-1801). Watercolour on paper. c.1770.*

This romantic watercolour shows the ruins of the best known, and last remaining, of Dunwich's eight parish churches: All Saints. Probably built by Richard Russell, it was, at 147 feet long (44.8m), just a little larger than Southwold's church, but lacking its height and volume. By the late 1750s All Saints had been abandoned. The sea was still seventy yards away (64m), but the decay of the building and the inability of the community of no more than a hundred souls to finance necessary repairs, had already resulted in its closure. Souvenir hunters hastened the destruction. One of them was Henry Negus of Harleston, who visited the church on 29 August 1770 with the intention of stealing memorial brasses from the floor. He was unsettled by the gloomy atmosphere, which pervaded the place: "When on my entrance the first thing which presented itself to my view was a majestic owl flying from the desk ... On the floor and pews is nothing but the worlds of that bird and dirt driven off the top, some part of which is exposed to the boisterous elements."

Victoria and Albert Museum

Dunwich had once been the major mercantile port of East Anglia, but it had always been at risk from the ever-changing coastline and the banks of loose sand that built up on the riverbed. In anticipation of trouble ahead the seamen would recite the following as the harbour mouth hove into view:

> *To Dunwich, Soul, and Walberswick,*
> *We pass in a lousy creek.*

Despite these famous hazards, trade and fishing remained the source of Dunwich's great prosperity. Vessels travelled as far as Iceland in search of sperling, and herring, sales of which were strictly monitored and taxed; and the city grew rich on the proceeds. In the reign of King Henry III the harbour mouth ran through land that belonged to one William Helmet who charged every vessel 4d for passage and the same again for anchorage. This was considered damaging to trade and so the town was given a royal grant of £47 10 shillings to remove the mouth of its harbour and thereby avoid the tolls.[1] However, the King's money was wasted: in January 1328 a strong northeasterly wind blocked the harbour mouth, and this was the beginning of Dunwich's steepest spiral of decline. Every effort to reverse the damage failed. The river Blyth burst out about two miles north, but became blocked again from about 1366. Another harbour mouth was cut and was in use until 1464; in the end, a total of four separate attempts were made to dig out a permanent haven before 1589.[2] Its position was critical for trade and, naturally, the townspeople of Dunwich wanted it to be as close to their town as possible, but those of Southwold and Walberswick insisted the haven should be between the two. Dunwich fought for its ancient rights, but its determination was tempered by the fact that an incalculable human effort and the huge sum of £300 had already been wasted in the digging of new harbour mouths. The town was greatly impoverished as a result. This lack of resolve must have been obvious and, in 1546, the people of Southwold and Walberswick forcibly opened the harbour at the site where it remains to this day. Dunwich sued the bailiffs of Southwold and the men of Walberswick for restitution but, after 10 years in the courts, they lost. Whilst they were busy fighting that battle, they were losing a more fundamental and important one on another front: the coastal erosion that had begun in the early thirteenth century was devastating the town. It was not only the power of the waves, but also the inability of the coastline to resist them, that was to prove a uniquely destructive combination. This was:

"... a coast destitute of rocks, or some artificial means of preservation [that] lies exposed to the constant assaults of the raging waves of the sea, which are observed to fret the high ground more than the low beach; as is manifestly apparent by Dunwich, Southwold, Easton, Pakefield, ... which have no sands lying off them to break the seas."[3]

The fate of the beleaguered inhabitants of Dunwich was well known in London and practical solutions were abandoned in favour of financial aid. This took the form of a

Saxon capitals in the walls of the church of the Hospice of St. James, Dunwich, Suffolk *by Thomas Hearne (1744-1817). Watercolour on paper. c.1786.*
Through fear of contagion this leper hospital, built c.1150, had been positioned outside the town. As a picturesque ruin it caught the attention of a number romantic artists who attempted to capture the tragic atmosphere of a town that had succumbed to the sea. This was accurately evoked by The Rev. Alfred Suckling who in 1848 wrote that "Dunwich is wasted, desolate and void. Its palaces and temples are no more and its very environs present an aspect lonely, stern and wild."   Fitzwilliam Museum, Cambridge

series of tax rebates and cash. In 1553 Queen Elizabeth I heard that Dunwich was "*daylie wasted and devoured*" by "*the rage and surgies of the sea*". As a relief fund, she granted it the proceeds from the sale of bells, lead, iron, glass and stone from the derelict Suffolk church at Ingate that amounted to £76 18s 4d. To this the Queen added the value of the lead that remained over the ruined chancel of St Edmund's, Kessingland.

In the end, the destruction of Dunwich included the loss of all eight churches, the town gates and hall, the crosses, the almshouses, hospitals, shops and private houses, the windmill, the prison and several cemeteries. The inhabitants must have been frightened and desperate, but Thomas Gardner seems to have been the only one to record the grim process of desolation properly. He was in Dunwich in December 1740 when the "*insulting waves*" pounded the cliff for days. It was a scene of wild confusion where foundations, naked wells, stone coffins and skeletons were exposed and the magnificent tower of All Saints was brought closer and closer to oblivion.

Even by the late fifteenth century the ancient city was fatally diminished and, although Southwold was the younger sister of Dunwich, Blythburgh and Walberswick, it eventually surpassed them in navigation, traffic and trade. Industry and good service had been recognised by Henry VII when in 1489 he had granted the town a charter that not only freed it from previous subservience to Dunwich, but made it a legal entity all of its own. In the charter he gave Southwold the privileges of the haven and it was probably at this point that it became known as the Port of Southwold rather than the Port of Dunwich. Henry VIII added to these privileges in the form of gifts, franchises and immunities, which proved to be a powerful incentive to the town's old established fishing trade. Ironically, it was this same monarch who was inadvertently to pitch Southwold's main industry into a decline: his break with Rome and the establishment of the Church of England meant that Catholic dietary restrictions were lifted and meat was allowed on the table when fish had frequently been mandatory. The 50 fishing vessels that operated from Southwold Harbour were obliged to supplement their decreasing income by trading in corn, timber, coal, butter and cheese. Some were engaged in whaling and brought raw blubber back to Southwold, where it was refined into oil in special pans, situated at Woods End Creek (Buss Creek), far enough away from the town to cause the least possible offence.

The very different circumstances of the neighbouring towns were highlighted when King Charles I began to raise money to finance a programme of shipbuilding. A tax of £8 was levied on Southwold but, despite its glorious history, Dunwich was asked for only half this sum. Not for long did the people of Southwold enjoy their ascendancy over the beleaguered city: in 1659 it was the turn of their town to be laid waste, not by water, but by fire.

All Saint's Church, Dunwich *by Bertram Priestman. 1920.*

Priestman was an artist who loved landscape and sky and found them in abundance when he came to the East Coast to paint. He was hailed as a "modern Constable", though in this instance he shared his inspiration with Turner who had *visited the remains of All Saints, Dunwich in 1824. Since the 1870s the ruins of the magnificent fourteenth century church had fallen, arch by arch, into the sea until just the tower remained. The steamship to the left of the composition emphasises the antiquity of the ruin that, for Priestman, was evidently an emblem of man's continuing struggle with nature. Despite the temporary gloom cast by a large cloud, holiday-makers enjoy the view. The tombstone to the left is the last to remain of hundreds that have already succumbed to the waves below. It is a poignant reminder that even the happiest sunny day is no more than a brief reprieve from oblivion.* Private Collection

THE PHOENIX BOROUGH

25 April 1659 was a Sunday. The days were lengthening, wild apples were in blossom and the wheatear had recently come to Gun Hill to feed on the gorse. The first haunting song of the nightingale could be heard at Henham and the swallows had returned to Southwold.[1] That morning the heavy bronze bells turned full circle in the church tower and it shook with the volume of the deafening peals. Uplifted by this glorious sound and the lengthening days there was a feeling of fresh hope in the Spring air. As the congregation sauntered to church, thorny wild roses snagged their plain woollen cloaks billowing in the breeze (see illustration on p.41). The bells fell silent and the congregation was seated, and it was probably the curate John Goldsmith who asked the people to give thanks to Almighty God for everything they had. For the majority this added up to very little. In fact the town was in a bad way: owing to the silting up of the harbour and the "*want of fishing*", poverty was rife. As a result of the Dutch wars there were many widows and dependent children amongst the 2,000 parishioners and, only five years before, Oliver Cromwell had been told that the borough was "*at present destitute*".[2]

Sea-faring folk are especially sensitive to changes in the weather, but none of them could have guessed that the gentle swaying of the trees was the first sign that a "*violent and boisterous*" wind was steadily gaining strength; a wind that was shortly to be Southwold's complete undoing.[3]

Overnight, in one of the buildings on East Cliff, a fire got out of control. Sparks and flames were fanned by what had now developed into a fierce gale, and the flames spread with terrifying speed. The alarm was raised and the people of Southwold tried desperately to halt the awful destruction. However, their fight against the inferno was pitifully inadequate: pails of water from the well in the Market Place did next to nothing to damp down the roaring flames as they tore through the timber frames of the houses and burst through the dry reed roofs. In the immediate path of the flames, courageous efforts must have been made to pull the thatch from the houses with the long-handled hooks stored in the church for this very purpose. Some must have tried to drench the walls of their wattle and daub houses using leather buckets filled from nearby water butts, whilst others tried to beat it out by wielding poles with mop heads full of water, known as maulkins. These brave efforts, however, were to no avail. Noise, fear and chaos were everywhere and, through the smoke, the people of Southwold watched, powerless, as 238 houses burned to the ground. It was cruel enough that 300 hundred families had been made homeless in just four hours, but worse was to come in the form of the economic collapse and the starvation that resulted from this disaster.

The town hall had been razed to the ground and so too the market place, the market house, prison, shops, granaries and warehouses. Fish stores, malt houses, tackle sheds, brew houses and other out-houses were also reduced to ashes. The fire had spread at such a pace that it was impossible to save even the movable goods. It was the loss of fishing nets that was the worst blow, and with all the corn, malt, barley, dried fish and coal gone too, the result was "*the utter undoing and impoverishing*" of the people.[4] Standing to the north of the town and protected by its yard, the church survived and we can be certain that hundreds of destitute people took temporary shelter there that night, sharing with one another the details of the tragedy.

Strangely, no visual representation of the Southwold fire survives, or indeed any first-hand account of it. Nonetheless, such tragedy was commonplace enough to inspire an unnamed writer to describe another conflagration that almost precisely anticipates Southwold's terrible destruction. His poem was written in black letter and was found hidden in the binding of a book in the library of The Royal Society:

> *But now beholde my great decay,*
> *which on a sodaine came;*
> *My sumptuous buildings burned be*
> *By force of fires flame;*
> *A careless wretch, most rude in life,*
> *His chimney set on fire,*
> *The instrument, I must confesse,*
> *Of God's most heavie ire.*
> *The flame whereof increasing still*
> *The blustering windes did blowe,*
> *And into divers buildings by*
> *Disperst it to and fro;*
> *So kindling in most grievous sort,*
> *It waxed huge and hie;*
> *The river then was frozen, so*
> *No water they could come by.*

News of Southwold's destruction spread quickly. As a result, immediate relief came from Yarmouth in the form of 20 combs of wheat, 20 of rye and £10 in cash[5]; and there must have been individual acts of charity that remain unrecorded. However, these were short-term solutions for a long-term problem.

On 4 May six local Justices of the Peace issued a certificate that they had "*taken a view of the sad ruines of the said towne*" and assessed the damage done by the fire to amount to the monumental sum of £40,000. It was quickly decided that the Bailiffs and Commonality of Southwold should apply to Parliament for Letters Patent to allow the collection of charity throughout England and Wales. In what must have been one of the very first nationwide fund-raising campaigns, parsons, ministers, lecturers, vicars and

Fire at the huts on Walberswick beach *by Richard Scott. Oil on board. 2003.*
Though there is no pictorial record of the terrible conflagration that devastated Southwold in 1659, we know its beginnings were small. This painting is a warning of the danger of an unguarded fire on a dry summer's night.

Author's Collection © Richard Scott

curates in every church throughout the land were asked to "*exhort and stir up*" their congregations to help the homeless of Southwold. Copies of the letters were sent to Mayors, Bailiffs, Head Officers, Chief Magistrates and Chief Constables in an effort to give the disaster maximum publicity and to pave the way for a nationwide door-to-door collection. In the country parish of Bidford in Warwickshire in 1661 the total raised was an impressive £5 and 2 shillings. In Harleston cum Redenhall on 17 August 1659 an even larger total had been achieved:

Recd. Of Mr John Hubberd, and Mr Fenn the briefe for Sourthwold wth fifteene ponds eleaven shillings five pence halpennye, and two od pieces of money to the value of foure pence collected in Harlston cum Reddenhall and Wortwell for the rebuilding of the said towne."

The results of this extraordinary relief effort allowed Southwold to make a hesitant recovery, but it was nearly a century before the "*languishing condition*" of the people was appreciably improved and the "*ruinous heap*" of the harbour was restored to its former splendour.

Fire was often a hazard in ancient, densely populated settlements built of flammable materials and this is how Southwold was before the eighteenth century when the use of bricks and tiled roofs became commonplace. Essential for cooking, for warmth and for a degree of light, a fire was maintained in every house. Accidents were bound to happen and they did, with devastating results: in Beccles in 1539, 1586 and 1662; in Lowestoft 1644, 1670 and 1717; in Bungay in 1652 and 1688; and in Ipswich in 1654. In 1666, only seven years after Southwold's own terrible conflagration, the Great Fire of London, which started in a baker's oven in Pudding Lane, was to raze the capital of the nation to the ground. There, fire followed the plague, but in Southwold the converse was true. Only four years after the town had been laid waste it was visited by "*a contagious infection*" of which 312 died.

These awful tragedies came at a time when the fortunes of Southwold were at low ebb and, in this regard, it shared the same fate as its once prosperous neighbour, Blythburgh. This former town had gradually declined after Henry VIII suppressed the Priory of the Blessed Virgin in 1534 with the final blow coming in 1676 when the fire that tore through the town resulted in damage estimated at £1803. Some of the inhabitants were unable to rebuild their houses, and some unwilling, and the place was virtually deserted. Only 21 houses survived the fire and the inhabitants were no more than 124.

Walberswick was once a hamlet of Blythburgh and, to some extent, it mirrored its fate, though fire had an even bigger part to play in its decline. Walberswick was burnt on at least four different occasions. First in 1583 and then, for a second time, in 1631 when the best part of the settlement was destroyed. Forty houses were consumed by fire and the human suffering must have been terrible. The tragedy was compounded when it was discovered that the fire had been set by arsonists, one of whom was a child. The diary of John Rous relates his pitiless end:

"Two women and a boy of sixteen executed at Bury, on the 18th July, for burning Walberswick. The boy upon his death, affirmed that his sister councelled and the other woman gave him fire."

In 1683 Walberswick was on fire for a third time, and in 1749 that small part which remained was also reduced to ashes. In this instance the circumstances are recorded and, as at Southwold, a fierce wind was to blame for the spread of sparks from a chimney fire. The burning thatch from the roof was carried 90 yards to the thatch of the Alms Houses and caught it alight. From there it blew over 130 yards to a cottage and several other dwellings, barns, stables, and outhouses. The heat was so intense that two green ash trees in the path of the fire were completely consumed and several fences and enclosures went the same way. The spread was halted by some tiled houses, which acted as a firebreak, otherwise every last bit of Walberswick would have been razed to the ground.

In Southwold new building materials and the open spaces provided by the greens – once thought to have been designed to prevent any further devastation – meant that it was never at the same degree of risk again. However, there remained a deep-seated terror of a similar disaster. In 1822 a fire engine was purchased for the town and a measure of its importance is shown by the fact that the corporation contributed the substantial sum of £36 to the cost. It was in use from time to time when isolated fires broke out. The diarist James Maggs recorded in 1857 that lives had been put in peril owing to the cheapness and widespread availability of 'lucifer' (friction) matches. In Walberswick in 1861 three cottages were destroyed when the children of a labourer called Knights were playing with them. One of them, terrified by the fire, hid in the attic and was saved just moments before the thatched roof fell in.[6]

Following their destruction neither Blythburgh nor Walberswick ever recovered their former glories. It was only Southwold that rose from its own ashes to assume its prosperous modern identity. Copyholders' leases had been destroyed and, consequently, they became freeholders; properly spaced development and improved fire-fighting technology meant that the town was no longer at serious risk. Ironically, it was not fire but water that was to prove the next real threat to Southwold and its power and volume was limitless, as it came from the sea.

Blythburgh church, Suffolk *by John Preston Neale (1780-1847). Watercolour on paper. 1808.*
The magnificent Church of Holy Trinity. The length of the nave is cleverly suggested by the shadow it casts in the afternoon sun. The village whipping post is positioned in front of the East Window. The artist was sitting in Priory Road when he made this delicate drawing. Victoria & Albert Museum

AN ELEMENTAL STRUGGLE

On the morning of 4 Sunday August 1577, between 9 and 10 o'clock in the morning, John Righton, the minister of Holy Trinity, Blythburgh, was reading the second lesson when a "*strange and terrible tempest of lightning and thunder*" broke through the side of the church and left a hole in the floor that was almost three feet deep. This was followed by another bolt that split the wall up to the revestry and cleaved the door in half. At the same time, the tower itself was hit by a lightning flash that split the timbers of the cradle supporting the bells and broke their chains. The entire congregation was traumatised and at least 20 parishioners were in the direct path of the first bolt and were floored by it. They were "*found groveling more than half an hour after, whereof a man and a boy were found dead; the others were scorched.*"[1]

The recovery of the wreck of the Thos. Betsey of Southwold *by Henry Davy. Watercolour on paper. 1839. The wreck of a cargo ship was brought ashore at Southwold and was the subject of a series of drawings by Davy, which are dated 1839. Note the lookout on the harbour arm and the tall net sheds beyond it. Walberswick church is just discernable in the distance. Salvage has been recovered from the wreck and is strewn all over the beach next to the mast and rudder.* John Tooke Esq.

At about the same time, in Bungay, the tempest took the form of a thunder ball, which entered the church of St. Mary and snapped back the necks of two of the congregation, killing them instantly. The terrifying force of the storm led the locals to believe they had been visited by Shuck, the spectral hellhound of East Anglia. A clergyman called Abraham Fleming described the scene in a paper entitled *A Strange and Terrible Wunder wrought very late in the parish Church of Bungay*:

"*Immediately hereupon, there appeared in a most horrible similitude and likenesse to the congregation... a dog as they might discerne it of a black colour ...together with fearful flashes of fire ... which ... moved such admiration in the minds of the assemblie, that they thought doomsday had already come.*"

A Ship Aground *by J.M.W. Turner. Oil on canvas. c.1828.*

This painting was finished less than four years after Turner's visit to Southwold and it is apparent from the conjunction of the land, sea and the rising sun that it was a sight he encountered on his travels along the East Coast. A ship has run aground within striking distance of a man-made haven and at first light a boat puts out to salvage the stricken vessel. The wooden pier to the left bears a striking similarity to that built on the south side of Southwold harbour in 1752 (see illustrations on pp.65 and 150). Until the first lighthouse was erected on California Sands, Southwold, in 1888, ships were frequently grounded and wrecked on the treacherous sandbanks to the north and south of Sole Bay. Tate Britain

The barque *Princess Augusta* of London stranded on the beach at Southwold in the morning of 28th October 1838.

The ship, weighing 308 tons, ran aground 400 hundred yards north of the North Pier of the old Southwold harbour on its way from St. Petersburg, laden with hemp and linseed. Though the vessel was completely wrecked, all the crew were saved. The vessel and cargo were salvaged by Benjamin Palmer and sold for £150 to John Magub and company. The beleaguered ship was secured with the use of capstans on the shoreline and the cargo was carried away on wagons as the townspeople looked on.

Before the building of the first lighthouse, the church tower and its high flagpole acted as a warning to shipping. In this instance it failed to prevent the Princess Augusta from running aground. The figurehead from the wreck is now on permanent loan to the Southwold Museum.

This print, issued by Day and Haghe, lithographers to the Queen, was taken from an original painting produced on the spot by Captain Henry Alexander and in his possession. It was published by John Berney Ladbrooke, a Norwich School painter and lithographer, who is believed to have been a pupil of his uncle John Crome. This is the only known work of art by Captain Alexander and it appears to owe more than a little to the influence of Henry Davy.

The National Maritime Museum

Lightning, deluges, gales, storms and flood tides are a perpetual menace in Southwold even to this day. In the past, however, when they came with little or no warning, the effects on both land and sea could be devastating. Wrecks were commonplace and, as a result, claim to them has always been a lucrative part of the manorial rights of the town.[2] There is no doubt that the pattern of these disasters was established long ago, but only in the eighteenth and nineteenth centuries did it begin to be properly recorded. The majority of wrecks resulted not only in loss of property, but also in pitiful struggles for survival. Frequently, these were acted out in Sole Bay and, whenever possible, Southwold's fishermen made brave attempts to save the beleaguered crews. In 1794 the *Philip and Ann* was beyond all help when she was wrecked under Easton Cliff; fifteen men and one woman perished in the waves. Only eight years later,

Above and opposite:
Southwold and Dunwich, *a pair of oil paintings by Thomas Smythe (1825-1906).*
The sea dominates the composition in both.
(Above) Southwold. *A fisherman's boat occupies the foreground with a distant view of the town behind it. Both St. Edmund's Church and the 'Casino' are clearly discernable. The sea is calm and fishing lines are being stretched out into the sea.*
(Oppposite) Dunwich. *The coastline of the ancient city has been disastrously eroded and most of it has fallen into the sea. In a vain attempt to halt the incessant destruction, crude wooden defences were built beneath the cliffs. In the picture two ladies and a child are taking the air whilst the sea crashes against the palings, hinting at the true potential of its destructive energy.*

Private Collection. Photograph: Burlington Paintings, London

the *Frederick* was lost off Southwold with all its crew. However, in January 1831 all on board the wrecked brig *Cumberland* were saved by the Southwold pilots John Montague and John Lowsey.[3]

As traffic on the sea greatly increased, so too did the number of disasters in the Bay and on Barnard Sands, which lie just north of Covehithe. There, in the early 1830s, a bearded hermit made a collection of figure heads from the numerous ships wrecked beneath the cliffs and turned it into a famous curiosity. In Southwold it was felt that the lives of fishermen were all too frequently put at risk in their rescue attempts and on 18 December 1840 a general meeting was held to establish a lifeboat for the town at a cost of £400.

The lifeboat station became active in August 1841 and the full threat of the weather on the East Coast was felt just a few months later. On 14 November a southeasterly gale gathered strength and blew for four days, during which no fewer than six ships had been wrecked. On the fifth day, the storm gathered even greater momentum only to subside immediately and be followed by a thick fog.

The calm after the storm is when the sea gives up her dead, and the majority of those who were washed up on Southwold beach were interred in its churchyard. In 1806 a Prussian officer was heading for England to deliver documents from the Emperor to his ambassador at the court of St. James. He was a passenger in a boat sent from the *Burletta* to the harbour where there was a postal facility in operation. On the way, the four-oared galley was upset on the sand bank and the messenger was drowned. His body

York Cliff, Southwold *by Henry Davy. Sepia on paper. 1835.*
A man is seated on the cliff top looking out to a sea teeming with traffic, there is a capstan in the foreground. Inadequate sea defences allowed the sandy cliff at Southwold to be badly eroded by heavy seas. On 31 October 1827 an unusually high tide coincided with a gale and the sea pounded against the cliff for days. According to Robert Wake the "sea [was] rolling tremendously" *against the cliffs and the* "Southwold people [were] thrown into great consternation."   The British Library

was decently buried in St. Edmund's yard in a quiet grave, but a long way from home.[4]

Sometimes the deceased were robbed of their identity by the tragic circumstances of their end. On 20 September 1843 the body of a sailor was washed into the harbour and James Maggs had the unpleasant task of searching his pockets for clues to his identity, though found none.[5] On 6 January 1853 the corpse of a man, naked except for a piece of flannel shirt marked 'XW', came ashore and was interred in Southwold.[6] Just five years later the body of an infant girl was found on the tide line, her tragic end the subject of morbid speculation.[7] The fate of those who drowned in the North Sea was chillingly articulated in a poem entitled *The Change* by the Suffolk poet George Crabbe (1754-1832):

There was a dreadful Storm at Sea
And bodies strewed the pebbly shore:
Behold them all from Misery free,
They feel the ills of life no more—
They are not rich, they are not poor;
They cannot think, they cannot weep:
Will you their happy State deplore,
The lasting, pure, unruffled Sleep?

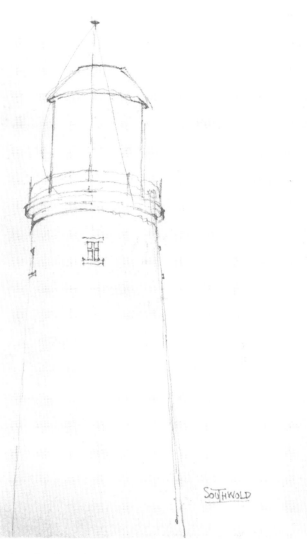

Storms and persistent gales not only cost lives, but also fouled the harbour mouth. This had been the undoing of Dunwich and naturally the people of Southwold were keen to avoid the same fate. By the end of the sixteenth century the fishing trade, on which the town's prosperity depended, was in a depressed state. A letter from the bailiffs to Milton, the secretary to the Protector, suggested that one of the reasons for the decline was the "*impairing of the harbour*". Thanks to human effort and a good deal of luck the situation gradually improved and by the mid-eighteenth century trade had increased to the point that something needed to be done to stabilise the haven. In 1746 the Borough of Southwold relinquished control of the harbour to a board of Commissioners who were later responsible for the building of the north pier in 1749 and the south pier in 1752. The permanence and safety they provided meant that Southwold was soon to become the headquarters of the Free British Fishery. Despite these ambitious engineering works the haven was repeatedly fouled and had to be dug out thirteen times between 1805 and 1818; continuing vigilance has been exercised ever since.

When Southwold harbour was threatened by the elements, so too was the fabric of the town. The low cliffs on which it was built had next to no protection to limit the pounding of the waves driven by North Easterly winds (see illustration on p.62). When

Southwold Lighthouse *by Charles Rennie Mackintosh. Pencil on paper.*
The artist's attention has been caught by the simple monumentality of the tower. One-and-a-half million bricks was used in its construction, which was completed in September 1890. It stands 101 feet (30.8m) high and the light from the lantern, weighing 18 tons (18.3 tonnes), is visible from 18 sea miles away. It was a highly effective aid to navigation and greatly reduced the incidence of wrecks on the East Coast. Today its function has been superseded by modern technology, but the lighthouse continues to be one of the focal points of the town. Photo © Hunterian Museum and Art Gallery, University of Glasgow, Mackintosh Collection

Crossing the Bar, Walberswick Sands *by Henry Moore (1831-1895). Watercolour on paper (see illustration on p.228).*

Painted from Southwold, the scene shows a fishing boat striking out to sea at dawn. Moore was the brother of Albert J. Moore (1841-1893), who is famous as a neo-classical painter. Both were inspired by the Pre-Raphaelites, but, in 1857, Albert turned to sea painting for which he is best remembered. Moore was one of the few who was "brave enough to paint the sea" in the words of the poet George Crabbe at Southwold. (See p.18). Abbott and Holder

Above:

The windmill (Walberswick) *by Edward Arthur Walton (1860-1922). c.1910.*

There was a succession of windmills on the high ground surrounding the flood plain of the river Blyth. In the 1830s there had been two on Southwold Common. Walberswick Mill was believed to be haunted by the ghost of a tall woman, whose skeleton was exhumed when the foundations of the mill were first dug. Edward Walton, who was head of the Life Department at Glasgow Art School, arranged a long-term tenancy of the Old Vicarage at Wenhaston in about 1900. Dundee City Art Gallery

Opposite:

Into Port *by Frank Brangwyn (1857-1956). Oil on canvas. 1894.*

A fishing ship returns to a harbour with two piers – evidently Southwold.

The vessel, with three masts, is of approximately 500 tons. It is a type that frequented the harbour and braved the German Ocean as far as Iceland in search of fish stocks. Brangwyn remembered these ships in a letter he wrote fifty years later to Cecil H. Lay (1855-1956) on 14th November 1946:

"Walberswick must have been a fine place when the whalers etc. used to sail out of the port, a busy place. I fear all is gone. The old piers etc. and the many sheds etc. Perhaps there is a good book written about these places ... if so let me know the publisher." The Witt Library, The Courtauld Institute of Art

these coincided with high tides the effects could be catastrophic. The highest tide recorded was on 3 February 1790, which flooded the marshes to a depth of 6 to 7 feet (1.8 - 2.1m).[8] On 1 November 1827 there was an another very high tide and the waves pounded the shoreline until 10 to 12 feet (3 - 3.6m) had fallen away from Gun Hill and left it undermined to the extent that large masses of the cliff collapsed during the following days. The walk between Gun Hill and New York Cliff lost some 6 to 7 feet (1.8 - 2.1m), and, on the beach, a boathouse built in 1818 for the use of the Queen's Preventative Service was washed away completely. As a result of these losses the first sea defences at the foot of Gun Hill were begun and finished a decade later. However, these were to prove ineffectual and were later described in Maggs's diaries as a "*wretched work of rotten stakes, miss-called a breakwater*". In 1849 the town was left unprotected and James Maggs recorded that there had been a very heavy swell and run from the sea that had coincided with a high tide and he observed that "*the sea must have swept a great part of our cliff away, if not the town*".

A lass that loved a sailor *by Walter Langley (1852-1922). Watercolour on paper. c.1890.*

A beautiful young woman awaits the return of the fishing boats from which she will unload the catch of herrings in to wicker baskets and salt them from the bags to her right. She leans on the long arm of a capstan used to pull the boats up the beach; there were several of this type at Southwold just north of the harbour mouth.

Although the sea is calm, the constant risk of drowning blighted the lives of fishermen and their families (see illustration on p.71). The elderly couple on the right have come safely to the end of theirs together. However, this young woman faces the very real prospect of a lonely widowhood.

Loss at sea was a favourite subject for Walter Langley. Although he worked in Newlyn, he made several visits to Southwold in the early 1890s.

Private collection on loan to
Penlee House Gallery and Museum, Penzance

Mending the nets *by Joseph Southall. Tempera. 1904.*

The lengthening shadows show that it is evening as father and son mend their nets on Southwold beach. The white smock indicates that the scene was painted on a Sunday. Southall was a strict Quaker and could not have failed to notice a parallel between the simple lives of the Southwold fishermen and those of Christ's disciples at the Sea of Galilee: "James the son of Zebedee and John his brother, in the boat with Zebedee, their father mending nets." (Matthew 4: 21). The shoreline, horizon and sweeping contours of their boat give a strong sense of perspective to this painting. On its heart-shaped stern is painted "S'WOLD STANNARD". The Stannards were a well known family of fishermen in the 19th and early 20th centuries. Evidently this is a portrait of Edward "Blondin" Stannard (b.1868) and his son Christmas, who was born 24 December 1891 and died in 1954. The Fine Art Society

Further erosion finally decided the Mayor and Town Council to send for a distinguished civil engineer to inspect the sea defences so that Gun Hill and the town might be saved. Only four years later, in 1853, the situation had grown acute. On the 23 February a high tide combined with a northeasterly wind had eroded Gun Hill as far as Long Island Cliff, scarcely leaving space for the bathing machines. The ground that supported the flagpole in front of New York Cliff was all washed away and there remained only about four-and-a-half feet (1.4m) in front of the Coastguard's Watch House. Gas pipes were cracked and left protruding from the cliff and there was a serious risk of explosion. Gun Hill was described as being "*much injured*" and

Up from the Sea *by Joseph Southall. Tempera on linen. 1920.*
This vigorous painting shows Southwold fishermen returning home from a fishing trip. The figures to the right represent three generations of a Southwold fishing family, and the boy in the foreground, the fourth. The long leather boots with thick wooden soles were studded with nails and were supplied by a cobbler called John Harrington in the High Street. They were perfect protection from the cold and wet, but in the event of capsizing or falling overboard prevented the wearer from swimming to safety. In 1920 a fisherman's wife called Victoria Palmer warned her new husband of the danger: "But I told him, lad, I said, them long leather legs'll kill you, bor." (See illustration on p.226). Castle Museum, Nottingham

the earth so loosened that there was a risk of losing it altogether. Groynes and faggot pilings were immediately installed at a cost of about £300 but proved to be ineffectual when the sea carried them away completely. An efficient breakwater or jetty was required; the estimated cost was £1200. In 1862 the beach was still inadequately protected and, according to cuttings in Maggs's diaries, just four days before Christmas all the picturesque fisherman's cottages were gone and "*destruction and desolation greeted you at every step*".

Even modern sea defences failed to resist the storms of February 1938 and, the most damaging of all, of 31 January 1953. The force of the northerly winds that day was so great that it generated a surge of water and a rise in sea level that, combined with a

Left:

Portrait of the Old Southwold Pensioner *by Charles Keene. Etching. Published by Sampson, Low, Marston & Co. Ltd.*

This is a portrait of an old ferryman who, when age and infirmity prevented him from working, was enabled, by the generosity of the artist Charles Keene (see p.200) and other friends, to keep his home and live in comfort for the rest of his life. Here we see him passing the time by mending nets.

Reproduced from *The Life and Letters of Charles Keene* by George Somes Layard 1892

Opposite:

Below East Cliff, Southwold *by Walter Crane (1845-1915). Watercolour. 1886.*

Before they were finally washed away in the storms of 1905, the fishermen's huts that lined the base of the cliff were recorded by the famous Aesthetic painter, designer and illustrator Walter Crane. The travel writer William. A. Dutt caught the atmosphere of the place in 1901. "... I am in the midst of a curious colony, consisting of a marvellous collection of wooden huts of all shapes and sizes, in which the Southwold beachmen and longshore fishermen are busy net mending, sail tanning and boat repairing ... these strange shanties, filled with briny and tarry sea stores and the flotsam and jetsum of many a winter's gale. This is a place to hear all the yarns of wreck and rescue ... that are worth hearing, and, maybe some strange stories of the old smuggling days." In the collection of St. Felix School, Southwold

Below:

The Ark at Dunwich *by Edwin Edwards. Pencil on Paper. 19 June 1872.*

A capstan is in the foreground of an eccentric group of fishermen's sheds and above them stands The Ark, an inn built for the use of the local seamen. Like the ramshackle houses and sheds on Southwold beach (see illustration opposite), those at Dunwich were eventually washed away completely.

Birmingham City Museum and Art Gallery

high tide, had devastating effects on the town. The waves surmounted the sea wall and flooded the low lying land, turning Southwold into an island to which access was impossible until the flood waters subsided 48 hours later. The bungalows in Ferry Road were particularly vulnerable and five people were drowned when their homes were inundated.

In an age when the threat of global warming is blamed for what seem to be unprecedented and violent weather patterns, some comfort can be taken from the history of Southwold's struggle with the elements. On 17 August 1931 huge hail stones fell out of the summer sky without the slightest warning. In the meadows cattle stampeded and windows were broken throughout the town; on the beach the bathers were left bruised and bleeding. What is coming next is anybody's guess, but it is unlikely to surpass the sensational display that took place in Southwold on 26 May 1832. James Maggs described it as follows:

"*A ball of electric fluid fell on Gun Hill where it spent itself in five different zig-zag directions ... leaving its parched traces in the grass for days ...and in a regular form ...had they been laid out by scale and compass could not have been more exact.*"[9]

73

THE DARK SIDE

Southwold has not always been a happy place; inexplicably, the suicide rate has always been high though at least cold-bloodied murder was rare, if non-existent.[1] Nonetheless, the darkest aspects of human nature were not always in check and the consequences were sometimes shameful.

There must have been something in the character or appearance of Ann Camell that set her apart from her neighbours in Southwold. In 1649 some of them, knowing full well the hideous potential of their actions, set upon Ann and made accusations of felony and witchcraft for the third time. Although she was indicted in Southwold, her case was taken to Westminster on the grounds that the charge accused her of "*practicavit diabolicas artes*", but was not more specific about her crimes. The prisoner pleaded not guilty and as part of her defence noted that she had been twice acquitted on similar charges. She was given bail on the surety of her husband, Thomas, and of Zachary Baggs "*a sufficient Citizen and Fishmonger of London*". Eventually her case was heard at the Suffolk Assizes, but her fate is unrecorded.[2]

Ann was probably a woman of some standing in the town and it is likely that she was involved in the fishing trade. The Camells were a family with a long connection to Southwold and had made their mark there; at one time, part of Victoria Street was known as Camell's Lane. Ann's husband Thomas may have been the same man who was bailiff of the town in 1603. Whatever his status, it was no protection against one of the baser forms of religious excitement ever to be sanctioned by government.

In 1644 Parliament had commissioned Matthew Hopkins, known as the Witchfinder General, to visit the Eastern Counties and to purge them of witchcraft. He was energetic and ruthless in the prosecution of his duties and secured his first conviction in Ipswich where Old Mother Lakeland was burnt on 9 September 1645. The day before she met her terrible fate, Hopkins set off for Aldeburgh where he instigated the hanging of seven witches. The process of trial and execution cost the town £10 and 7 shillings, of which

---

Opposite:

Matthew Hopkins Witch Finder Generall *from* The Discovery of Witches *by Matthew Hopkins 1647.*

Two witches are examined by Matthew Hopkins, using one of his favourite techniques of discovery, which was to keep the prisoners awake for days in the centre of a large room with an open door to allow imps access.

On the left is Elizabeth Clark, an old beggar woman with a wooden leg who, in desperation, confessed to having imps in the form of a white kitten called Holt, a fat spaniel Jarmara, a black rabbit known as Sacke and Sugar, a polecat called Newes, and a greyhound with a bull's head known as Vinegar Tom. The other old woman accused of witchcraft confessed to having imps known as Ilemauzar, Pyewackett, Pecke in the Crowne, and Griezzell Greedigutt. She was convicted on the grounds that "no mortal could invent" such names.

The simple character of this print belies the awful truth. The naming of imps was tantamount to a confession of witchcraft and, for these desperate women, the door to the left of the hall led only to the gallows.

The Bridgeman Art Library

the Witchfinder received £6 and the hangman just the 7 shillings. Hopkin's favourite technique of discovery was to strip the victim and search for the concealed teats on which the devil's imps were suckled. These were probed with three-inch pins. If this process yielded nothing then the accused was "swum". During this awful process the thumbs and toes were tied crossways and the victim tossed into a convenient pond. If the body floated it was taken as proof of guilt, and if it sank, of innocence.

One of the worst cases of mob violence in Suffolk was of that against the octogenarian John Lowes, fifty years vicar of Brandeston, who was accused of witchcraft in 1645. During his inquisition he was kept awake for days and run about till breathless, after which he was "swum" in the moat at Framlingham Castle. He floated. On this evidence he was convicted, obliged to read the burial office on his own account, and was hanged whilst the townsfolk looked on.[3]

The Witchfinder, his accomplice John Stern and female "searcher" Mary Philips, riding on horseback, had passed very close to Southwold when they visited Halesworth. There a cooper, Thomas Evererd, and his wife Mary, are said to have "freely confessed" to bewitching beer:

"That the obnoxiousnesse of the infectious stinke of it was such and so intolerable that by the noyisomnesse of the same and tast many people dyed ... they also confessed to many other mischiefes ... damnable sorceries and that they also had their impes to whom they gave suck."

No matter how this confession was secured it led to the conviction of Mr and Mrs Evererd, and they were just two of eighteen men and women who were convicted at Bury St. Edmunds on 27 August 1645 and hanged.

In Southwold it was probably the voices of a few moderates that prevented the Witchfinder from wreaking awful havoc there. Nonetheless, there can be little doubt that it was knowledge of Hopkins's atrocities that inspired the persecution of the luckless Ann Camell. At the very least she knew that some of her neighbours wanted her dead and she was certainly in terror of examination by torture and the virtual certainty of being hanged or, if the budget allowed, burned at the stake.

Thankfully, the enthusiasm for these dreadful practices waned and, eventually, the Witchfinder himself was accused of witchery. Following his own methods of detection, his thumbs and toes were tied, he was "swum", floated, and was hanged in front of a crowd at Mistley-cum-Manningtree and was buried there on 12 August 1647.

What distinguishes the East Anglian witch trials from the majority of subsequent atrocities is that the victims shared the same environment, ancestry, religion and language as their persecutors. It is extremely unlikely that any of the condemned had much knowledge of the Wicca or any of the old religions, least of all Satanism. What really made them a target for their tormentors was that they were different. Age, ugliness, eccentricity and depression distinguished them and race rarely, if ever, sparked this kind of violence and evil. However, during the late eighteenth century black people were not an uncommon sight in England and the colour of their skin made them an obvious target for persecution. The tragic fate of a black soldier called Tobias Gill casts a dark shadow over the Blyth valley even to this day.

During the mid-eighteenth century smuggling and loss of revenue was at its height and the government was determined to eradicate it.[4] As a deterrent, the distinguished soldier and local dignitary, Lieutenant General Sir Robert Rich (1685-1768) of Roos Hall near Beccles, had stationed his detachment of Fourth Dragoons at Blythburgh. Exactly what practical part this old soldier played in its command is not known, but the troop was unruly, ill-disciplined and unpopular with local residents. Several incidents of crime and bad behaviour were reported in the *Ipswich Journal*; some of which may, of course, have been exaggerated by those with an interest in contraband.

The worst of these took place about a mile from Blythburgh in June 1750 when a local girl was murdered.[5] A musician from the 4th Dragoons was arrested and the *Ipswich Journal* took up the lurid story:

"Tobias Hill [sic], a black, one of the drummers in Sir Robert Rich's regiment was committed to Ipswich gaol, the coroner's enquiry having found him guilty of the murder of Ann Blakemore of Walberswick."

Tobias, nicknamed 'Black Tob' was described as tall and muscular, charming when sober and belligerent when drunk. At his trial at the Bury assizes part of the evidence against him was that he had been banned from several local beer houses. However, the real substance of the indictment was that Tobias had been discovered in a drunken stupor next to the body of the dead girl; he vigorously denied the murder, but his pleas were ignored. Eventually Tobias was convicted and was sentenced to death, his body then to be hung in chains on the spot where Anne Blakemore's body had been found. On 25 August 1750 the *Ipswich Journal* read:

"At Bury assizes, Toby Gil [sic], one of Sir Robert Rich's drummers received the death sentence for murder of Anne Blakemore of Walberswick, next Monday is appointed for his execution which will probably be at Ipswich and he is to be hanged in chains near the place where he committed the murder."

The Judge was surely no stranger to murder or, indeed, to the passing of the death sentence, but he was roused, presumably by prejudice, to declare:

"I never before desired a power of executing the legal penalties, but if I had such a power I would exercise it in this case."

During the twenty days between sentence and execution it was decided that Tobias should be hanged at the place where Anne Blakemore's body had been discovered. On 14 September 1750 he was dragged to Blythburgh where a gallows had been erected. Tobias continually pleaded his innocence until the London Mail Coach was seen in the distance. In a last desperate attempt to save his life he asked the hangman to fit a halter round his neck and attach it to the coach so that he might run for his life. This was refused and Tobias was eventually put to death in front of a large group of onlookers. One of the spectators, a certain Mr Bokenham, was seated in his saddle to take better advantage of the view. When, suddenly, Tobias's body dropped to the end of the rope, the horse bolted. Bokenham was thrown from his saddle and killed.

The musician's body was hung in chains at the Four Ways until it eventually disintegrated, and the bones were interred where they fell. The gibbet stood for another fifty years as a grim reminder, not so much of Tobias's guilt, but that of his accusers. Shavings of the gallows were collected as a cure for toothache and eventually the beams rotted and collapsed. The nails that had secured them were gathered as talismans and one of the timbers, carved with Tobias's initials, was incorporated in a barn at nearby Westwood Lodge.

Immediately after Tobias's death, the mood of the vengeful mob turned quickly from elation to remorse. It was noted that no marks had been found on Anne Blakemore's body; indeed there was no evidence that she had been murdered by anyone, least of all Tobias Gill.

Although a free man it is hardly surprising that Tobias was a denied a fair trial. Black people would be bought and sold like animals for another fifty-seven years before, in 1807, the slave trade was finally abolished. As far as Sir Robert Rich, knight and 4th baronet, Member of Parliament for Dunwich, and Groom of the Bedchamber to King George II[6] was concerned, the conviction of one of his musicians, a black, was little more than a minor embarrassment and rumours of wrongful conviction, nothing more.

Locally, Tobias's death was quickly considered to be a gross miscarriage of justice and pathetic attempts were made to commemorate him. The track from Blythburgh that meets the "*great road from Ipswich to Beccles*" (now the A12) was called 'Toby's Road' and the place where he died 'Toby's Walks', in homage to his restless ghost.

Opposite:
Negro trumpeter, 1st troop of House Guards *by David Morier. Oil on canvas. 1750.*
Although black people were not uncommon in the military in the eighteenth century, representations of them are very rare. This picture, painted the year Tobias was hanged, evokes his striking presence. Although Tobias Gill is usually described as a drummer, this was a generic term for military musicians that included trumpeters.
© Royal Collection 2006

78

The Battle of Sole Bay 1672 *by Willem van de Velde the Younger (1633-1707).*
Several versions of this dramatic oil painting were made but this is the best. The Royal James *is seen in the foreground with a fire ship alongside. Note the tattered rigging, holed by chainshot from the enemy cannon. It was a scene of terrible carnage: 900 men lost their lives aboard the* Royal James *alone and the sea was* "red with their blood".
The Dutch Maritime Museum

THE BATTLE OF SOLE BAY

A priceless treasure of silver plate, gold and jewellery lies deep on the seabed off the coast of Southwold.[1] Around it are littered 100 heavy guns and the bones of those who died on the *Royal James* during the bloody battle of Sole Bay on 28 May 1672. These grim relics are almost all that remains of one the fiercest confrontations in British marine history.

The Anglo-Dutch wars, 1652-1654, 1664-1667 and 1672-1674, were fundamentally a clash between two great maritime nations over trade. The east coast of England being particularly vulnerable to invasion, the people of Southwold were among the first to be made aware of the seriousness of the situation. On 11 November 1664 a Royal commission was sent to "*…our loving friends the bailiffs of the town of Southwold*" from the Court of Whitehall saying that the King willed and required that all possible assistance be offered during the war. Quarters were to be provided for the sick and wounded from any of his Majesty's ships and fit places of security were to be maintained for prisoners until "*they shall otherwise be disposed of*".[2] Early warning systems were meticulously maintained: lookouts operated from the steeples of churches and sea coal filled the iron fire-baskets that topped a series of stone beacons all along the coastline. Troops on horseback were always on the headlands ready to give warning when invasion threatened, and trainbands of citizens were formed into an unofficial Home Guard. When the enemy fleet was sighted it invariably heightened the sense of fear that had swept the entire country.

The high ground and tower of Southwold church had been a useful vantage point for the Lord High Admiral of the Fleet, His Royal Highness James, Duke of York (1633-1701) and brother of King Charles II (see illustration on p.85). When prevailing winds were in the right direction Southwold Bay, known as Sole Bay, provided a safe haven for the fleet and its harbour could be used for maintenance and minor refitting. The town was convenient for supplies and hospitality and the fleet gathered there on several occasions. It was decided, with our allies the French, that an attempt should be made to engage the Dutch in a sea battle as far away from their own coastline as possible, where they would be unfamiliar with the mud and sandbanks that characterise the East Coast.

On 18 May 1672 a confrontation with the enemy seemed imminent and the French and English fleets were combined to make up 101 ships. The total number of hands on all sides has been calculated as 34,530.[3] The Comte d'Estrees was admiral of the French fleet – the White Squadron. The Duke of York, on the *Royal Prince*, commanded the centre or Red Squadron, and the Earl of Sandwich (1625-1672) headed the Blue Squadron on the *Royal James*. The scale of the accommodation for these Royal and aristocratic commanders is indicated by Sir William Lowser, a cousin of King Charles II, who described the Earl's quarters on board one of his previous commands, the *Naseby*:

"*The Admiral's table was better served on sea, than those of many princes are in their dominions. The plate was all of silver, of prodigious greatness, laden with great pieces of roast beef. Other dishes were massier than the greatest wash basins ...*"[4]

The equally splendid Dutch fleet, made up 186 ships including 91 men o' war, had been sighted off Orford Ness keeping a keen eye on the activities of the English by means of scouts. Based on the information these provided, the fleet slipped away in the middle of the night and were only faintly visible on the horizon at dawn. The British fleet led the chase with the French behind and the wind was favourable and the sea smooth. Simple preparations on board were a signal to the crew that battle was unavoidable. Hammocks and chests were put in holds and all "*trumpery*" including cabin furnishings was thrown overboard. Despite their fear, the men were good tempered and cheerful and seemed confident of success. Though all decks had been cleared, the action was not to come for several days. Instead, a game of cat and mouse followed, and the night was full of confusion. Distractions were staged by means of sounds, signals, false fires, and blue flames, which were shot up in the darkness to bewilder the enemy; shot from the Dutch fleet whined through the air. Dawn was accompanied by thick fog. Although the ships were invisible to one another, the psychological warfare continued with the use of lights, bells, musket fire and drums.

On 20 May the wind changed and the Dutch were soon three leagues to stern of the allied fleets; wind and high seas made the use of guns impossible. The Dutch had tried to lure the allies into dangerous waters but were unsuccessful. The British fleet decided instead to drop anchor in Southwold Bay and to get badly needed provisions and to rest. Some of the ships lacked their full complement and so the men of the town were press-ganged into service. These unpleasant arrangements had to be made in quick time as there was news that the Dutch fleet, commanded by Admiral Michel de Ruyter, was out once more. The movements of the enemy had confused the English: On 25 May Haddock, who was captain on the *Royal James*, believed that they were "*very near ready*" and saw no need to leave Southwold for some days by which time preparations would be complete. The Earl of Sandwich warned of the danger of being trapped in the surrounding shoals and sands but his warning was virtually ignored. An unfavourable wind, meant that they were delayed in Southwold Bay for too long and lost the advantage of their position to the Dutch. The Earl's caution was ignored and the Duke of York said that it was a counsel born of fear rather than prudence. Nonetheless, the Earl was shortly to be vindicated.

The Earl of Sandwich at the Battle of Sole Bay *by Robert Smirke (1752-1845). Oil on canvas.*
The First Earl of Sandwich was second in command to The Duke of York at the battle of Sole Bay in 1672 and it cost him his life. In this picture the Royal James *is on fire and the mast and rigging have been shot down. The crew is pleading with Lord Sandwich to leave the sinking ship. This is an idealised scene in which the Earl is shown as fit and slim. In fact he was rather corpulent and was unable swim. When, finally, there was no option but to jump from the burning ship into the sea it was these factors that contributed to the Earl's death.* Private Collection, USA

James, Duke of York *by Henri Gascar (1653-1701). Oil on canvas. 1672.*

The Duke of York appears in the guise of Mars, the god of war. The armour that lies at his feet reinforces the image of the warrior. Rich arrangements, gold and jewellery are typical of Gascar's work but here they are a powerful endorsement of the Duke's high rank as heir to the throne.

James was Lord High Admiral for his brother Charles II from the latter's restoration to the throne in 1660 until 1673. This position is indicated by the depiction of the fleet in the background with the Duke's flagship Royal Prince, *which may be based on a lost painting by Willem van de Velde the Younger. Its flags indicate a royal visit to the fleet in late 1672. The Duke was in personal command at the battle of Sole Bay in 1672 and it seems certain that this portrait was made to commemorate it. He succeeded his brother as King in 1685 but his Catholic sympathies led to his overthrow during the Glorious Revolution of 1688. When the Duke of York was in Southwold during the Dutch Wars he stayed at Sutherland House at the west end of the High Street. The Duke of York was a duke of fifth creation and became King James II in 1685. It was 265 years before Southwold was to be visited by his successor, a Duke of York of seventh creation, who was crowned King George VI in 1937 (see illustration on p.238).*

The detail above shows the imposing profile of the Royal Prince *from which the Duke of York commanded the fleet off Southwold at the Battle of Sole Bay. Note the carved ornaments including lanterns and the royal cypher applied with pure gold leaf.*   The National Maritime Museum

In the early hours of dawn on 28 May the entire fleet was woken by the news that the enemy was close. After a sleepless night the Earl prepared for battle, dressing with great care. His hair was tied back with a ribbon and he wore a large plumed hat. A jewelled watch and several rings added to the richness of his arrangements. These included a blue sapphire, a white sapphire engraved with the Earl's crest surrounded by the Garter, a carnelian engraved with an antique head and another supporting a tiny compass that was more decorative than functional. Round his body was the rich blue sash of the Order of the Garter and the star blazed on his chest. The jewelled collar and George scintillated at his neck. As his secretary Valevin pinned the insignia to his chest, Sandwich explained that he had been accused of cowardice by the Duke of York and that he was determined to reclaim his reputation. When he left the cabin he said, in an attitude that was to be echoed by Nelson at Trafalgar in 1805, "*Now, Val, I must be sacrificed.*"

The Dutch had set sail slowly and silently to make a surprise attack but had been detected by a French frigate, which had successfully raised the alarm. Unfortunately, the bulk of the allied fleet were completely unprepared, indeed the *Royal Prince* was in the process of having its sides cleaned of seaweed and shells. As the sun rose the Dutch fleet made an awesome sight as it appeared over the horizon with the wind in its favour.

Confusion was everywhere. The smaller support craft and fire ships were near the shore. Worse still, a number of seamen were busy enjoying every aspect of hospitality that Southwold could provide, so a bailiff was sent round "*to see them put out of the ale houses and the tippling houses*".[5] The sailors were warned, on pain of death, to return to their ships because the enemy was close at hand. The thought of fighting a battle with a hangover was just too much for some who "*skulked away and hid about the town*" but most were stirred by the beating of drums and tumbled into their boats, rowing hard and fast back to their ships. Orders were piped with the boatswain's whistle and sails were hoisted and anchors raised. When the first action began some of the ships were scarcely under weigh, but most managed to get going without cutting their cables. For the first hour-and-a-half the fighting was of terrifying intensity and the countryside was covered in smoke and the smell of gunpowder. The people of Southwold stood watching on the cliff and shoreline, the sound of the guns "*shook them in their houses and their standing places [and] held them, as it were well-bound by excitement and panic*".[6] In total there were 4,300 pieces of cannon available for use in the allied fleet alone. The noise was so terrific that it could be heard in the English Channel between Dover and Calais and it is said that Sir Isaac Newton detected it in Cambridge.[7] In all the terrible din and confusion the inhabitants of the town became less certain of the outcome of the battle. They formed themselves into a "*strong guard*" and prevented the country people from returning back over the bridge so that the enemy might be offered a "*warm reception*" if they stepped ashore.

Caught unprepared, the ships were forced close up to the coast and, owing to lack of wind, they were difficult to manoeuvre. The French fleet misunderstood the signals and went south, whilst the Duke of York's squadron headed north. The Earl of Sandwich also headed north and took the first brunt of the attack. De Ruyter was a said to have borne down on them "*like a torrent*". They were armed with "*perilous fire ships*" the size of fourth- and fifth-rate frigates. The Dutch seamen had apparently been spurred on to acts of courage with bribes and menaces and with lurid stories of the fate of the defeated.

The Duke of York's ship the *Royal Prince* was an obvious target and at one point she was surrounded. The English expected her to be boarded but, instead, the Dutch intended to disable her and then to set the ship on fire. Shortly, two fire ships were seen coming through the smoke, being towed by a rowing boat because of the lack of wind. One fire ship was quickly sunk and the other driven away, but the Dutch were unrelenting and the *Royal Prince* had suffered badly. Bullets, cannon balls and chain-shot had torn down her rigging. A single shot had missed the Duke of York but killed his captain, and he had been spattered with blood and brains. Before eleven in the morning the topmast was shot through, her rigging was in tatters and 200 of her men were dead. The Duke of York fled to the St. Michael and hoisted his standard, but when the Dutch saw the flag they turned their attention to attacking it. No sooner had the Duke's pilot given directions than he was killed with a single shot.

When the smoke cleared the *Royal James* could be seen towards the north of the battle. It was singled out for unrelenting attack. Captain Van Brakel bravely bore down on her in a smaller ship called the *Groot Hollandia* and was soon entangled in her rigging, the flood tide jamming the enemy ship right under the figure head of the *Royal James*. Sandwich fired on them with musket balls in such numbers that it made the sea "*boil as if full of whales*". The wounded "*writhed upon the slippery decks; blood poured down the scuppers and stained the sea*".[8] Of the *Royal James's* crew, 300 were already dead and Captain Haddock wounded, but the spent tide allowed Sandwich to extricate himself from the *Groot Hollandia*. This change of fortune was short-lived: a fire ship commanded by Van de Rijn came out of the smoke in the direction of the *Royal James*. In moments it had grappled the *Royal James* and set fire to her in the light breeze. Of the 1,000 original crew only 100 survived. Sandwich, wounded by shards of wood, stood upon the burning deck whilst his officers begged him to leave. In reply he ordered the men to save themselves as best they could. By midday the ship was untenable and the people of Southwold watched it burn away. There was a fear amongst the observers on both land and sea that there would be an explosion when the fire reached the ship's powder magazine, but there was none; the gunners had fired all their ammunition. At two in the afternoon the *Royal James* was a mass of flames and by four it was reduced to the level of the hull. By the time darkness fell and brought calm and quiet to that terrible day in May only the odd ember pinpointed the location of the wreck before it finally sank to the bottom of the German Ocean (now known as the North Sea).

The fighting continued throughout the afternoon, both the English and the Dutch fleets were out of line and locked in individual confrontations that lasted until 5 o'clock. The Duke was obliged to transfer to *The London*. The fighting slackened and the fleets were drifting towards Aldeburgh. As they gradually separated an occasional shot was fired until night closed over the scene. The next morning it was thought that the battle would be renewed (see illustration opposite). The French, untouched and unharmed, joined the allies, but a wind had made the sea rough and a further engagement was rendered impossible.

Despite the fact that the battle of Southwold Bay was one of the fiercest in our history, the result is often described as inconclusive, though the losses to the English side far outweighed those of the Dutch; the French were almost unscathed. The loss of the *Royal James* was by far the greatest loss, not only in terms of the ship itself, but also in the number of men who died defending her. A number of other vessels were severely battered. Of the *Henry* and the *Katherine* a shipbuilder said, "*I find such a spectacle for damage of masts, yards and rigging as I never yet saw so bad*". The *Victory* was so shot through in the hull that it took on nearly seven feet of water.

The Dutch had one ship taken, another sunk, and others were badly damaged; the loss of life, however, was not enormous. Van Ghent was killed and a captain died of his injuries; and De Ruyter's son was wounded. The greatest devastation occurred when the *Groot Hollandia* engaged the *Royal James*. Then Jan van Brakel was wounded, and his two lieutenants were killed together with 150 of the sailors. English losses were very heavy and amounted to 900 on the *Royal James* alone. The officers and volunteers who died were Sir John Cox, Francis Digby, and Frescheville Holles. The greatest loss of all was the Earl of Sandwich himself, and the Dutch might have claimed a victory by virtue of that alone. Several memorials were made to the battle. Though the French took little part in the action, ironically, it was they who were to issue a commemorative medal. Cut by Mauger it featured the profile of Louis XIV.[9] In 1759 at Hinchingbroke, the Earl's seat, a stained glass window by William Peckitt of York, decorated with a scene from the battle, was fitted. It cost of £117 11 shillings.

Happily, a comprehensive visual record of the battle remains in the form of a map of the hostilities. At the National Maritime Museum, there is also a series of very fine drawings by Willem van de Velde the Younger that are closely related to the battle of Sole Bay. Their dramatic climax is the painting, now in the Dutch Maritime Museum, of the plight of the *Royal James*. The Garter sash, which was found on the Earl's body, was preserved in the family for 300 years until it was stolen by a visitor to the house in the 1970s.

After the battle, the sea was slow to give up her dead and a bounty of a shilling per body was offered in the hope of speeding the recovery. However, it was not until 10 June

---

Opposite:
The day after the Battle of Sole Bay *by Willem van de Velde the Younger. Pencil on paper.*
The sinking of the flagship the Royal James *and the considerable loss of life and damage to the battleships meant that the fleet was seriously demoralised. There was talk of engaging the enemy again, but bad weather prevented it. Van de Velde's little drawing has somehow captured the aimlessness of the combatants the day after their terrible ordeal.*   The National Maritime Museum

that Sandwich's bloated corpse was recovered off Harwich – still wearing the Garter sash, star and the jewel. In the pocket of his coat were found the sapphire rings. The body was embalmed and a lavish funeral was followed by an interment in Henry VIII's chapel Westminster Abbey. At this moment the family motto "*After so many wrecks I find a port*" must have seemed especially poignant to the chief mourners. In Southwold his death became associated with a popular ballad called *The Drowned Lover*:

> *As I was walking down in Stokes [Southwold] Bay*
> *I met a drowned sailor on the beach as he lay*
> *And as I drew near him, it put me to stand,*
> *When I knew it was my own true love by the marks on his hand.*

The will of the 47-year-old Earl was proved in September 1672. The value of his substantial personal estate was reduced by £4,000 to take account of the treasure of plate and jewellery that went to the bottom with the *Royal James*.

PIRATES AND MARAUDERS

The East Coast has always been vulnerable to attack because it was potentially the first stop for a succession of sea raiders and pirates who came from the continent by sea. The grim reality of this threat was graphically evoked by Roland Parker in his *Men of Dunwich*:

"A brisk day and half a night's sailing; half an hour of strenuous rowing up a tidal river; silent approach to sleeping villa or village; a few minutes of bloody pandemonium; then away to the boat with the carcases of several pigs and sheep, a couple of trembling slaves, and any other loot... down the river once more and out on the open sea, pulling hard in the direction of the rising sun, to cease rowing when the offshore wind bellied out the sail."

The mouth of the river Blyth was just such a tidal river and it was there, in Southwold, that a thriving fishing community had been long established. By the beginning of the thirteenth century local landowners and prosperous fish merchants had richly furnished their church.This, and the availability of livestock, wells, ships at anchor and ease of escape, meant that Southwold was especially attractive to the sort of sea raiders described above. A high proportion of the many cases of piracy in Southwold Bay between 1299 and 1318 concerned 'Flemings', the term then used for the inhabitants of what are now Holland, Belgium and North Eastern France. As early as 1173 they had set sail with the specific intention of plundering the property of those who shared in their ancestry, common interests and even friends.[1]

Lookouts, beacons, troupes of archers, and guns were positioned on the cliff tops at Dunwich and Southwold as deterrents against the raiders.[2] At Blythburgh, in 1451, a conder was erected giving "*signals of boughs*" to shipping, and in 1490 an archery butt was installed at the expense of four shillings and four pence. The only road into Southwold was protected by a drawbridge and archers practised on the church green.[3] A fort was built at the end of Buss Creek and a fire beacon was positioned on Eye Cliff (Gun Hill); and with the invention of gunpowder a series of batteries was positioned there. In 1547 the need for seven horse soldiers caused the sale of most of the church plate and by 1745 the town's parapet of two nine-pounder guns was augmented by the half-a-dozen eighteen-pounders that remain there to this day.

The few available accounts of piracy in Sole Bay make it clear that the threat was serious. In 1300 the Earl of Gloucester's ship put in at Southwold whilst its owner was on the King's service in Scotland. There it was plundered, attacked and sunk.[4] It is likely that the threat of pirates was the reason the Earl of Gloucester applied to King Henry III for permission to convert his house in Southwold into a castle. It is said to have stood on the east side of what is now Skilmans Hill (see illustration on p.32).

"*Foreigners*" were blamed for these crimes, though they were not always the culprits. The escalating problem was also linked to the dereliction of Dunwich, which had resulted from the fouling of the harbour by the sea. It was there, especially, that desperation had turned honest seafarers into thieves and it seems the risk of hanging was worth taking when balanced against the certainty of slow starvation.

Preventative measures meant that attacks on the harbour became increasingly difficult and, consequently, pirates turned their attention to the open sea and foreign ports. In 1561 William Garston of Walberswick and Thomas Gray, master of *The James* of Walberswick, complained of piracy at the highest possible level. They wrote to Mary, Queen of Scots to tell her that whilst they were in haven in Westmoney in Iceland they were "*cruelly underset*", and invaded by some "*Scotchmen*" who robbed them of goods to the value of £2,800. On 19 August of the same year Her Majesty had returned to Scotland to face serious difficulties of her own and it is unlikely that the she had time to consider those of Walberswick, in the separate kingdom of England. The fishermen were obliged to resort to more practical measures to avoid a repetition. One solution was for merchant ships to sail in groups, but even combined forces were not always enough to prevent bloody confrontations and heavy financial losses. The problem was sufficiently acute in 1619 for the Bailiffs of Yarmouth to invite the people of Walberswick to contribute to a fund to suppress piracy on the southern seas. However, the townspeople asked to be excused on the grounds that there were no merchants living in the town and that its inhabitants were "*very poor*".[5]

Certainly poverty and starvation were circumstances in which the hopeless turned to piracy, but it was also one of the few options for those on the outside of society. For escaped convicts and mutineers a short and hazardous life on the high seas was infinitely more attractive than a long and miserable captivity. In 1722, the Welsh pirate Bartholomew Roberts wrote:

"*In honest service, there are commonly low wages and hard labour; in this [piracy] plenty and satiety, pleasure and ease, liberty and power. Who would not balance credit on this side, when all the hazard that is run for it, at worst, is only a sour look or two on choking? No, a merry life and a short one, that's my motto.*"[6]

The same point of view was held by the tiny minority of slaves who were lucky enough to make a successful bid for freedom. One of their masters, John Crabbe, brother of the poet George, was captain of a Liverpool slave ship belonging to his father-in-law. It was to no avail that George wished his brother every success in his new trade; John and his crew were overwhelmed by their human cargo, set adrift in an open boat, and were never heard of again. Desperate slaves who had liberated themselves in this way were often in command of a sturdy ship and piracy must have been the only immediate prospect of survival.

On the south side of Southwold's church, near the path, there is a stone erected to the memory of one David May who was murdered by pirates in the Bay of Florida in June 1819; his body was never recovered. It bears dramatic testimony to the fate of those who were baptised at St. Edmund's font but never returned to be buried in the churchyard outside.

JACK bringing a PIRATE in

Justice. "You must swear this Fellow stopped you, on the Kings Highway an
that this Swaberly Lubber put me in Bodily Fear? No no your Worship that won't do
Gallery, Damn'him he attempted to Rob me, but not put me in Bodily Fear.

Publish'd Jan.18.1804.by LAURIE & WHITTLE, 53,Fleet St

330

RT.

in Bodily Fear." ___ Sailor. "What! I swear

his Shatter'd Riggings and his broken Stern

Jack bringing a Pirate into Port. _Coloured print. Published by Laurie and Whittle, 53 Fleet Street, London on 18 January, 1804._
The caption reads:

Justice: "You must swear this Fellow stopped you, on the King's Highway and put you in Bodily Fear."
Sailor: "What! I swear that this Swaberly Lubber put me in Bodily Fear? No no your Worship that won't do, look at his Shatter'd Riggings and his broken Stern Gallery. Damn! him he attempted to Rob me, but not put me in Bodily Fear."

For obvious reasons images of pirates are rare. This amusing print makes light of what had been a serious problem on the East Coast of England for centuries.
The three men hanged from a gibbet is a grim reminder of the fate of those convicted of piracy. The gallows was seen as the only effective deterrent against it. In Southwold in the sixteenth century a gibbet was erected on the south side of Buss Creek, where it was clearly visible from the sea.
                                        The National Maritime Museum

Some were lost in war, some were shipwrecked or accidentally drowned whilst others fell victim to pirates. Occasionally honest seafarers were recruited to piracy through fear for their lives, but this put them immediately outside the law. In the case of David May only he and his captain and two shipmates resisted their attackers and they paid dearly for it. The story of both the victims and the aggressors has been pieced together by Mary Trumpess, one of May's family, and is highly detailed and affecting.

David May was the mate on an East Indiaman, the *Ann of Scarbro'*, under Captain Sunley. The *Ann* was a merchant brig with two masts and square rigging and her cargo was coffee and sugar valued at $20,000 and $10,000 respectively. She had set sail for Falmouth in 1819 on a journey that would normally have taken eight to twelve weeks. Born in Southwold in 1788, David May was the third son of a family that had a long tradition of seafaring and had taken every sort of natural catastrophe in its stride. It was not Atlantic storms and towering seas that merchant seamen feared most, rather the ever-present threat of piracy.

On 28 June 1819 *The Ann* was on its third day at sea when, 60 miles off the coast of Florida, a small vessel approached them, signalling for help. *The Ann* dropped her sails and lowered a rope, the men on board the yawl immediately drew pistols and cutlasses and overwhelmed her. The leader of the pirates, a stocky, pockmarked Irishman who went under the name of John Atwick took the crew below, one by one, and demanded money. There was none because it had all been spent on the valuable cargo. Each crewman was given the choice between defecting to the pirates or immediate death. Understandably most capitulated but Captain Sunley, David May, William Quince the carpenter and John Hall the cook resisted. Captain Sunley was shot through the heart and David May just below the eye. Their bodies and those of the other two men were pitched overboard together with a seaman who was ill and therefore an encumbrance to the pirates.

The cargo was transferred to the main pirate vessel, *The Lawrence* – also known as *The Black Joke*. Before separating into three groups, the pirates ran the *The Ann* ashore on a rocky island to give the impression that it had been wrecked and Atwick headed for Charleston. There he claimed that the coffee was part of the cargo of an abandoned ship but the authorities became suspicious and Atwick was charged with piracy and two counts of murder and convicted. Before sentencing, the judge described the crime as:

"*of the blackest die…The victims of your cruelty were unoffending and merited no punishment. Prepare yourself for your impending fate*".

The preparations that Atwick made were audacious enough to exceed the judge's wildest imaginings. After praying with a Catholic priest and warning the large crowd of spectators to think twice before they acted once, Atwick suggested to the hangman that the noose had been inexpertly tied. On Atwick's suggestion two half hitches were made to the rope and, once it had been approved, the condemned man was hanged from it. The body remained suspended for half-an-hour and was then buried nearby.

Back in Southwold there was no body and no grave to comfort the grieving May family. David's father died just over two years after his son and his tombstone serves as a memorial to them both. On it David's widow described her husband's dreadful fate in rhyming couplets, outlining the many dangers faced by all those who left the safety of Southwold's harbour for the open sea:

Not yet have ceased to flow a widow's tears,
O'er scenes remembered midst the lapse of years.
On foreign seas he fell, but not by storm
When boisterous winds the heaving waves deform,
Nor by the rock beneath the tide concealed,
Nor by the sword which warring natives wield,
But by the foe received in friendship's guise.
By hands of treacherous pirates lo! he dies.
Thou too art mortal hastening to thy grave
Believe on him who ever lives to save.

These lines are inscribed by his widow as the last melancholy tribute of affection.

A Pirate's Head *by Edward Gordon Craig. Carved and painted wood and cloth. c.1897.*
Ellen Terry's son, the artist, actor and stage designer, Edward Gordon Craig, was in Southwold in 1897. It was then that the sideshows and itinerant actors working on the beach proved to be a powerful inspiration in his work (see p.168).   Tom Craig Esq.

TURNER IN SOUTHWOLD

Turner was one of the supreme interpreters of the sea and all its moods in his or any other time. On the east coast of England he was able to immerse himself completely in the elements and it was here that he found what fascinated him most: sublimely beautiful landscapes and the drama of the ever-changing ocean.

The German Ocean, now known as the North Sea, was famous for its treacherous sandbanks, undercurrents and fearsome storms; the perpetual struggle against the violence of the elements was part of everyday life. Coastal fortifications, cliff-top ruins and tales of sunken cities made romantic foils for the vast East Anglian skies, but even in the finest weather the search for inspiration was arduous. Happily, Turner had a wiry and resilient constitution and was more than capable of walking 25 miles a day in blazing sun or rain. Against these he wore a greatcoat and, invariably, carried a faded umbrella, the hollow handle of which could easily be removed and made into a fishing rod, whilst the maggots for bait were kept warm and lively in his pockets.

It was probably the success of Turner's series of engravings *Picturesque Views of the Southern Coast of England*, published between 1814 and 1826, that inspired him to plan a similar series, which was to be called simply *The East Coast of England*. Turner was already familiar with the coastline having sailed around it when he was on the way to Edinburgh by sea in August 1822. Whilst on board ship he had made a number of sketches, including a view of the cliff and townscape of Southwold. It may have been this journey that persuaded Turner, in 1824, to travel northwards along the coast of Suffolk. He could well have afforded a coach and horses, but the coastline is divided by all manner of obstacles. Dunes, cliffs and estuaries meant that the traveller was often obliged to retreat inland and this route would have kept Turner from what he had come for, the coastline and the sea. Evidently he decided to walk. As well as the famous umbrella, he carried watercolour paints, pencils and series of pocket sketchbooks.

The long trudge up the pebble beach in the direction of Lowestoft brought Turner close to the haunting ruins of a church perched precariously above the sea. It was standing on what was left of the eastern corner of the once thriving Saxon cathedral city of Dunwich. From the thirteenth century, coastal erosion had begun to destroy this prosperous port with its several churches and chapels; by the time Turner arrived nearly all of it had gone. What remained were the ruins of the Franciscan Abbey and leper hospital; almost all the rest had succumbed to the ceaseless pounding of the waves.

Opposite:
Self-portrait *by Joseph Mallord William Turner. Oil on Canvas. 1799.*
Turner was twenty-four when he painted this, his last self-portrait. The frontal pose accentuates the intensity of Turner's determined gaze. He was forty-nine when he passed Southwold on his journey from Aldeburgh to Lowestoft. Next to nothing is known about how long he spent there; the only evidence being the series of pencil drawings, which are part of his bequest to the nation. Copyright Tate, London 2005

Dunwich, Suffolk *by J.M.W. Turner. c.1824.*
This painting demonstrates man's continuing struggle with nature. The ruined city of Dunwich is seen at the top of the cliff and All Saint's Church is evidently doomed to fall into the waves. The ruins of Blackfriars Abbey are to the right of the composition. Yet, despite the bleakness of the scene, the indomitability of the human spirit is represented by the fishermen, putting out in rough weather. Their kinsmen watching from the beach suggests that a ship is in trouble further out to sea.

© Manchester Art Gallery

Kill Cock Cliff, Southwold *by J.M.W. Turner.*

The flagpole and Queens Preventative Station with single canon are at the centre of the drawing. The same house with distinctive bow-fronted fenestration appears in Davy's drawing (see illustration opposite). Boats and a capstan are at the foot of the path beneath it.   Copyright Tate, London 2005

Although the derelict church of All Saints was still standing (see illustration on p.43), it must have been obvious to the congregation that its days were numbered. The straight-sided bell tower stood alone in a landscape that was wasted and desolate and, as a result, had become an emblem of spiritual isolation and mortality. Turner did not view the scene as one of utter hopelessness. As a reminder of man's continuing struggle with nature he painted the crew of a small boat bravely putting out into a threatening sea (see pp.98/99).

Although few finished works illustrate the artist's hike up the East Coast, some surviving sketchbooks (in the Turner bequest to the nation) show that he used his pencil and paper as the traveller uses a camera today. A fantastically prolific artist, Turner dashed off hundreds of delicate drawings, labelling a few of them with their locations; one, a sketch of Walberswick (see illustration on p.102), is a view of the village and to the left the ruined church of St. Andrew can clearly be made out. Another view of the beach shows a litter of wicker herring baskets and a distant view of Southwold and its

Opposite:

Kill Cock Cliff, Southwold *by Henry Davy. c.1840.*

This is the site of the Queen's Preventative Station where the excise men operated a lookout for smugglers and a small cannon was mounted on the cliff. On the beach an upturned boat has been converted to a shed. The sea is busy with traffic. A capstan used to haul boats up the beach is to the right of the composition. It is said that the Excise men used the sandstone top of the tombstone outside the church porch to sharpen their cutlasses. The canon and distinctive fenestration of the house to the left of the flagpole are clearly visible in Turner's sketch of the scene taken below the cliff.   John Tooke Esq.

Four drawings of Southwold and Walberswick by J.M.W.Turner. Pencil on paper. 1824.

© Tate, London

Left:
Walberswick with the fifteenth century church of St. Andrew to the left and the village to the right. Below is a scene of herring baskets and floats for nets. Below that Southwold Haven and fisherfolk and their boats.

Below:
The steps up the cliff to The Queen's Preventative Station with fishermen's huts to the left. Below, another scene of beached boats and the capstan used to pull them there.

Opposite, above:
The church of St. Edmund, Southwold. *Turner was evidently fascinated with the complex architecture of the church. The woodwoses and grotesques under the west door have been abbreviated to simple dots that, in the drawing, serve to suggest the depth of the arched doorway. Individual studies of the stone window frames, distinctive porch and flèche appear to the right of the sheet. To the left of the drawing a few lines suggest the profile of the river and are captioned "Over Blyth".*

Opposite, below:
The profile of Southwold seen from Gun Hill. *The guns, with muzzles lowered, are in the foreground. St. Edmund's Church fixes the position of South Green Cottage and South Green House, with the distinctive windows of Marine Villa (now called Little White Lodge) to the right. Another study of the church and its flèche appears on the same sheet. Above is a view of ships moored in the harbour with St. Andrews, Walberswick, in the distance.*

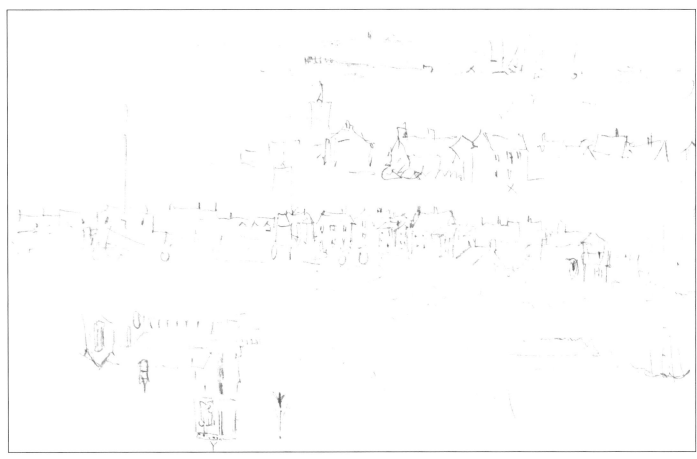

church. On the preceding pages in the sketchbook there are two views of Blyth Haven, the man-made harbour separating Southwold from the village of Walberswick. A number of drawings in the same sketchbook, which were previously catalogued simply as 'scenes on the East Coast', can now be identified properly as views of Southwold (see illustrations on pp.101, 102 and 103).

In the town a number of artists were already busy making prints and drawings for sale to the summer visitors and aristocratic families who had taken houses by the seaside. Henry Davy (1793-1865) was one such artist. Now that Southwold's architecture has changed, Davy's minutely observed drawings of the marine villas, cliffs and open greens are useful in pinpointing the location of some of Turner's sketches. The imposing fifteenth century church of Saint Edmund stands to the north of the old town and attracted Turner's attention. Until now the drawing he made of it was known simply as *A Church on the East Coast*, but the distinctive 100ft (30.5m) bell tower and the long roof with its pretty flèche make the subject quite unmistakable. So too is the delicate clerestory of eighteen closely-set windows and the fine Suffolk flushwork used to decorate the exterior of the church. None of these complex architectural details had escaped Turner's enquiring eye and, from the perspective of the drawing, it is possible to work out exactly where in the graveyard he stood when making it.

By Turner's time Southwold was a busy little trading town that had profited from the disastrous erosion of Dunwich. Substantial merchant and fishing vessels used its harbour and there was always hectic traffic on the sea. With at least two hotels and several bathing machines, the foundations of Southwold's modern identity were firmly in place. The quietly distinguished architecture, open greens and busy beaches have brought myriad artists to the town. Some were entranced by what they found and some were completely stultified; perhaps Turner was one of those who wanted more drama than Southwold could provide and that is why these delicate drawings remain the only certain evidence of his fleeting visit to the town.

The breaking wave *by J.M.W. Turner. Gouache on paper. c.1832.*

Exactly where this painting was made is unknown but it evidently dates from the time when Turner's fascination with the sea was at its height. It was this fascination with the ever-changing surface of the water that attracted Turner to the East coast in 1824. This painting is all the more remarkable for having been made before the advent of photography and 'freeze frame' technology. The modern concept of abstraction would not have been understood or endorsed in the nineteenth century, even by an artist as experimental as Turner.

HENRY DAVY:
A SOUTHWOLD PANORAMA

In the late eighteenth and early nineteenth centuries travel was arduous, if not downright dangerous, and students of topography often chose to satisfy their curiosity by collecting prints and drawings. Not always framed, they were often kept in racks or bound in volumes where, in a world without photography, they helped to generate the growing interest in architectural history and the natural sciences.

Probably the most notable topographical artist working in East Anglia in the early nineteenth century was John Sell Cotman. Born in Norwich to a rich silk mercer in 1782 he was educated at the local free grammar school. Later he trained as an architectural and landscape painter before moving to London where he made the acquaintance of Turner, Girtin and De Wint, who had also painted in Walberswick. In 1811 Cotman published his first series of etchings made up of 24 plates of ancient buildings in various parts of Britain. This was followed in 1817 by a volume of 50 plates entitled *Specimens of Norman and Gothic Architecture in the county of Norfolk*. Although Cotman taught drawing in Yarmouth and painted throughout East Anglia there is no certain evidence that he visited Southwold. However, we do know that he came very close to the town to paint the derelict church of Covehithe and it is more than likely that he extended his journey by an extra mile or so to visit his friend and talented pupil, Henry Davy.

Born in Westhall on 30 May 1793, Davy was a farmer's son, though his maternal grandfather was a physician called William Gibson who had lived at Willingham Hall. Having been apprenticed to a grocer in Halesworth, Davy went to study under Cotman

in Great Yarmouth and by 1815 was making etchings from his own drawings. In 1818, the very same year that Cotman had published a collection called *A Series of Etchings Illustrative of the Archaeological Antiquities of Norfolk*, Henry Davy published a volume that was to complement it exactly: *A Series of Ten Etchings illustrative of Beccles Church and other Suffolk Antiquities*. In 1819 Davy went to London to continue his training under George Cooke, but it was not long before he was working in Bury St. Edmunds and searching for much needed patrons. Between 1817 and 1823 he exhibited 23 pictures at the Norwich Society of Artists. On the proceeds of all this hard work he was able to marry at St. Peter's Church, Ipswich on 30 November 1824; Sarah was the daughter of James Bardwell, a master mariner and stationer from Southwold. Henry and Sarah settled in Southwold for five years and two of their 16 children were born there. Davy established himself as an art master and, in 1828, he issued a circular from West Green announcing his intention to give "*Instructions in Drawing and Sketching from Nature*".

Davy had been working on a series of 70 etchings called *The Architectural Antiquities of Suffolk* since 1817, and these were finally published in Southwold in 1827. The Dukes

Southwold looking from the Gun Hill by Henry Davy. Pencil on paper. c.1825.

Despite being much altered, the architecture and topography of this panoramic view of the town remains instantly recognisable. To the extreme left is the house known today as Wellesley Cottage. Next door to it is Dartmouth Cottage, which remains virtually untouched. The drawing predates the building of Regency House by the Reverend Henry Uhtoff in 1828. Just beyond the site of it, the top of the church tower can be seen; to the right is Tamarisk Villa (May Place), once the property of Archdeacon Philpot, and subsequently owned by the Southwold historian, Robert Wake. The Red Lion Inn, then known as The Queen's Head is seen without its ugly extension; alongside it is Sole Bay Cottage, and South Green House. The house with the bay window and that with the pitched roof have since been pulled down to make way for a pair of houses faced with pale brick. To the right is the profile of the house built for Edmund Barber called Marine Villa (now called Little White Lodge). The British Library

Southwold, Suffolk *by Henry Davy. A print published by the artist in 1820 and dedicated to The Hon. Lady Rous.*

In the foreground on Eye Cliff (Gun Hill) is the reading room built in 1801. Groups of fashionable people promenade there. To the left sheep and cattle share a compound and just beyond it are the pans of Southwold Salt works and the small windmill that was used to drain them. The associated bath house is just to the right of them.

Author's collection

of Norfolk and Grafton, the Marquesses of Salisbury and Bristol, the Earls of Gosford and Stradbroke, Lord Henniker, Sir Charles Blois, the Bishop of Salisbury and John Sell Cotman are just a few of the 155 patrons who helped to finance the publication of the etchings. Even with backing, Davy ran into financial problems and, as a result, only 20 plates were issued. The finished album, bound in tooled leather, was accompanied by an historical index that gave brief descriptions of every scene. Evidently, subjects were included not only for their beauty but for their rarity and antiquity; the ancient Jewish synagogue in Bury St. Edmunds is one of them.

Since Davy lived in Southwold it is hardly surprising that the album contains a number of scenes of the town and its surrounding villages. The imposing 100ft (30.5m) tower of St. Edmund's Church, circled by birds, with the sea in the distance, is depicted with an almost surreal clarity. Although Davy emphasised its dominating presence he was quick to point out that Southwold's church was only a chapel of ease for the older parish of St. Margaret of Antioch in Reydon.

The exterior of St. Edmund's Church had survived virtually intact, though by the early nineteenth century others were in ruins. Although Davy must have regretted their decay it is undeniable that this added enormously to their romantic charm. The churches of St. Andrew in Walberswick and Covehithe, shared not only the same patron saint but also the same state of dereliction when Davy etched them in 1826. In explaining Covehithe's decline Davy echoed the sad predicament of village churches throughout most of Suffolk in the first half of the nineteenth century:

A North West View of Southwold, Suffolk *by Henry Davy. Hand-coloured print dedicated to Mrs. C. Acton. Published by the artist in 1826.*

Davy was working in Reydon with Southwold in the distance. Buss Creek is full of water and is spanned by Mights Bridge. St. Edmund's Church dominates the horizon, and on Southwold common there are two windmills. To the left of the composition is the Lowestoft Road and just beyond it the Bear Inn, Reydon. A horse and rider are coming from Blythburgh and a covered coach from Reydon. In the foreground is a gamekeeper's gibbet and harvesters lean on their scythes; it was evidently late summer when the preliminary drawing was made. Author's collection

"*These splendid ruins attest to the former wealth and populousness of a place, which now ranks amongst the poorest and meanest parishes in the country.*"

However, the converse was true in Southwold, where the profitable fishing trade had to share the honours with the town's status as a fashionable watering place. In high season it was not only the sea that attracted visitors to the town, but also the views from Gun Hill, the battery of guns after which it was named and the pretty octagonal reading room, 'The Casino' on St. Edmund's Hill, which had been built in 1801.[1] Davy recorded the scene in July 1828, presumably in preparation for the famous etching that he published in partnership with Thomas Griffiths of London the following year. It was dedicated to Sir George Crewe of Calke Abbey (see illustration on p.149). The Crewe family were landowners in Derbyshire, but sometimes resided in Southwold and are commemorated with a monument in St. Edmund's Church.

Those who could afford to maintain marine villas and residences throughout the year included high-ranking members of Suffolk society. Following a grant of land from the corporation in 1810, large houses had been built on Gun Hill for both full-time residents and visitors. The baronet Sir Charles Blois of Cockfield Hall near Yoxford owned Centre Villa. Adjoining the 'Red Villa' was Mrs. Hunt's lodging house, which was tenanted in season for nearly 40 years running by the much-loved benefactress Caroline Acton (see

Mills on Southwold Common *by Henry Davy. Pencil on paper. 28 October 1823.*
In the background is Red Mill and in the foreground is the Great Town Mill first erected there in 1798.
Both were highly susceptible to damage from the north-easterly winds and their predecessors were
frequently blown down completely. In the distance the tower of St. Edmund's Church is seen, complete
with flagpole on the top. Both windmills were fenced to prevent accidental injury.   The British Library

illustration on p.112). The Rev. Henry Uhthoff lived in South Green Lodge and the Rev. T. Sheriffe from Henstead owned Lenny House. It was he who was responsible for the development of Centre Cliff Houses for the "*accommodation of lodgers*". A number of these elegant Regency buildings were also to attract Davy's attention, amongst them those of Sir Charles Blois (see illustration on p.111) and Mrs. Acton.

A change in circumstances is the likely reason for Davy's decision to leave Southwold for Ipswich in 1829. There he lived with his family at Whitton Road in the area of St. Matthews, later moving to 16 Globe Street [later renamed St George Street]. Whatever the reason, it was clear where his heart lay when, in 1829, he submitted three watercolours to The Royal Society of British Artists's exhibition entitled: *Southwold*, *A Scene of Southwold Beach*, and *Gun Hill, Southwold*.

Evidently Davy was in need of money by 1833 and he had a number of creditors. His printer Deck settled for some of Davy's personal property, which was auctioned on 16 April 1833. It included paintings, books, engraved plates for etchings and a number of rather modest household effects suggesting that the family was living a very frugal lifestyle indeed. Life in Ipswich had been hard for Henry Davy and it is possible that the proximity of his parents-in-law made Southwold a more attractive place to be. He was back there in 1835 when he painted a watercolour of boats and tall ships and in 1838 when he recorded a charming scene that included the flowers in Captain Kilwick's garden. His mother-in-law, Mrs. Bardwell, continued to live in Market Place, where she was a bookseller and dealer in stamps until at least 1839.

A House on the Gun Hill, Southwold, now the property of Sir Chas. Blois Bart *by Henry Davy. Pencil on paper. 25 October 1823.*
This building, originally built for the Benjanfield family has survived virtually without alteration. It is called Centre Villa and once belonged to Sir Charles Blois of Yoxford.
Only a porch has been added and even the unusual windbreaks on each side of the house remain intact.

The British Library

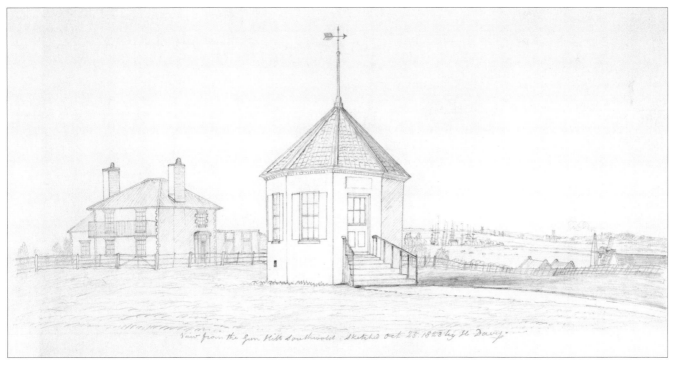

View from the Gun Hill, Southwold *by Henry Davy. Pencil on paper. 25 October 1823.*
In the foreground is the octagonal reading room called the 'Casino'. It appears narrower than it is today; an illusion brought about by the subsequent lowering of the roof and disastrous alterations to the windows. Beyond it is Stone House, built for the Sperling family and later acquired by Onley Savill Onley. It was probably he who extended it by adding the two bays. Coach houses were built in 1879. Ships are moored in Southwold harbour and beyond them St. Andrew's Church in Walberwick can just be made out.

The British Library

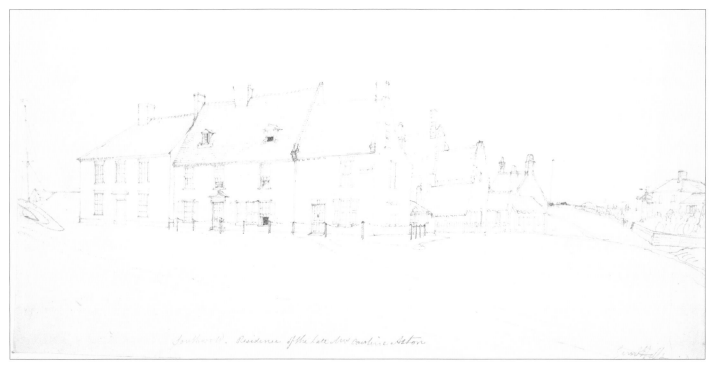

Southwold – Residence of the late Mrs. Caroline Acton *by Henry Davy. Pencil on paper. c.1825.*
Only the house on the extreme left, known as the Red House, then the home of the Reverend James Carlos, and that on the far right, known as Centre Villa, have survived since this delicate drawing was made. The building at the centre was a lodging house belonging to Mrs. Hunt. The philanthropist, Mrs. Caroline Acton tenanted the house, each season, for nearly forty years. In 1872 it was pulled down to make way for the large Italianate residence of Councillor William Hotson. The British Library

Although Davy styled himself as an architect, very little is known about this part of his career. There is no record of him serving his articles at the Royal Institute of British Architects and very few of his architectural designs have survived. Two of them were for work to be undertaken in Southwold. One was the plan for the alteration of a building in Market Place, and the other a design for two tiers of 12 free seats in the church; as Southwold's already expanded population fluctuated seasonally, there was a pressing need to increase the number of seats for the summer congregation, which numbered nearly 1,000 "hearers". In 1836-7 a new gallery of benches, largely intended for children was put up under the tower arch. Although Davy's scheme is not dated it is highly likely that it was the very one that Dr Wake denounced only a few years later as:

"*the unsightly gallery which, by encroachment after encroachment, has pushed out his threatening shelves almost midway towards the choir, and intrusively extended them, even against the very mullions of the trellised windows on the northern and southern walls*".

In the second half of the nineteenth century the gallery was removed when the old organ was sold and replaced by another.

If Davy had plans to publish further editions of topographical prints they were never realised. It is not clear how his career developed after 1830, although it is known that he accepted special commissions, continued to teach in Southwold and that a number of individual etchings were issued after 1835.

The Piers, Southwold, Suffolk *by Henry Davy. Pencil on paper. 6 July 1824*
The north pier was constructed in 1749 and the south in 1752. The latter supported cranes for unloading fishing and merchant ships, a rope with block and tackle, and two winches. These piers were built as a result of an Act of Southwold Borough in 1746 that allowed funds to be raised by a body of commissioners drawn largely from neighbouring country gentlemen. The British Library

Black Shore, Southwold. Walberswick in the Distance *by Henry Davy. Pencil on paper. 1 August 1825.*
The scene, where Carnsey Road meets the river Blyth, is still recognisable even though none of the buildings, with the exception of St. Andrew's Church, Walberswick have survived. Those to the left of the composition are the coalbins and granaries built by Francis Wayth in 1816 and were used as storage for the cargoes landed by merchant ships visiting the harbour. Vessels are moored opposite The Fishing Buss, now called The Harbour Inn. The British Library

A House in Park Lane, Southwold *by Henry Davy. Watercolour on paper. 1837.*
This building, now 16-18 Park Lane, is one of the oldest and most tantalising buildings in the town. Dating from the first quarter of the seventeenth century it is probably a rare survivor of the fire of Southwold. Although it was once called Manor Farm it is actually a type of Suffolk town house built in the artisan Mannerist style. The front, now washed with paint, has kept its mullioned and transomed windows, though all other ornament has been stripped away. A new roof has covered the attic windows. The British Library

A remarkable collection of topographical watercolours of Suffolk purchased by the British Museum from a Mrs. L.E. Davy of Ufford on 13 November 1852 shows that his most productive year was 1842. The watercolours are bound in six large volumes and are arranged by the old administrative divisions called 'hundreds'. A very few are by Davy's contemporaries but the majority of the 1319 separate watercolours and drawings are in his own hand. The volume entitled *The Hundred of Blything* contains 33 of his watercolour drawings of Southwold, including views of York Cliff, North Cliff, the Swan Hotel, Blackshore, the old houses in Park Lane, the windmill, the racecourse, the lime kilns on the common and a wreck on the beach. There are also detailed studies of the smuggler's tavern at Reydon called *The Bear*, the nearby Wolsey Bridge and the cliffs at Easton

Bavents. Davy also made watercolour drawings of the churches at Reydon, Walberswick, Blyford and Wangford and the remains of the Chapel of St. James in Dunwich.

The volumes contain a number of preliminary sketches for his more famous paintings and etchings, but most are highly finished works of art. The majority are signed and dated to the day and from this we know that Davy liked to sketch and paint in high summer. Perhaps it was the full sunlight that allowed him to work with such meticulous attention to detail and to achieve a glacial clarity in his work.

What is known of Henry Davy suggests a modest and methodical man whose character was not conducive to a financially successful career as an artist. He died, apparently intestate, on 8 February 1865. There was no obituary to accompany the notice in the *Beccles and Bungay Weekly News* six days after his death, only a note to say that he was an artist and was much respected. He is buried in Ipswich cemetery under a stone that commemorates both him and his wife.

Apart from the collection of drawings cited above there are very few examples of Davy's work in our public collections. He was best known through the published etchings on which his posthumous reputation rests. When the material now kept in the British Library has been properly evaluated, perhaps then Davy will finally be acknowledged as one the most singular topographical artists of the nineteenth century.[2]

Three boats beached at Southwold *attributed to Henry Davy. Pencil on paper. Dated 24 October 1838. These small vessels may have belonged to the larger fishing ships that were the foundation of Southwold's economy. They are labelled with the name of the mother vessel, the harbour of registration, and the name of the owner: "Sarah, Southwold, Corbell Cole"; "John and Mary of Southwold, Robert Land"; and "William and Rachel, John Crickmore, Southwold". On 19 May 1839, the year after this drawing was made, the pilot cutter* John and Mary *picked up the* Eliza of London, *which had been abandoned by her crew and towed onshore at Easton. It was subsequently purchased by R.R. Boniwell Esq. Corbell Cole and Robert Land were listed as burgesses of Southwold in 1837.* Mr and Mrs Brian Webb

SOUTHWOLD AND THE ANTIQUARY

On 20 May 1824 a group of men came from London to Southwold and committed what now seems to be an act of unmitigated vandalism. Lying to the south of the town and over the river at Walberswick was a group of tumuli, known locally as the 'Fairy Hills'. They were believed to be the remains of a Viking settlement and perhaps it was romantic speculation of this sort that had first excited the destructive curiosity of the mysterious visitors and led them to uncover three "*urns*" containing the bones of the "*illustrious dead*". In the process of the dig almost all historical context was destroyed and the new owners of these ancient artefacts left with little more than meaningless souvenirs and the quickly abating excitement of their discovery. Today even the urns have passed into oblivion and all that remains of value from this regrettable episode is the insight it provides into the antiquarian attitudes of the time.

In the late eighteenth and early nineteenth century, interest in the past had never been greater and, concurrent with a sense that antiquities and history were a communal possession of the public, there was an appetite for sensational discoveries. An enhanced sense of national identity meant that there was a patriotic obligation to make antiquarian studies freely available to all. A re-evaluation of domestic antiquities had come about from a preference for the sublime and the picturesque and, as a result, much greater value was placed upon our ancient monuments, Gothic ruins, churches and mediaeval castles. The nation was getting to know its past as much through the publication of engravings as through topographical literature.[1] In Southwold these were brilliantly effected by the painter and engraver Henry Davy and the historian Thomas Gardner (1690?- 1769), author of the first history of the area, published in 1754, under the full and informative title of*: An Historical Account of Dunwich, antiently a city, now a borough; Blithburgh, formally a town of note, now a village; Southwold, once a village, now a town-corporate; with remarks on some places contiguous thereto, principally extracted from several antient Records, Manuscripts &c which were never before made public.*

Little is known about Gardner's early life, though he seems to have had strong connections with Walberswick and may have lived there for a while. Certainly two of his children were baptised in St. Andrew's Church: Renshaw in 1723 and Georg in 1724. It was as a salt officer in Southwold that Gardner earned a living, until he became deputy controller of the harbour; by 1738 he was also inspector of the town workhouse.

Gardner's antiquarian interests were personal rather than professional. He was a product of the mercantile middle class, which, largely self-educated, was the backbone of The Enlightenment. An early interest in local history was fired by the oldest inhabitants of the area who told him about life in the early seventeenth century and, in particular, about the lost city of Dunwich. This inspired the young man to visit the

The section and elevation of part of the rail of the rood screen in St. Edmund's, Southwold *by George Wardle (ob. 1910). Pencil and watercolour on paper. c.1862.*
Wardle toured the churches of East Anglia making meticulous record drawings of the painted decorations that had survived the destructive purges of the Reformation and the Commonwealth. The screen had been the focus of antiquarian interest for some while before Wardle made this beautiful watercolour drawing. It was the subject of an article entitled 'On the remains of the painted decoration in Southwold Church, Suffolk' by C.L. Blackbourne in 1859. In it the screen is described as one of the richest examples of painted decoration in Suffolk, if not in the whole of England. The Society of Antiquaries, London

borough where he discovered a sublime and romantic landscape, heightened by the presence of ancient ramparts:

"... *foundations of fallen-down edifices, and tottering fragments of noble structures, remains of the dead exposed and naked wells divested of the ground about them, by waves of the sea.*"

A N
HISTORICAL ACCOUNT
O F
SOUTHWOLD.

(1)

(2)

Copper plate engravings from the first page of Thomas Gardner's Historical Account of Southwold. *1754.*
To the left is shown a halfpenny token issued by the Borough of Southwold in 1667 for the relief of its poor. To the right is the matrix of a late mediaeval seal engraved with a horse's head and the date 1490. It was found in Southwold and may have been made to mark the first year of the town's incorporation by Henry VII.

C H A P. I.

A. 1. THIS Place, in elder Time, was called SUWALD, SU-WALDA, SUDHOLDA, SOUTHWAUD, and SOUTHWOOD; pro-bably from a Wood growing near; for the weftern Confines ftill retain the Appellation of *Wood's-End-Marfhes*, and *Wood's-End-Creek*.

(1) THE Arrows in Saltier piercing the Crown feems to allude to the Martyrdom of *Edmund* King of the *Eaft-Angles*, by the Pagan *Danes*. And being between two Dolphins naiant, fhews the Town of Note for the Fifhery. But whether the E has Reference to the Name of that Saint whofe Buft with a radiated Crown is the Creft to thefe Arms, and to whom the Church here was dedicated, or to fome latter crown'd Head, I refer to the Opinion of the Curious. The S is the initial Letter of, and fignifies the Appellation of the Corporation.

(2) THIS Seal with the Horfe's Head, infcribed *Henricus Dei Gra. Rex Anglie et Franc. Dux Lan.* 1490, was found at *Southwold*. The Front thereof was deaurated, and the Reverfe adorn'd with a Plate of Silver, and bearing Date with this Corporation's firft Charter, requires a ferious Confideration to judge of its Propriety.

B b 2   2. SOUTH-

Evidently there was precious little left of Dunwich by the time Gardner visited, and even less remaining of its records, which he found "*ransacked*" except for the common court books that were "*too close confined for inspection*". Nonetheless, he was fascinated by what he saw and embarked on making a collection of available facts, which he arranged under appropriate headings, including 'Fairs and Markets', 'The Forest', 'Rivers and Ports', 'Churches', 'Hospitals', 'Mayors and Bailiffs and Members of Parliament', 'Charters' and, finally, 'The Destruction of Dunwich'.

Because the history of the sunken city could not be written in isolation, Gardner expanded his research to encompass Southwold and the final text of 260 pages included 73 devoted to the borough. The focus of the book, however, remained a narrow one and Gardner was obliged to finance, print and distribute it himself. The list of 189 subscribers is impressive and included the newly deceased Frederick Prince of Wales (1707-1751) who was the intelligent, intellectual heir of King George II, the 4th Earl of Shaftesbury whose predecessor had been at the battle of Sole Bay, as well as five members of the recently founded Society of Antiquaries of London.

Gardner lived in what is now 21-23 Park Lane, and it was from his life and work in the town that he acquired his knowledge of its past. In his introduction he outlined Southwold's ancient history and eventual supremacy over Dunwich. An account was given of the town's exemption from taxes previously owed to Dunwich, its original charter from Henry VII in 1489 and those granted by his successors. This was followed by a history of the church and chapels, a detailed account of the evolution of Southwold Haven, the bequest of William

A copper plate engraving from Thomas Gardner's Historical Account of Dunwich. 1754.

It shows various small coins, antique seals and seal rings dating from the thirteenth to the fifteenth centuries. Some were found in Dunwich and others had local connections. The plate was dedicated to Thomas Martin (1697-1771) a Fellow of the Society of Antiquaries. Martin's thirst after antiquities was said to be as great as his thirst after liquors. Despite his disreputable past and dissolute character he was esteemed by the new generation of East Anglian antiquaries, among them Gardner.

Godell in 1509, the great fire of 1659, and the Battle of Sole Bay in 1672.

Thomas Gardner's history is an extraordinary collection of facts, some of which were set down as much to amaze as to inform, nonetheless, they are invaluable today because they were gleaned from sources now obscure or completely lost. Gardner's achievement is all the greater considering that he was living in an age with few of the amenities that we take for granted today; he was a determined researcher and took as much care in the transcription of original documents as he did in recording, from living memory, Southwold's topography, including the drawbridges, beacons, batteries and fortifications that have since disappeared without trace.

In the process of accumulating facts, Gardner made next to no attempt to interpret them. However, he recognised the value of small but vivid details. One such was the accidental discovery of a macabre relic in the church: a velvet cap worn by the corpse of Thomas Elliot who had died in 1641. Despite being buried for 96 years it was found to be in remarkably good condition.

When reading Gardner, one senses a man, conscious of his humble background, who was both modest and sensitive. Twice widowed before he died in 1769, Thomas Gardner was buried on the south side of St. Edmund's Church near the nave. His tombstone reads:

> *Between Honor and Virtue, here doth lie*
> *The remains of Old Antiquity*

119

However, it was not Gardner's tombstone but his book that was to be his greatest monument.

The converse was true of Gardner's successor, James Maggs (1797-1890), until his *Southwold Diary* was finally published posthumously, nearly a century after his death.

Born at the *Blue Anchor Inn*, Walberswick on 9 February 1797, James Maggs was lame, which disbarred him from a career at sea. His widowed mother, recognising the special importance of a good education for the disabled boy, sent him to a school in Wenhaston from the age of seven.[2] At the age of 14, Maggs was articled and later went to work for James Jermyn who lived in Reydon. This appointment was to prove formative since Jermyn's interests were literary and antiquarian, and it was probably from him that Maggs developed a passion for the past. By 1816 Maggs had been appointed to a position at Dedham Grammar School, but he quickly moved to London to take up work at the Grey Coat School in Westminster. By 1817 he was back in his own parish with the intention of opening a school in Walberswick, though in 1818 he decided that Southwold would be the better place. After many years of teaching and running a boarding house for summer visitors, James Maggs finally settled on a career as an auctioneer.

From the age of about 21, Maggs had begun to accumulate a collection of notes, cuttings and ephemera about Southwold that included the town properties, mills, harbour, quay, salt works, inns, and schools. Records of wrecks, crimes, suicides, executions,

Opposite:
St. John, a panel from the roodscreen at St. Edmund's Church Southwold *by George Wardle. (ob. 1910). Watercolour on paper.*
The Apostle carries a chalice from which emerges a dragon. Almost all the original silver from St. Edmund's Church, including three pairs of chalices in silver and silver gilt, was sold in 1547. That which is carried by St. John shows what they may have looked like (see p.33).
The Society of Antiquaries, London

Left:
Detail of St. John *by George Wardle.*

significant obituaries and entertainments were included in the diaries, which were kept from 1818 to 1876. These volumes are of inestimable value and when, in 1973, Yvonne Hatton gave them to the Southwold Archaeological Society, their preservation was assured. They were made more widely available when, in 1984, the Suffolk Records Society published a small edition in two volumes, edited by the late Alan Bottomley.

Throughout his life Maggs amassed facts, but he also liked to collect things and had a typically Victorian penchant for the antique and the curious. In Wrentham, in 1865, there was an exhibition to which he brought a number of oil paintings including *The Old Mill* (Easton Bavents) and the *Cherry Tree Inn* (Stoven). In 1888, just two years before he died, he contributed a number of "*curious items*" to a similar show, though it was his portrait that attracted the most attention because he was well known for his "*passionate love of collecting and preserving local traditions and records of events.*"

During the time that Maggs was compiling his collection, his efforts were being paralleled by a Fellow of the Society of Antiquaries, Joseph Sim Earle (1839-1912). Earle was the son of a wealthy timber merchant who lived in Kensington Palace Gardens, which had been known as 'Millionaire's Row' from the early 1860s. Earle's antiquarian tastes developed from his close friendship with the Rev. Edmund Farrer and it was from sailing together up the East Coast and excursions inland that Earle's fascination with the area was kindled and he began to collect related material. This included 121 books on Essex and 174 on Suffolk. However, a growing library was not enough and it appears that when he was not sailing, Earle was buying up everything related to the two counties: prints and engravings, maps, postcards, restoration appeal notices, letters, trade and visiting cards, newspaper cuttings, obituary notices, brass rubbings and sale catalogues. These were supplemented with a number of watercolours that held a special fascination for Earle, and included several by the Southwold artist Henry Davy (see p.106). When Earle died his collection was left to the Society of

Antiquaries and comprised a considerable amount of material relating to Southwold.[3]

Some of the archive amassed by James Maggs was made available to the Mayor of Southwold and local historian, Robert Wake, when he was writing *Southwold and its Vicinity*, published in 1839. His book was not only a history of Southwold but also a natural history of its environs. In this regard it has something of the character of a Victorian museum, where archaeological finds jostle with fossils and specimens of flora and fauna. Ironically, its value today is not so much in Wake's view of the past, but in what he wrote about his present. The evolution of the borough from a fishing port into a fashionable watering place had begun in the late eighteenth century and these changes were a recent memory. Wake not only detailed the development of the town and its permanent residents, but also described the activities of those fashionable visitors who came to Southwold in the summer to promenade on Gun Hill:

"*Let him turn his eye and fix ... on the pleasure parties on either side of him. Smiling faces and fairy forms... while he sits and saunters upon the cliff ...will pass and repass like summer clouds and almost as light and fantastic. The well-backed benches, near him and in the distance, are occupied by the lolling yet talkative gentry...*"

Robert Wake was happy to acknowledge his debt to James Maggs, but he was much less comfortable in his obligation to Thomas Gardner. On more than one occasion he criticises Gardner for factual error and omission on grounds that are highly suspect[4] and sometimes his tone can only be described as snobbish and spiteful:

Left and opposite:
Outline drawings of panels from the screen in St. Edmund's Church, Southwold *by George E. Fox. Left: the Archangel Michael, carrying a sword and scales. Right: Potestates or Powers, the sixth order of angels in the celestial hierarchy, with a devil subdued, on a chain. Pencil on paper. 1885. Michael wears a sunburst crown and a jewelled morse at his neck and his body, with the exception of face, hands and feet, is feathered.*
Powers has no crown but wears a richly decorated turban and aigrette of osprey feathers.
These fine drawings are the product of hours of the closest scrutiny and they allow us to understand the rood screen in a way that would be very difficult today. The Society of Antiquaries, London

"*The printed history, or 'Historical account of Dunwich, including Blythburgh and Southwold' by Thomas Gardner published in 1754, is not remarkable either for the extent or accuracy of its contents. The author was a salt officer, that is, resident revenue-officer, appointed for the collector of duties of the saltworks in Southwold, possessing some antiquarian taste, but to judge 'ex pede' of no gigantic literary talent.*"

In the mid-nineteenth century antiquarian tastes were encouraged by a network of museums and scholarly societies including the Suffolk Archaeological Society. Some, inspired in part by Ruskin's *Stones of Venice* of 1851, were established for the preservation of our national heritage. In 1853, the year that William Morris went up to Oxford, the fourteenth century window of Christ Church was torn out and replaced with a 'Norman' version devised by Sir George Gilbert Scott. Over the next quarter of a century Morris was not only to witness disastrous "improvements" of this sort, but also the decline that resulted from sheer neglect. In 1868 Morris and his family were in Southwold and the pitiful state of Blythburgh church could not have escaped his notice. Ten years later he read of Sir George Gilbert Scott's plans to 'restore' Tewkesbury Abbey and protested against it with a vigour born of a new sense of conviction. Morris immediately proposed a defence committee that included Carlyle, Ruskin, Burne-Jones and Philip Webb. It was a congregation of the greatest sages of the nineteenth century and from it emerged the Society for the Protection of Ancient Buildings, known affectionately as "Anti-Scrape". Morris, as secretary, set out its aims and, in doing so, articulated some of the antiquarian attitudes of the future:

"*What I wish for therefore is that an association be set on foot to keep watch on old monuments ... and by all means, literary and other, to awaken a feeling that our ancient buildings are not mere ecclesiastical toys but sacred monuments of the nation's growth and hope.*"

It is possible that Morris had been first alerted to Southwold's heritage, and its attractions as a watering place, by his colleague and friend George Young Wardle (ob. 1910). Wardle had been there in 1862-3 as part of a long tour to make record drawings

and photographs of the fittings and decorations of the East Anglian churches. Three years later Wardle was employed as bookkeeper and draughtsman to Morris, Marshall, Faulkner & Co, later Morris and Co., of which company he was general manager from 1870-90. Perhaps it was because of his knowledge of East Anglian architecture that he, William Morris and Philip Webb drew up the statement of aims of the Society for the Protection of Ancient Buildings. The Society of Antiquaries owns a remarkable collection of Wardle's drawings and they are interesting not only as a record of mediaeval decoration, but also because they were made for the practical purpose of providing William Morris with sources for his fabric and stained glass designs.

Wardle was followed to Southwold by a Fellow of the Society of Antiquaries, George Edward Fox (1833-1908). Although his interest in the decoration of Suffolk churches paralleled that of Wardle, his was exclusively academic. Born in Norwich in 1833, Fox travelled extensively in Italy, studying for his future career as an artist architect. Making use of the experience he gleaned there, Fox carried out extensive schemes for the decoration at Eastnor Castle, Warwick Castle, Longleat and for tombs in the Duke of Bedford's mausoleum at Chenies. Fox was at the centre of the artistic community in London and was a friend of the artist Sir Lawrence Alma-Tadema. It was for Alma-Tadema that he designed a grand pianoforte and matching chair. After retiring from his professional career, Fox focussed his attention on his antiquarian interests and made a special study of the painted roofs and screens of Norfolk churches. His drawings of the rood screen of Southwold and the ceiling of Blythburgh church made in 1878 and 1885 are part of a superb collection belonging to The Society of Antiquaries (see illustrations on pp.32, 33, 35, 122 and 123). They are meticulously observed and skilfully drawn, and the jewel-like intensity of their colouring goes a long way to evoking the lost splendour of Southwold's mediaeval past.[5]

Eustace Edward Grubbe (1847-1933), Mayor of Southwold in 1911, is remembered for being "a gentleman in both manners and position ... and an old and tried friend of the the town," but less well known for being an enthusiastic antiquary. Conscious of his kinship with James Giles (1718-1780) – the famous 'china painter' and glass enameller from London – Eustace began to make a comprehensive catalogue of the

---

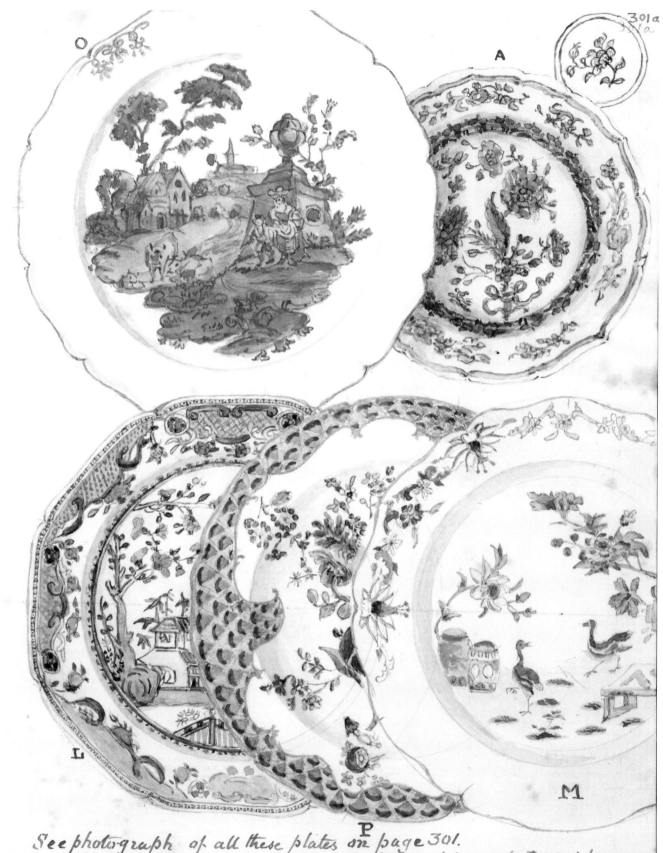

301a
a

See photograph of all these plates on page 301.

A. An oriental blue & white plate. Came from the Halls, & belonged to J.C.G. in her very early days. She gave it to me in 1889. On the right of the drawing of this plate (above) is a sketch of the mark beneath it, reduced in size the real size ~~being~~ of the diameter of the outer circle being 1 7/8 in. As to the plate itself - diam. is 6 5/8 in: diam. of pediment 3 3/8 Height ~~8 inches~~ 1 5/16 in.

L & M are oriental plates, & belonged to desert services in use in Dr Hull's house at Pemb. Coll. Oxford, when he was Master. Both were given to me by J.C.G. in 1889. There is no mark on either. As to L - diam: is 9 1/4 in; diam of ped about 5 in. Height 1 1/16 in. M's diam. is 8 3/4; Di. of ped. 4 7/8; height 15/16 in. I know of no other piece of the service to which L belongs but L.H.H. has a plate like M in his house at Churcham.

O & P belonged to the Rev. Geo. C. Hall, on whose death they were allotted (with another plate of each pattern) to L.H.H, who gave them two to me in 1901 or 1902. O is very richly gilded & is a beautiful specimen of chelsea china. There is a very collection of porcelain proudly displayed at his house at 22 Park Lane. Grubbe drew these and every other heirloom, including silver, jewellery and glass, in meticulous detail in watercolour, heightened with gold. With them are photographs of Grubbe's collection of topographical oil paintings of Southwold including views of the ferry, two landscapes by Thomas Smythe and a number of Grubbe's own watercolours of buildings in Southwold, now quite gone. The album, known as the 'black book', in which these colourful record drawings are contained is still in the family. Eustace Grubbe was in frequent correspondence with the Society of Antiquaries in London and was made a Fellow in 1908. There, one of his oil sketches of an ancient stone mortar is preserved to this day. His sixth son, Lawrence Carrington Grubbe, inherited his father's talent for painting and drawing and was a locally respected artist at the turn of the nineteenth century.

With the expansion of society and communications in the late nineteenth and twentieth centuries, Southwold entered a new phase of popularity and with it came a deeper fascination with the past. Interest in its history was fostered by The Southwold Archaeological Society founded in 1932 and the intimate and charming museum in Victoria Street, which was established at the same time. It remains very popular with visitors who come to see a wide range of exhibits including fossils, seaside souvenirs and paintings by a number of the distinguished artists who have worked in the town.

In recent years there have been numerous publications of varying degrees of scholarship. Some are little more than sensational journalism and others, like *Southwold River* (1990) by Rachel Lawrence are evidently the result of years of painstaking and dedicated work. Shorter studies include *Mardles from Suffolk* by a Fellow of the Society of Antiquaries, Ernest R. Cooper. This was published when Cooper was living on East Cliff in 1932; it is a gathering of numerous amusing anecdotes about Suffolk and Southwold in particular. The author's chatty, humorous style should not be allowed to distract from the impressive range and depth of his research. Ernest Cooper's papers now belong to the Southwold Archaeological Society.

In the bibliography at the back of this book I have tried to include the best of the many books about Southwold, however, a special tribute should be made to Norman Scarfe who has added so much to our understanding of Suffolk's past and to the late Alan Bottomley, resident of Southwold and master at Eversley School, for editing James Maggs's diaries in such a meticulous and informative way. His *Short History of The Borough of Southwold* remains unequalled.

John Tooke, a man of local descent, has, in the tradition of both Maggs and Earle, been collecting books and ephemera associated with Southwold. His work with removals and house clearances has enabled him to rescue all manner of documents from destruction and, as a result, he has accumulated a unique and valuable collection, rich in newspaper cuttings, photographs and postcards. John was always ready to show this remarkable archive at his home, and has now generously deposited part of it with the Southwold Museum, where its value has already proved to be enormous.

A watercolour detail of the mantle of St. Philip from the rood screen of St. Edmund's Church, Southwold *by George Wardle. c.1862.*
Two swans, emblematic of purity, grace and the Virgin Mary, share a nest built amid flowers. The Society of Antiquaries, London

This is the age of digital photography and video and, as a result, historians of the future will not need to rely exclusively on the work of visiting artists to piece together a visual impression of Southwold as it is now. However, the letters and prose that proved indispensable to understanding our predecessors have been supplanted by the telephone, text messages and emails. Paradoxically, we are living in an age when the visual memory of the past is secure, but the legacy of our thoughts and feelings is ephemeral; historians and antiquaries of the future are losing with one hand what they are gaining with the other. Today the lives of the people of Southwold are spent in an age with a dazzling technological present, but a fast-fading past.

PEN TO PAPER

To be able to bring the greatest genius of English literature into Southwold's orbit might easily be dismissed as an historian's impossible fantasy, but for me it has become all but a complete reality. Part of Shakespeare's acting career was with a troupe of itinerant players called 'The King's Men' who performed in Dunwich on 10 October 1608 and again in October 1610. The actors probably travelled from London the quickest and most efficient way: by ship, heading for Southwold Haven. Little is known about these visits except to say that 'The King's Men' would have discovered that the inhabitants of Dunwich were very poor. In fact some were starving and were supplementing their meagre diet by gathering the wild sea peas growing on the cliffs. Somehow the actors' fees were scraped together and when 'The King's Men' accepted the invitation to come to Dunwich they must have been on their guard, knowing that the audience was not an easy one to please. Eleven years earlier, in December 1597, Mr Allen, scrivener, grudgingly paid their predecessors, 'The Queen her Majestie's Players', 6 shillings *"and [was] yet much discontented"*.[1]

If indeed Shakespeare came to within literally a stone's throw of Southwold then he tops an impressive, but by no means comprehensive, list of writers: Daniel Defoe, reputedly the inventor of the English novel, and his successors Thomas Hardy, Jerome K. Jerome, Sir Henry Rider Haggard, Henry James, Edward Thomas, George Orwell, Penelope Fitzgerald, P.D. James and Esther Freud; the story writer and distinguished antiquary M.R. James, the poets Edward Fitzgerald, William Morris, Algernon Swinburne, Walter de la Mare, John Masefield, A.E. Coppard, Ruth Pitter and John Betjeman; the philologists George Borrow and John Bagnell Bury; the thinker and early pioneer in the scientific study of sex, Henry Havelock Ellis; the philosopher Bertrand Russell; and the travel writer Julian Tennyson. For all of them Southwold had a special personal significance, but for just a few it proved a truly powerful inspiration.

By the early eighteenth century communications had improved and travel by coach had developed from being a dangerous chore into something of a pleasure. As a consequence, several guidebooks were published.[2] Daniel Defoe (1661?-1731), adept at all the skills of journalism, wrote one of the more famous guides to the United Kingdom, entitled *Tour through Great Britain*, published in 1724. In the October, he lodged opposite the church in Southwold and found it to be a quiet place:

> "*I found no business the people here were employ'd in, but the Fishery ...*
> *for Herrings and Sprats; which they Cure by the help of Smoak.*"

A successor to Defoe's guide was *Suffolk Garland*, published in 1818. In it there is a flattering description of Southwold written by an unnamed poet ten years previously:

> *Southwold, all hail! peace to thy billowy shore;*
> *In vain may tempests rage or ocean roar,*
> *Thy verdant cliffs still bless the seaman's eye,*
> *Thy genial gales still health and ease supply:*
> *Still may thy sons, on active gen'rous train,*
> *Guide the frail bark in safety thro' the main;*
> *And home returning, with delight and joy*

Opposite:
William Shakespeare *by Martin Droeshout (1601-1650?). Engraving.*
It is virtually certain that Shakespeare was part of 'The King's Men' when the troupe of actors played to the people of Dunwich. Shakespeare was inspired by the sea and powerfully evokes its destructive moods and changes in The Tempest. *However, it is the opening lines of* Sonnet 60 *that a shoreline like that at Southwold becomes a powerful* memento mori:

Like as the waves make towards the pebbled shore,
So do our minutes hasten to their end;   The National Portrait Gallery

Embrace the faithful wife, the blooming boy.
Yes, their's the bliss domestic love imparts,
Unknown to sordid minds and venal hearts.
Though Vice, with giant strides, throughout the land
Extends her sway, and boasts supreme command,
When far removed my lingering fancy strays
O'er the memorials of departed days,
Southwold shall rise to memory ever dear,
For worth and virtue yet are cherished here.

These, the first of a steadily increasing number of guidebooks, outlined the attractions of Southwold and, as a result, a number of visitors returned each year to enjoy the summer sun. Their visits were mirrored by the annual flight of migrant birds to and from Southwold. In 1724 Defoe had noted that "*a prodigious multitude of swallows*" had covered the church roof and several houses nearby. Clusters of their descendants had also caught the eye of George Crabbe (1754-1832) when he was writing *Smugglers and Labourers*:

> *As on their neighbouring beach yon swallows stand,*
> *And wait for favouring winds to leave the land;*
> *While still for flight the ready wing is spread:*
> *So waited I the favouring hour and fled.*

Crabbe was born in Aldeburgh and it was there that, as a result of an unhappy upbringing, he developed into a man of imperious character and strong passions, heightened by an addiction to opium. Although he was a natural writer, he also had a facility for mathematics, which, together with his great physical strength, made him an unlikely poet. Crabbe was a practical man and, after holding several inferior offices, he was, like Thomas Gardner in Southwold, promoted to saltmaster of the town. His younger brother Robert, "*a most worthy person, gifted with many attainments beyond his rank*" settled in 55 High Street[3] in Southwold and there he worked as a sign writer and glazier. When the poet was living at Glemham the brothers met every Monday at the *White Hart* in Blythburgh to "*exchange the news of the week*" over "*tea and a glass of punch*", though sometimes he made the full journey to stay with Robert in Southwold.[4]

When George Crabbe was in Suffolk, the sea and coastline were on his doorstep and he described both with great force and fidelity in his poetry.

> *Turn to the watery world! – but who to thee*
> *(A wonder yet unview'd) shall paint – the Sea?*
> *Various and vast, sublime in all its forms,*
> *When lull'd by zephyrs, or when roused by storms,*

Its colours changing, when from clouds and sun
Shades after shades upon the surface run;
Embrown'd and horrid now, and now serene,
In limpid blue and evanescent green;

One of Crabbe's most devoted friends and admirers was the writer Edward Fitzgerald (1809-1883). They both originated in Suffolk and shared a deep affection for the county. Fitzgerald was born in Bredfield and, after a short spell in France and going up to Cambridge, he settled in nearby Woodbridge. It was there that he made his translation of the *Rubaiyat of Omar Khayyam* and on it his reputation was founded.

The driving force of his life was not love but friendship and he recognised the importance of maintaining it. In nearby Dunwich he was part of the glittering artistic circle of Edwin (1823-1879) and Ruth Edwards and spent the summers of 1876, 1877 and 1878 with them. It was there, in 1877, that he met Charles Keene (1823-1891); they enjoyed each other's company from the very start. Keene remembered their conversations:

"*We met every evening and talked belles lettres, Shakespeare, and the musical glasses till midnight.*"[5]

Relationships with those who lived further away were kept up by post: Fitzgerald wrote wonderful letters to William Makepeace Thackery, Alfred Tennyson, Samuel Lawrence, and the Suffolk painter Thomas Churchyard.

Fitzgerald loved the sea and, from 1865, he kept a sailing boat called *The Scandal* on the river Deben. He sailed past Southwold on his way to Lowestoft, where he was part owner of a herring-lugger. More and more of the summer was spent on the water, mostly off the Suffolk coast, though, on occasion, he would sail to France and Holland. The master of the herring-lugger was a man called Joseph Fletcher, known as 'Posh'. For several years after they met in 1864, 'Posh' became the centre of Fitzgerald's emotional life. It was probably on one of their idyllic sailing trips together that Fitzgerald was inspired enough to write the following:

The German Ocean will dimple with innumerable pin points, and porpoises rolling near the surface sneeze with unusual pellets of fresh water-

Can such things be,
And overcome us like a summer cloud,
Without our special wonder &

Oh this wonderful, wonderful world, and we who stand in the middle of it are all in a maze...

The poet Algernon Swinburne (1837-1909), see illustration opposite, became an admirer of Fitzgerald's *Rubaiyat* after he had chanced upon a copy being disposed of cheaply at the bookseller Bernard Quaritch. They had more in common than a love of exotic poetry: both of them loved the sea, indeed Swinburne was once described as the "*laureate of the sea*". Such was its power over him that it partially took the place of the drink and dissolution that had threatened his early life. It was then that he began to refer to it as "*my mother sea*".

Swinburne was rescued from himself by a man called Theodore Watts-Dunton (1832-1914) who, from 1872 onwards, became not only his saviour but his intimate friend. When Swinburne's excesses were bordering on life-threatening depravity, Watts-Dunton removed him from his lodgings to the comparative safety of a house in Putney called 'The Pines'. There, a strict regimen of rest, proper food and exercise turned round the life of the poet and extended it to the age of 72.

Watts-Dunton has been described as "*genteel*" and "*suburban*", but to Swinburne his dominant character meant that he became known as 'Major'. Trained as a solicitor, he had known East Anglia from his childhood. Watts-Dunton went to school in Cambridge and made regular visits to the East Coast to bathe. Swinburne's mother, Lady Jane, had been born at Barking Hall in Suffolk, the daughter of the third Earl of Ashburton. It was to this fact that Swinburne attributed his affection for the East Coast. Certainly, it was a return to his roots, but it was the health giving effects of the sea water that Watts-Dunton believed would benefit his talented but highly-strung friend. Swinburne was in Southwold[6] in late September and October of 1875, and again in 1876, and there can be little doubt that it satisfied a deep-seated need in him to swim:

"*I begin to get impatient for it, and feel the want of bathing before summer is out.*"

Swinburne's address in Southwold in 1875 was South House, Middle Cliff. He was evidently bored by the local topography when he wrote to William Michael Rossetti on 26 of September:

"*I am here for a fortnight or so longer on a coast which for four days I found as dull as any place can be to me where I have the sea, but on the fifth (this morning) I have found a place that would have delighted Shelley—a lake of fresh water only parted from the sea by a steep and thick pebble-ridge through which a broad channel has been cut in the middle a little above the lake, to let off the water in flood-time; half encircled to the north and west by an old wood of oaks and ash-trees, with a wide common beyond it sweeping sideways to the sea. It is so unutterably lonely that that I thought instantly how like this new beautiful wood must be in winter to Dante's wood of suicides. I would not break a leafless bough there for anything.*"[7]

Swinburne's sister Alice accompanied him on at least one of these holidays in Southwold. Together they enjoyed the "*Wide sands where wave draws breath*". She

Algernon Swinburne *by William Bell Scott (1811-1890). Oil on canvas. 1860.*
Swinburne was attracted to the East Coast by the sea and stayed at both Southwold and Dunwich. He
was deeply inspired by what he found there, which led to him being called the 'Seagull Poet'. Swinburne
also enjoyed the physical presence of the water and bathed naked whenever possible. In Southwold
this was only permitted at the North end of the town before 6am.

Master and Fellows of Balliol College, Oxford

remembered the same lake and wood as where he first read her excerpts from his poem *Erechtheus*, based on a Greek tragic style, in which a daughter is sacrificed by her father for the sake of Athens. In a letter to Swinburne dated 9 June 1887 she wrote:

"*Erechtheus always reminds me of Southwold, especially of that dear little wind-blown wood by the inland sea, (which is only divided from the open sea by a bank of pebbles) where you read us some of it for the first time.*"[8]

After a morning's walk down the coast, Swinburne was to find similarly gloomy inspiration for his poem *By the North Sea* in which he describes the terrible fate of Dunwich and the dramatic ruins that remained of its glorious past. The crumbling tower and cemetery of All Saints Church are recognisable in the following verses as are the grisly exhumations from its cemetery, effected by the constant erosion of the cliff below:

Here is all the end of all his glory—
Dust, and grass, and barren silent stones.
Dead, like him, one hollow tower and hoary
Naked in the sea-wind stands and moans,
Filled and thrilled with its perpetual story:
Here, where earth is dense with dead men's bones.

Naked, shamed, cast out of consecration,
Corpse and coffin, yea the very graves,
Scoffed at, scattered, shaken from their station,
Spurned and scoured of wind and sea like slaves,
Desolate beyond man's desolation,
Shrink and sink into the waste of waves.

Tombs, with bare white piteous bones protruded,
Shroudless, down the loose collapsing bank,
Crumble from their constant place detruded,
That the sea devours and gives not thanks.
Graves where hope and prayer and sorrow brooded
Gape and slide and perish, ranks on ranks.

One summer Watts-Dunton, in the company of Swinburne, took a house in Dunwich. There he had a chance meeting with his childhood hero the philologist and writer George Borrow (1803-1881), who lived at Oulton Broad but was then staying at *The Swan* in Southwold.[9] Watts-Dunton recorded it as a semi-fictional interlude called *A Day with 'Lavengro'*.

Watts-Dunton's career was inevitably overshadowed by his famous friend Swinburne, though he wrote numerous essays and reviews on a wide variety of subjects including

Victor Hugo, William Morris, Alfred Tennyson and his great friend Dante Gabriel Rossetti, whose own links with Southwold are described in the following chapter, Paradise Lost.

In the early 1880s Swinburne and Watts-Dunton were ready for a change from Southwold and Dunwich and heard of a very "*aesthetic*" place on the Norfolk Coast, near Cromer, whose name "*sounded delicious*". Consequently it was not to Southwold they came that summer but to Poppyland.[10]

Swinburne's contemporary and close literary friend was the author Thomas Hardy (1840-1928). Unlike Swinburne, Hardy was not drawn to Southwold by love of the sea but by one of their mutual acquaintances, the Hon. Florence Henniker. She was the daughter of Richard Monckton, first Baron Houghton, who was noted as much for his extravagant hospitality as for his varied list of friends, which included politicians, poets, authors, artists, actors, explorers, and members of fashionable society. In 1882, at the age of 27, Florence married The Hon. Arthur Henniker-Major, the younger son of Lord Henniker of Thornham Hall in Suffolk. Inheriting many of her father's traits, she soon established a coterie of literary friends of her own; not the least of these was Thomas Hardy. Florence Henniker was author of six novels and three collections of short stories, but it was not so much for her literary skills that Hardy was attracted to her, rather as a great thinker and for her far-reaching compassion. Thomas Hardy first met Florence Henniker in Ireland in 1893 and she aroused strong emotions in him from the start. Mrs Henniker was happily married and Hardy was not, and because of this the relationship was always imbalanced. Evidently, a sense of realism tempered Hardy's ardour, which had begun to cool by 1896. Nonetheless, they remained close friends and he always thought of her as "*one rare woman*".

After Hardy's first wife, Emma, died in 1912, Mrs. Henniker invited him to the house she had taken on Gun Hill called Southwold House. He arrived on 22 April 1913 to meet his old friend Florence Dugdale there. Miss Dugdale was 39 years younger than Hardy but, despite their differing ages and the fact that Hardy was already married, they had begun a love affair in 1907. Florence Henniker must have been aware of this and perhaps that is why Hardy decided to sleep

Thomas Hardy by Harry Furniss (1854-1925). Pen and ink on paper. c.1900.
An amusing caricature of the famous author at about the time he was in Southwold and staying at The Swan. During his time in the town Hardy was in love, but he still had time to enjoy the sunshine, fresh air and the splendid architecture of the church.　　The National Portrait Gallery

at The Swan. Hardy was preoccupied by his emotional life during his time in Southwold and, as a result, there is little written evidence of his visit except the routine letters he wrote to friends from Southwold House. One of them is a postcard of the church sent to his sister Mary on 23 April, on which he drew her attention to famous flint flushwork decoration. The only hint that he enjoyed his stay is to be found in a letter written to his friend Edward Clodd in which he wrote: "*Cloudless weather here, and splendid air*". Although Hardy was gone from Southwold by 8 May we can be certain that the visit made an impression on him, not only because of his deep affection for Mrs. Henniker, but because he had shared the visit with Florence Dugdale: they were married less than a year later in February 1914.

If love was in the air for Hardy so it was for Walter de la Mare (1873-1956) when he came to Southwold in the summer of 1894. He had not seen the sea since his early childhood and travel to Southwold was within the modest budget of a young man. However, it was not the German Ocean but a young lady called Constance Elfrida Ingpen, known as Elfie, who proved to be the main attraction for de la Mare. In the beginning, for propriety's sake, his first visits alternated with hers but, later, she was chaperoned by her brothers and sisters and the two were able to be there together. At the time, de la Mare was unhappily employed by the Anglo American Oil Company; a city job that was not only stressful but prevented him from writing. However, the prospect of escaping to Southwold and seeing his beloved Elfie raised his spirits to a fever pitch. With the writing of drama on his mind, de la Mare told Elfie that they would have "*grand ideas*" in Southwold. Not long after, he did indeed write a play, *Mrs Urquhart*, about a haunted house by the sea. It may be that he had Elfie in mind for one of the parts since one of the pet names he invented for her was 'Phantom'. In time, Southwold proved to have shaped de la Mare's life in two important directions: it was there that he finally won the affections of Elfie and that he confirmed his ambition to be a writer. Southwold was the beginning of a dazzling literary career that was to earn him the Companion of Honour, the Order of Merit and a place for his ashes in the crypt of St. Paul's Cathedral.[11]

One of the most luxuriously tortuous writers to have been inspired by the East Coast was the American Henry James (1843-1916), and he was attracted to it by a remarkable series of coincidences. On 3 July 1897, at Bournemouth, he had been reading the letters of Edward Fitzgerald and had come upon the name of 'Saxmundham', which he found had a "*strangeness and handsomeness*" to it. That very afternoon he had met a rugged boatman from Suffolk – from Saxmundham – whose brother had been Fitzgerald's beloved boatman, 'Posh'. On returning home he found a letter from Saxmundham from an American cousin asking him to come to stay with them at Dunwich. Taken by this thrice-encountered coincidence James immediately packed his bags and went. The visit was the inspiration for the chapter called *Old Suffolk* that started as a magazine article and was later reprinted as one of James's *English Hours*, a series of travel sketches, beautifully illustrated by an American artist, the friend and biographer of Whistler, Joseph Pennell. The perpetual struggle with the sea proved a powerful inspiration for James:

"The coast, up and down, for miles, has been, for more centuries than I presume to count, gnawed away by the sea... which moves for ever, like a ruminating beast, an insatiable, indefatigable lip."

In 1932 Eric Blair, better known as George Orwell (1903-1950), chose, as his pen name that of the river that flows into the sea at Felixstowe. He was to cross it innumerable times on his way to Southwold, which had been his parents' home since he was 18. The first house they lived in was 4 Stradbroke Road, from there they moved to 3 Queen Street, before they finally settled in Montague House in the High Street in 1933. Southwold, a quiet middle-class town on the East Coast of England, was an unlikely place for the future author of *Down and Out in Paris and London* to announce his intention to be a writer. In August 1927 he returned from service in Burma to tell his parents that he had resigned his hard won commission in the army in order to realise his ambition to be an author. They were horrified. Despite this, Southwold was to play an important role in his literary career. He left his parents' home there in 1927 and returned to it from Paris in 1930, hardly any closer to his goal, and with less money than he hard started out, but it was in Southwold that he began to write the first drafts of *Down and Out in Paris and London*. This has come to be known as Orwell's 'Southwold period'; it was a domestic interlude during which writing outweighed all other considerations except the search for inspiration. From Southwold Orwell set off, sometimes just overnight and sometimes for weeks, to go 'down and out'. This was a time when he lived deeply contrasting lives. One was led at the reserved, respectable seaside home of his parents and the other in doss houses, in the squalor of the East End and in the hop fields of Kent. These dualities were to be found not only in his circumstances but also in his friends and, between 1930 and 1933, the difference between the life of Southwold's Eric Blair and the mask that was George Orwell was most obvious.

If Suffolk was not enough for Orwell it certainly was *"everything"* for Julian Tennyson (1915-1945). In 1938 he published *Suffolk Scene*, which goes far beyond what was expected of a simple county guide, striving to identify the essence of a landscape and its people. Tennyson, great-grandson of the poet, was introduced to Suffolk by his parents when he was 15 and he was shortly to discover that it provided him with all he needed. Indeed, he once admitted, when writing at Ancient House, Peasenhall, that he never wanted to go any further East than East Anglia. Sadly, he was obliged to when, after joining the Irish Rifles in 1939, he was sent to Burma where he was less lucky than Orwell. Aged just 30, a fragment of shrapnel, the size of a fingernail, pierced his skull and killed him, thereby putting to an end a literary career that had promised to be dazzling.

Like Henry James before him, Julian Tennyson reflected not so much on the beauty of the sea, but on its destructive power:

"Oh, so slowly does it beleaguer us! Could you see it in summer, drawling up the beach, brushing the shingle with its coquettish lips, so gentle, so harmless, so indolent, you would scoff at the idea of evil lurking in that serene and imperturbable bosom."

Suffolk Scene remains a fitting monument to its short-lived author, but it is not the only one. His father, Sir Charles Tennyson, who lived in Park Lane, Southwold, set a glass window, engraved with the martyrdom of St. Edmund, in the church as a memorial to the wife and sons who pre-deceased him: Ivy, Penrose and Julian (see illustration on p.21).

Sometimes it is not the sea, but the society of Southwold that has inspired resident writers. By the third quarter of the nineteenth century prosperity had returned and, for some, it was a place of leisure. Inevitably, there were intrigues and scandals, and interest in them was heightened by the rank of their participants. In 1874 anonymous authors published a scurrilous novel called *Shingleborough Society,* which was followed three years later by *Nettlestings.* The portrayal of Southwold life was only thinly disguised, so thinly that some of the inhabitants recognised themselves. The authors were also to betray their own identity and had no option but to leave town. It is possible that these rather silly books were the original inspiration for the novelist Penelope Fitzgerald's own beautiful little novel *The Bookshop*, published in 1989. Based on the time when she worked in a haunted bookshop in the High Street in Southwold, it is a touching story of a woman who wanted to start her own business in a town on the East Coast called Hardborough. What started out as a relatively modest ambition turned into a battleground not only with supernatural forces but also with snobbery, envy and prejudice.

Even today Southwold and its surroundings continue to inspire its resident writers, including Michael Palin, P.D. James and Esther Freud (see illustration opposite).

Occasionally Southwold has provoked spontaneous lyricism from unexpected directions, and one such is the script for a talk given by Eric Phillips on B.B.C.'s radio programme *Holiday Hour* (The Light Programme, 13 February 1955):

"*The sun blazed down that afternoon at Southwold. Stone and red brick alike glowed in the strong light. The gardens were a riot of crimson roses and blue delphiniums. And in the evening, after sundown, the pale blue sea was changed to a darker blue and was flecked here and there with pin-points of opalescent fire. There are some moments that you know you will never forget all – this was one of them.*"

Opposite:
Esther *by Lucian Freud. Oil on canvas. 1982-83.*
A portrait of Esther Freud by her father Lucian before her highly successful career as a novelist was launched with the publication of Hideous Kinky *in 1992. This was the first of five novels, the last of which,* The Sea House, *derives its plot and title from the buildings on the Walberswick side of Southwold Harbour. Lucian Freud's own connections with the area are outlined on p.241.*
By kind permission of the artist. © Lucian Freud

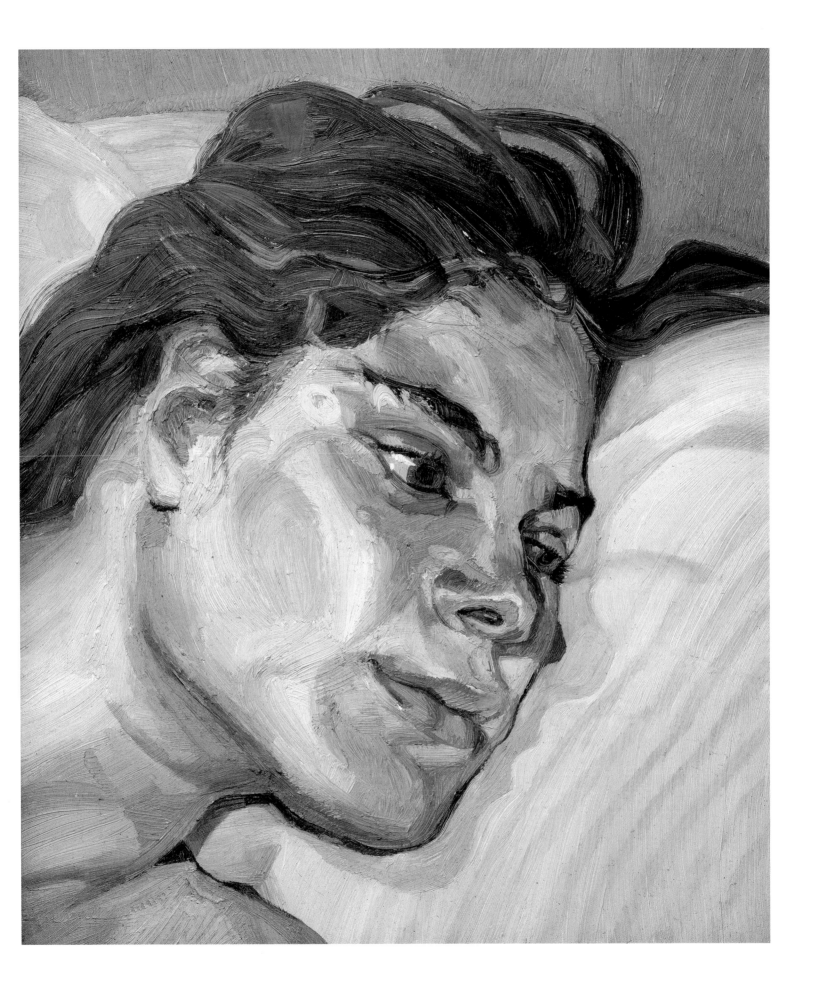

PARADISE LOST

"A figure cut out of a missal ... an apparition of fearful and wonderful intensity" was how, in April 1859, Henry James described William Morris's wife Jane.[1] The daughter of an Oxford groom, she had entered the orbit of the Pre-Raphaelites in about 1857 when Dante Gabriel Rossetti (1828-1882) and William Morris (1834-1896) were in Oxford working together on the Oxford Union murals. It was Rossetti who first persuaded her to sit for them and it is likely that he was in love with her from the beginning. Nonetheless, Rossetti kept faith with Elizabeth Siddal to whom he was married in 1860. The next best thing to having Jane as his wife was to place her at the centre of the Pre-Raphaelite circle and her marriage to William Morris in 1859 assured it.

The young artist Graham Robertson said *"Hers was one of the world's faces – unique"*. Despite her great beauty, after her wedding to Morris Jane did not appear in Rossetti's work again until 1867, when their intimacy was heightened. The following year the Morris family, which now included their daughters Jenny and May, spent the late summer in Southwold. Morris gives a retrospective account of that visit when he was there again in 1895. On 19 July he wrote to his close friend Georgiana Burne-Jones:

"Blythborough was what we went to see... The place is close to Southwold on the little tidal river Bly at the end of the marshland valley, where they were busy with their second hay crop. Little spits of sandy low upland covered with heather and bracken run down to the marsh, and make a strange landscape of it; a mournful place, but full of character."[2]

Morris may have remembered Southwold in vivid detail because he stayed there with his young family at a time of deep emotional upheaval. Rossetti was in secret correspondence with his wife Jane and the tone of his letters reveal that a passionate love affair was well under way. It was probably because Mrs. Morris was in Southwold that Rossetti had it on his mind. On 21 August 1868 he referred to it in a letter to their

---

Opposite:

The Blue Silk Dress – A Portrait of Janey Morris *by Dante Gabriel Rossetti. Oil on canvas. Planned in 1866 and finished in 1868; the year Mrs. Morris was in Southwold.*

The painting is inscribed "Jane Morris AD 1868 D.G. Rossetti pinxit. Conjure clara poeta et praeclarissima vulta, denique pictura clara sit illa mea." [Famous for her poet husband, famous for her face, may my picture add to her fame.] This remarkable portrait was finished the year that the Morris family was in Southwold and when the love affair between Janey Morris and the painter was at its height. In front of Mrs Morris is a vase containing white roses and hops. On the pages of the open book is a striped carnation and at her side a vivid red one. In the language of flowers these mean "Keep my secret" "Injustice" "Alas for my poor heart" and "Refusal". Whilst in Southwold Mrs. Morris kept up a secret correspondence with Rossetti and no doubt similar emotions were articulated in their letters to one another.

The Society of Antiquaries, Kelmscott Manor

friend Charles Augustus Howell, who had been staying in Southwold with his wife Kitty at the same time as the Morris family:

"I wish I could get to Yarmouth ... it is barely possible that I may, with William, next week which he has at his disposal and will go anywhere with me ... but I rather incline to Southwold, as a very quiet place, in spite of what you say. It is provoking to get there when everyone else is gone, but I have been seeing doctors till now."[3]

By *"everyone"* he must really have meant Jane Morris in particular. If Southwold was quiet, then the urbane Howell was probably suffering from boredom, only slightly alleviated by the fact that he was, in his own words, acting the *"postbox"* between Mrs. Morris and Rossetti. Rossetti makes covert reference to one of the letters he wanted Howell to give to Jane before she left Southwold on 24 August. Howell had already moved from Southwold to Lowestoft and Rossetti was probably trying to dissuade him from returning specially in order to deliver it to her in secret.

"Don't trouble about what I send you unless it is convenient. I couldn't think of giving you a long job over it. No really don't as there is nothing of importance."

Rossetti had not been well and believed that his brain had been affected through overwork. It is possible that this was the beginning of the mental collapse he was to suffer four years later in 1872. His mood made the thought of the journey to Southwold daunting. Rossetti had it in mind to travel by train and asked Howell for advice about the *"least miserable way"* of getting to Southwold from the nearest station, which was Darsham. He was also exercised by the thought of finding decent lodgings and asked Howell: *"Didn't Topsy [Morris] have a house to himself? Could this be got?"* A letter to William Allingham four days later, shows that Rossetti was still undecided:

"I'm going to start away somewhere, but fancy seaside. There's a deadly-lively (or very quiet) place called Southwold, in Suffolk, where the Morris's, Howells and others have been lately. I think perhaps of going there."[4]

This lack-lustre description of Southwold is not Rossetti's own and probably derives from Howell's disappointment with the town. Careful reading of these letters reveals that Rossetti never arrived in Southwold on this occasion or, indeed, on any other.

Opposite:
William Morris *by George Frederick Watts (1817-1904). Oil on canvas. 1870.*
This portrait was painted not two years after the Morris family had visited Southwold. Owing to Jane's affair with Dante Gabriel Rossetti, Morris's spirits had been low for some time. On 15 April 1870 Morris wrote to her:
" I am going to visit Watts this afternoon although I have the devil of a cold in the head which don't make it very suitable."
National Portrait Gallery

Dante Gabriel Rossetti *by William Holman Hunt. Oil on panel. 1853.*
This remarkable portrait was made not long before Rossetti met Jane Morris for the first time in 1857. It is probable that he fell in love with her then. The intensity of Rossetti's stare is explained by the fact that he was making Holman Hunt's portrait whilst he sat for him. Nonetheless, it reveals the passionate nature that Mrs. Morris found impossible to resist. Although Rossetti knew of Southwold from his friend Augustus Howell (see opposite) its main attraction was the knowledge that Jane Morris had spent the summer of 1868 there. Although he made detailed plans to follow her it is virtually certain that he did not.

Birmingham City Museum and Art Gallery

144

Charles Augustus Howell *by Frederick Sandys. Coloured chalks on paper. 1882.*
Charles Howell, infamous in the English art world from the 1860s to the 1880s, was a glamorous figure with unscrupulous morals. Georgiana Burne-Jones remembered him as "one who came amongst us in friend's clothing ...but inwardly was a stranger to all our life meant." He was a friend of both Swinburne and Rossetti and the trio were a common sight in the 1860s when they enjoyed "the acrid putrescence" of London life. When Howell was in Southwold in 1868, he was entrusted with the task of passing love letters from Rossetti to Mrs. Morris. However, the greatest service he did Rossetti was during the following year when he retrieved a manuscript of poems from Lizzie Siddal's grave in West Highgate Cemetery.

Ashmolean Museum, Oxford

Although the Morris family holiday in Southwold should have been full of sunshine and domestic bliss, it was not. Perhaps Morris had finally to accept that he had failed to take his marriage with Jane from youthful romance and idealism to a relationship based on mutual respect, confidence and intimacy.[5] Certainly the melancholy feelings he was experiencing then were acute enough to inspire the beautiful, yet mournful, stanzas for

October in his epic poem *The Earthly Paradise*. The "*wold*", its "*grey church*" and bells, are easily recognisable references to Southwold.[6]

> *O love turn from the unchanging sea, and gaze*
> *Down these grey slopes upon the year grown old,*
> *A-dying mid the autumn-scented haze,*
> *That hangeth o'er the hollow in the wold,*
> *Where the wind-bitten ancient elms enfold*
> *Grey church, long barn, orchard and red-roofed stead,*
> *Wrought in dead days for men a long while dead.*
>
> *Come down, O love: may not our hands still meet,*
> *Since still we live to-day, forgetting June,*
> *Forgetting May, deeming October sweet?*
> *O hearken, hearken! Though the afternoon,*
> *The grey tower sings a strange old tinkling tune!*
> *Sweet, sweet and sad, the toiling year's last breath,*
> *Too satiate of life to strive with death.*
>
> *And we too; will it not be soft and kind,*
> *That rest from life, from patience and from pain;*
> *That rest from bliss we know not when we find;*
> *That rest from love which n'er the end can gain?*
> *Hark how the tune swells, that erewhile did wane!*
> *Look up, love! Ah cling close and never move!*
> *How can I have enough of life and love?*

Rossetti was obsessed with Jane Morris's face until the day he died from chloral addiction and ill health in 1882. Morris had accepted the estrangement of his wife with stoicism and concentrated on his social activity and conservation work. He founded The Society for the Protection of Ancient Buildings in 1877 and it was on its behalf that he returned to Suffolk in July 1895 to report on the sad condition of Blythburgh church.[7] Twenty-seven years had passed since Morris had been to Southwold, but he found that he had remembered it perfectly. The following year the great Victorian polymath was dead.

Opposite:
Colouring of the roof, Blythburgh Church *by George E. Fox. 1878.*
Although Morris was worried by the condition of the church by 1895, this part, the ceiling, looks to be in a good state of repair. It originally blazed with bright colours and the visual impact of the angel's wings was heightened with the application of silver foil. Now the roof is almost all that has survived of the original decoration. It is now subtle and muted and in perfect harmony with the rest of the church.
The Society of Antiquaries, London

Blythburgh Church, Colouring of Roof

George 2nd 1819

13 feet

9 in. Aspect

HAPPY HOLIDAYS

In 1762 John Kirby published one of the first guide books to Suffolk called *A Traveller's Guide and Topographical Description of the County of Suffolk*. In it he gives the first indications that Southwold's future prosperity would depend not so much on fishing the sea but the seawater itself:

"The town of Southwold has become a bathing place within 20 years, and is well attended, but the beach is not as good as Aldeburgh. It has some good inns and buildings."

In 1809 Southwold had just two bathing machines, but its other attractions as a holiday destination were expanded upon in a pamphlet dated 1823 that had something of the nature of an advertisement:

"This ancient Town & Burgh so delightfully situated on an eminence at the very margin of the sea and enjoying in the greatest perfection and purity the cool & vivifying breezes from the wide expanded ocean is daily filling with visitors. The inhabitants have generally reduced the price of their lodgings considerably in order to meet the depressed state of the times. ...The town is daily supplied with an abundance of meat, fish and vegetables of the best quality & on the most reasonable terms; in short the real or imagined valetudinarian may meet with every comfort here... Every accommodation is offered either for hot or warm bathing..."

Eye Cliff, Southwold *by Henry Davy. Watercolour on paper. c.1828.*
On what is now known as Gun Hill, holiday-makers enjoy the view of a sea teeming with traffic. Ladies and gentlemen with children and dogs walk past the flagpole and amongst the cannon from which the place derives its name. Beyond is the pretty reading room, which, owing to its octagonal shape, was known as the "Casino". Beyond is Stone House then belonging to Onley Savill Onley Esq. It was there that the portrait painter George Richmond stayed as his guest in 1861. Beyond the last cannon is a path towards the sea that ends close to the north pier of the harbour, first built in 1749.
This is the original watercolour drawing from which Davy took the famous print, dedicated to his patron and sometime resident of Southwold, Sir George Crewe of Calke Abbey. The National Maritime Museum

At the time the pamphlet was distributed, sea bathing had become of great importance to the prosperity of coastal resorts like Southwold. Huge publicity attended George III's sea bathing at Weymouth with his family and inspired many of his subjects to follow suit. However, bathing was seldom indulged in for pleasure and few people learned to swim, but it was still possible to benefit from the health-giving effects of seawater dips. Doctors prescribed them as a cure for every kind of ailment and a "*sanitary reaction*" and an "*improvement of tone in the finer vessels and animal functions*" was the result that was wanted.[1] All that was necessary in order to gain these benefits was a single dip, but in the process it was necessary to maintain the highest levels of propriety and modesty. Even though the bather remained fully clothed throughout, the process was a very private one and the only way to keep it that way was to hire a bathing machine, and the services of its attendant. These 'machines' were small wooden sheds on wheels with an entrance at both ends. The door on the seaward side

Glasses round *by Charles Keene. Sepia on paper. c.1870. Probably the preliminary drawing for a cartoon in* Punch.

A fashionable urban gentleman, his hat secured against the wind with a silk lace, meets two seamen with a telescope. There has always been a degree of tension between the residents of Southwold and its affluent visitors. In 1893 the magazine Pall Mall *observed, "It must not be supposed that the place is free from all nuisances. There is the 'Summer Man' as he is called, with loud check knickerbockers and an affection for golf".* Evidently this drawing was made on one of the wooden piers at Southwold harbour.

The Fine Art Society

THOSE DREADFUL BOYS!

Algernon. "AND, DEAREST, IF THE DEVOTION OF A LIFE——" *(At this moment his hat is knocked over his eyes by a common Star-fish, or Five-fingers (Asterias rubens), thrown, with considerable force and precision, by one of those* infern ——*high-spirited little fellows her younger brothers,* TOMMY *and* BERTIE *!!!*

Those dreadful boys! *A cartoon for* Punch *by Charles Keene. Published 18 June 1870.*

An intimate moment is disturbed when siblings throw a starfish at the lovers who are standing next to the capstan on the Walberswick side of Southwold harbour. (See illustrations on pp.56 and 65).

© Punch archives

Scene on the beach *by Charles Keene. Watercolour on paper. c.1877.*

A well-dressed lady with a parasol negotiates the hire of a bathing machine on the beach at Southwold. Once the fee has been established, the machine will be reversed down the beach into the chill water to facilitate bathing. The customer will need to undress in close proximity to the operator. The issues of class and sexuality raised in this amusing drawing anticipate the coarse humour of the twentieth century seaside postcard. At the turn of the nineteenth century the bathing machines were operated by Smith and Palmer, who boasted that "sanitised" bathing dresses and outfits were provided and that every machine was equipped with a looking glass, shoe horn and brush.   Courtesy of the Fogg Art Museum, Harvard University Art Museums

Bequest of Meta and Paul J. Sachs, 1965.183

was shielded from view by a pair of canvas curtains. Inside, the bather would undress, put on a cumbersome costume that covered the whole body and the machine would then be wheeled into the sea. Below the level of the water was a suspended wooden floor with sides of canvas that provided even greater privacy and security. If required, the "*gentle and encouraging*" attendant would help the bather into the chill water, as near horizontally as was possible. It was not recommended that the dip should last any longer than the point when "*a grateful thrill, and the fast flowing animal exhilaration had been achieved*" and that the process of drying and dressing should be as quick as possible. Over indulgence was not recommended, as it may be "*injurious to the health of the subject, as indiscreet intimacy is to friendship*".

If sea bathing was thought to be therapeutic, then sunbathing was not. A pale complexion was attractive in a woman and a tan was considered vulgar. Immodesty of any kind was unthinkable. In Southwold in the late 1830s the law upheld public decency and propriety. Bathing was permitted only at the north end of the beach beyond the town boundary post, before six in the morning. Anyone "*found bathing or indecently exposing his person, within sight of any person passing along...*" was to be fined five

The Beach at Walberswick *by Philip Wilson Steer (1860-1942). Oil on wood. c.1889.*
A family and their dogs enjoy the sunshine and sea views. This vibrant painting is typical of the compositions that Wilson Steer made when he was at Walberswick. Flat plains of colour are accentuated by the human form and the effect is dazzling. However, Steer's work was not appreciated in his own time. In fact, it generated a storm of abuse so violent that he considered giving up painting forever.

shillings. No matter how hot the weather, hats and skirts were *de rigueur* and men wore shoes, socks, long trousers, starched long-sleeved shirts and a jacket and tie (see illustrations on pp.154-155, 157 and 175).

Extra modesty and comfort could be bought at a price by visiting the public baths, which had been established at the south end of the town by Edmund Preston of Yarmouth and were run by a *"discreet and orderly couple"*. Hot, cold and tepid water could be had there and the seawater, a by-product of the salt industry conducted on the same site, was said to very pure.

By the end of the nineteenth century attitudes had softened a little and bathing had

152

Girls running, Walberswick Pier by Philip Wilson Steer (1860-1942). Oil on canvas. 1888-1894.
This is perhaps the most famous of all the paintings made in Walberswick and Southwold. The precise location of the scene is a mystery and it may, like so many of Steer's oil paintings, have been drawn from different sources and finished in his London studio. At this time Walberswick Pier was cluttered with capstans and the huts of the lookout men (see illustrations on pp.8 and 9). © Tate London, 2002

given way to the joys of swimming. It still took place at the north end of the town but costumes for men and women were less inhibiting and were considered by some to be all too alluring. The bathing machines remained for many years, but their use gradually declined. A faint memory of them was kept alive until very recently in the form of the wheeled huts that stood just south of the old pier, but their real heirs are the brightly-painted beach huts that stretch the whole length of the promenade. By the 1890s pontoons were anchored off the beach as an incentive to the hesitant swimmer and they provided an excellent vantage point from which to look back at the pretty town and its prettier visitors (see illustration on p.160).

Southwold beach *by Sir Walter Westley Russell (1867-1949). Oil on canvas. c.1897.*

Children are enjoying a bucket and spade holiday with their mothers. For modesty's sake they are fully clothed and hats are worn to prevent the skin from developing a vulgar tan. Behind them is the wooden pier on the north side of the harbour and sailing boats are returning to the haven.

Russell, a friend of Philip Wilson Steer, worked regularly on the Norfolk coast and was an occasional visitor to Suffolk. This may be the picture of the same title that Russell showed at the New English Arts Club in 1897. F. Starr Associates, New York

Even today those who have spent a holiday in Southwold tend to return each year and as its popularity increases, so does the demand for accommodation. There are several hotels where fully-catered service is available, but many families prefer to take short holiday leases on houses all around the town. This was true in the early nineteenth century when the first large influx of summer visitors arrived, and by the 1830s Southwold was already being developed. In 1829 The Rev. Thomas Sheriffe had built the neoclassical building Centre Cliff Houses specifically to accommodate the summer visitors. The white stuccoed front, columns surmounted by shells, and decorative ironwork make it the most attractive to have survived. Those that could afford it kept holiday homes in the centre of town, the most enviable position being on Gun Hill where the sea views were the best. When not in use, these elegant Regency houses were lent to family and friends. One such is Stone House, which belonged to the Squire of Sistead, Mr. Onley Savill Onley; in 1861 he generously lent it to the painter George Richmond (1809-1896) and his family.

However, the house, which was intended for sheer pleasure, turned out to be the scene of an all too familiar holiday nightmare. Mrs. Richmond had the misfortune to spill an inkpot down the "*spotless*" watered sea-green wallpaper in the drawing room. Paying for the damage was not an option and the family were appalled by their predicament. Apparently there "*was silence and there was lamentation*" but it was Richmond who provided the first ray of hope. He shook his head doubtfully and said: "*Well, I have done a little painting now and again and with your permission, dear Lady, I will try my hand at this.*" He went into the little town and bought white paint and green, and applied coat after coat until the ink was completely covered. Laughing at last, the famous portrait painter declared, "*The greatest work of art I have ever accomplished – is it not?*"

In those days the holiday-makers from London were encouraged to travel by sea on ships owned by the General Steam Navigation Company. They left for Southwold on Mondays and Thursdays, returning on Wednesdays and Sundays. Published timetables were available and the fares were reasonable for what were powerful and fast-moving ships. Apparently the accommodation on board was considered remarkably good, the views of the passing coastline attractive, and the sea air, a welcome relief from the smoky capital, was almost as great an attraction as the sea itself. When the steamer had eventually anchored, the holiday-makers were collected in large boats and rowed to land in return for a fare of 2 shillings each.[2]

There has never been a shortage of things to do in Southwold. In the early nineteenth century it was fashionable to promenade on Gun Hill in groups that were described by Robert Wake as "*pleasure parties of smiling faces and fairy forms*". Whilst liveried servants attended the gentry, others went to 'The Casino',

George Richmond, R.A. by William Blake Richmond. Reproduced from 'The Richmond Papers' by A.M.W. Stirling 1926.

156

A pair of paintings, evidently of the sands at Walberswick, by Septimus E. Scott (1879-1965). Oil on canvas. c.1900.

Mothers with their children are enjoying brilliant sunshine by the side of the German Ocean. There are no bathing machines in sight on what appears to be the beach beyond the south pier of Southwold harbour.

Septimus Scott was a popular book illustrator and British poster artist.   Christie's, London

157

the little reading room, to see the daily newspapers; an elegant amenity reminiscent of the world of Jane Austen's novels. Public benches were set out and provided views of a sea teeming with commercial traffic. Boat races were also popular and, despite a hesitant start, the Southwold regatta, first held on 23 August 1835, became firmly established. In 1842 the boats made a pretty sight with coloured sails and flags and they were not the only attraction that year: the sky above Southwold blazed with coloured fireworks on three consecutive nights. During the next six years the regatta was popular enough to signal an annual holiday for the residents of the town. All the shops were closed, the high street was hung with flags, the bells rang throughout the day, and the battery on Gun Hill was fired over the sea.

" 'Let's go along and see Eeyore' said Piglet. So the three of them went, and after they had walked and walked and walked, they came to a part of the forest where Eeyore was."

An illustration for A.A. Milne's The House at Pooh Corner, *by E.H. Shepard. 1928.*
Shepard's wife had died under anaesthetic in September 1927. Naturally, his thoughts returned to the sunny days of their courtship at Southwold and his memories of the scene were incorporated in the now famous series of drawings. The lonely pines on the hill, surrounded by prickly gorse, was a place where the doleful donkey, Eeyore, lived, like Shepard, quite alone.

16.VII.1905

c/o Miss Roberts
10 South End
Southwold

My dear Artie

Our time here is nearly up, more's the pity, as we are going home on Tuesday. And I have been so busy I have had no time to reply to your very welcome letter with its brilliant drawing which shows you know Southwold beach pretty well and that you too have been a student of nature.

These family men with perambulators do get a look in sometimes I've noticed. We are all artists at the seaside. Well we are going back as I say on Tuesday & I have cricket on Wednesday at Harborne and on Thursday Norman and May are to come and have tea with us, would you and Georgie come too? we should be so pleased if you would Georgie hasn't been for so long to see us. There are endless pictures to be done here but I have only done one little thing and a drawing or two. They talk of widening the harbour and making docks at Walberswick. I hope they won't, it would be ruined. Never was such sunshine as we have had day after day no rain at all. Farewell and may we all come here again for a long stay. Our love to you all Yours affectionately Joz

"We are all artists at the seaside".
An illustrated letter from the Birmingham artist Joseph Southall to the painter and jeweller Arthur Gaskin, who knew Southwold well. Written from South End on 16 July 1905.
It shows a young man with family responsibilities distracted by two girls who have swum out to one of the pontoons anchored off the beach near the pier (see illustration on p.257). Another observes the scene from the safety of a bathing machine. Southall evokes the sadness that invariably clouds the last few days of a happy holiday in Southwold: "Our time here is nearly is up, more's the pity, as we are going home on Tuesday … Never was such sunshine as we have had day after day, no rain at all. Farewell and may we all come here again for a long stay."
Stephen Wildman Esq.

Opposite:
Along the Shore *by Joseph Southall. Tempera on silk. 1914.*
Fashionable holidaymakers are caught in a sudden gust of wind. The conjunction of bathing machines, a rowing boat, and a modern yacht suggests that this scene was painted at the north end of the beach near the pier. There Messrs. Smith and Palmer were proprietors of the well-equipped machines, as well as being the owners of several comfortable rowing boats and the makers of model yachts for use on the nearby lake (see p151).
Southall's juxtapositioning of the modern and the classical was not well-received at the time: "[his] goddesses are more convincing in their fairy-tale charades than when they strike the same attitudes in Edwardian clothes in Corporation Street, Birmingham or Along the Shore", wrote The Times. *The painting was exhibited at the 1920 Oldham Spring Exhibition, where it sold for 60 guineas.*
Joseph Southall came to Southwold every year at the same time and it is virtually certain that this painting was made in July 1914; only weeks later this seaside idyll was shattered when war was declared on Germany on 4 August 1914.

Gallery Oldham.
Bequest of Mrs A.E. Southall in 1948
© Estate of Joseph Southall

The Bridge *by Philip Wilson Steer. Oil on canvas. 1887.*
In this picture, clearly inspired by Steer's visits to Walberswick, a man and a woman meet on the 'Kissing Bridge' at sunset. Their relationship is enigmatic and a hazy evening light adds to the mystery. The river flowing out to sea may be a metaphor of their future together. Although the bridge arched in the middle it straightened as it met the ground at its eastern end (see illustration opposite and on p.223). The local historian and friend of Steer, Carol Christie, remarked that the bridge was a favourite subject for artists because it " 'came in' so beautifully against the old Harbour bar with the fishing boats near and the nets hanging to dry from their masts". In about 1900 it carried a sign saying "Dangerous" and was eventually moved into the marshes. (See opposite.)

For those who preferred their sport on land, the corporation sponsored horse races on the common from 1820, though some of the more conservative residents were pleased when this ceased in 1833. More exotic amusements were provided by a variety of travelling entertainers. In August 1839 a ventriloquist was competition for the troupes of actors who were making their annual visit; in September 1845 James Ewing's display of waxwork effigies of the Royal family was something quite unique. So too was the troupe of Ethiopian singers who performed for one night only, in April 1847,[3] adding to the variety and eccentricity of the entertainments.[4]

A lantern party on the Kissing Bridge, Walberswick *by Bertram Priestman (1868-1951). Oil on canvas. Dated 1927.*

Like the Ferry over the river Blyth (see illustrations on pp.214 and 215), this bridge was the favourite subject for "shoals" of artists who came to Walberswick to paint. By 1911 it had been moved to this position, over Dunwich Cut, known locally as The Went. Priestman has intensified the oriental character of the bridge by including Chinese lanterns in his beautiful composition. Priestman had a house and garden in Walberswick from 1914 to 1927 and it was there that he taught Edward Seago (see illustration on p.212).

Private Collection

An annual round of fairs and circuses contributed to the lively atmosphere of the town and the origins of some are very ancient. In 1227 Southwold was granted a royal charter for two fairs to take place on the eve and days of Saints Philip and Jacob. These were superseded by those that took place on the feasts of Holy Trinity and St. Bartholomew. Today their character is very different from their ancient predecessors, but they continue to provide excitement and amusement. Once the fairs were a place where all manner of business went on, including the sale of luxury goods and the exchange of employment, however, since the early twentieth century the focus has moved from commerce to a wide range of entertainments. Enjoyed by both residents and summer visitors alike,

163

Chinese Lanterns *by Bertram Priestman. Watercolour on paper. 1919.*
This lyrical scene of children carrying paper lanterns was painted in the afterglow of a summer night.
There is hardly enough topographical detail to pinpoint the location, though there is little doubt that it is
Walberswick. An oil painting by Priestman of the same subject painted at the "Kissing Bridge" is on p.163.
Private Collection

these happy events attracted itinerant operators who brought sideshows, colourfully painted swing-boats and steam-driven carousels. The activity and excitement they generated inspired a number of artists including Alan Gwynne-Jones, John Doman Turner and possibly Alfred Munnings to capture the ever-varying scene.

The arrival of circuses and menageries always attracted attention. They included the usual range of performing animals, lions, bears and ostriches and dancing dogs. On one occasion the operators tried to persuade an elephant to cross the Blyth from Walberswick by means of the steam ferry but it balked at the idea and had to be walked round to Southwold via Blythburgh instead.

The presence of summer visitors drew actors to Southwold and the performances they gave varied in complexity from sideshows on the beach, to full scale productions under canvas. In 1897 a small troupe of actors was rendered destitute when its manager absconded with the earnings. Happily Ellen Terry's son, the actor and theatrical designer Edward Gordon Craig (1872-1966) was there, and their fortunes changed for the better when he

164

organised a production of *Villon* specifically for their benefit. The painter and designer James Pryde (1866-1941) had a leading roll and so indulged a taste for dressing up, which, in Southwold, had been limited to the rôle of Pierrot (see illustration on p.169). These colourful and lively productions anticipated those that have been given by the Southwold players, under the direction of Jill Freud (the inspiration for Lucy in C.S. Lewis's *Narnia*), every year since 1984. Summer sunshine and a rich variety of entertainments were the basic ingredients of a wonderful holiday and helped to establish the rosy view of Southwold that prevails even to this day. It is one that was poignantly evoked in *East of Ipswich* by Michael Palin.

In 1883 the satirical magazine *Punch* found "delightful" Southwold a place ideally suited to doing next to nothing but eat:

A Song of Southwold

I can lie on my back and look up at the sky,
And I see the swift sea-gulls sail solemnly by;
While I've nothing to think of but what there's for lunch,
And how yonder fair face should be pictured in Punch.

There is fish to be eaten – although, with a frown,
I find out that the best of it goes up to town:
Yet with heartfelt delight will the epicure say,
He is simply sublime is the shrimp of Sole Bay!

There is little to do; I can go for a sail,
And I try to catch fish, and most probably fail.
So I lie down again, and this time with a pipe,
And feel thankful that country greengages are ripe.

There's the Common, where young men and maidens can play
That eternal Lawn Tennis from dawning of day;
As they brandish the rackets, and struggle, and run,
I've the best of the game looking on at the fun.

Or I wander to Walberswick, place of delight
To the artists who paint it from morning till night;
But I sit on the pier and I relish the view,
Without messing my fingers with cyanine blue.

Little Southwold's the place to get rid of black Care,
Which "post equitem sedit" let HORACE *declare;*
There are no town amusements, but swift the time passes,
By wild wavelets "πολυφλοισβοιο θαλάσσης" [of the loud-roaring sea].

Southwold by Philip Wilson Steer. c.1889.

The shorthand sketchy outlines and dislocation of the figures is highly original and the colours have a brilliance that goes beyond the impressionist paintings of Monet that Steer had seen in London. Although Steer's paintings look spontaneous, most of them took several years to complete. The benches and distinctive white railings suggest that this is a view from Centre Cliff. A group of ladies and children are observing one of the many regattas that took place off the coast of Southwold in the nineteenth century. © Tate London, 2002

However, there have been just a few visitors who remained completely immune to Southwold's charms, the correspondent for the magazine *The Builder*, who visited on 24 January 1891 was one of them:

"The town is a tolerably large one of its class, but straggling, unpicturesque and dirty … it lies low and has nothing attractive in its general appearance, and presents a steep shingle beach, one of the most uncomfortable type of beach for a watering-place lounge. The new houses that have been built on the north end of the town front, in answer to the need for accommodation, are mostly of the ugliest and most uninviting type … Southwold, excepting the air and the church, is rather a disillusion."

166

Visitors to Southwold *by William Bowyer (b.1926).Oil on canvas. 1987.*
A hot summer's day has brought trippers to Southwold in both cars and coach parties. Three are standing on Centre Cliff admiring the Regency architecture surrounding them. Sunlight from the west shows that this is late afternoon.   © William Bowyer, 2006. Photograph: Messum

Just two years later, in 1893, the magazine *Pall Mall* voiced misgivings about the plans to build a promenade pier in Southwold and the quality of visitors it might attract to the town,

"May the gods avert the advent of such a pier or the watery gods devour it should it come! Up to the present Southwold has been mercifully spared from such an affliction."

By the turn of the nineteenth century Southwold's full potential for being a fashionable holiday resort had been realised by powerful commercial interests.

In competition with the Southwold Railway, of which more later, the East Coast Development Company brought holiday-makers to Southwold by sea. In 1900 a daily service was provided by an elegant paddle steamer of 743 tons called the *Southwold Belle,* which had cost £28,500 to build. Despite this hefty investment, the fare from London was just nine shillings return and, apparently, there was rarely a charge for excess luggage. The fun began as soon as the holiday-makers had embarked at Fresh Wharf, by London Bridge. The cabins and lounges of the *Southwold Belle* could accommodate 900 passengers and were luxuriously furnished in "*velvet plush*". Teas and dinners were enjoyed as the ship paddled down the river past Gravesend, Southend and on toward the open sea past Walton, Felixstowe and along the Suffolk coast. The Company waxed lyrical about the journey:

"*No matter how melancholy, how overwhelmed the sufferer may be, in the freshness of the breeze and the brightness of the sun, and the glorious sheen of the ocean, he begins to enter once again into the gladness of nature and to experience how sweet life is; and new hope rises within him as he realises that the better part of his body is still healthy, still capable of enjoyment, and putting forward some power of good.*"[4]

This is the mood in which some of the passengers disembarked at the East Coast Development Company's pier, from there it was possible to ride to their lodgings in little carriages drawn by goats, though most people preferred the buses that had been laid on for the purpose. Some went to rented houses, some to The Swan and others to the Marlborough Hotel that once dominated the south end of Marlborough Road; it was fitted to the highest level of luxury by Maple of London. Those who could afford it wanted the best of everything and it was to be found, opposite the pier, in the form of The Grand Hotel. Built in 1901 by the architect Charles H.M. Mileham, it was furnished in the Chippendale taste by the fashionable decorator and cabinetmaker James Shoolbred of London. Inevitably, Shoolbred's interiors tended towards the middle-class and claustro-phobic. This was a firm that supplied every type of furniture including light fittings and clocks in the latest fashions, including the Mediaeval, Stuart, Louis Seize and Japanese styles. The firm's reputation had been enhanced at five International Exhibitions, and especially when it supplied Queen Victoria at Windsor and furnished the Prince of Wales's private room at the Wyndham Theatre in 1899. As a supplier of safe and bourgeois

furnishings, Shoolbred was immortalised by E.M. Forster in *A Room with a View* and the following passage is redolent of the interior of Southwold's Grand Hotel:

"From the outlook it should have been a successful room, but the trail of Tottenham Court Road was upon it. He could almost visualise the motor vans of Messrs. Shoolbred... arriving at the door and depositing this chair, those varnished bookcases, that writing table."[5]

The East Coast Development Company had not only built the pier and the Grand Hotel but also boasted of having installed a new electric lighting system and water works for the town. This kind of investment required a good return and the company was always keen to paint the rosiest picture possible of a place that not only enjoyed sunshine and low rainfall, but was famous for the curative powers of the sea and its breezes:

"To the city dweller it is a new world, a veritable Eden whose pure, fragrant, ozone-laden atmosphere and genial reposeful homeliness afford as surprising a contrast to their usual environment as light to darkness or joyous youth to oppressed and irritable old age."

Obviously some required even more than this to keep them happy and so Southwold's many and varied attractions were itemised in a 64-page pamphlet, full of photographs, which was given to every passenger on the *Southwold Belle*. As well as *"the royal, ancient and fascinating game of golf"* there was cricket, lawn tennis and football. Freshwater fish could be caught in the river Blyth and sea anglers could make use of the promenade pier. Duck, snipe, widgeon and teal could be bagged in the surrounding countryside, though some might prefer to take wildfowl with a punt gun ...

Like all coastal towns, Southwold's holiday life was hurriedly suspended during the Second World War; the High Street stood empty on August Bank Holiday in 1940. Both residents and visitors were right to be cautious. The battery on Gun Hill had been buried, nonetheless, the town and harbour quickly caught the attention of the enemy, who used

---

Opposite above:
The hall at the Grand Hotel, Southwold *by T. Raffles Davison. Published in* The British Architect, *December 1903.*
As the name suggests, the Grand Hotel, with its 100 bedrooms, supplied its guests with every modern luxury, including central heating and a safety elevator. The hall is furnished with comfortable fauteuils in the Louis XVI taste and palms are growing in Chinese porcelain cachepots, supported on wooden guéridons. The electric light fittings are shaded in the Arts and Crafts taste. Perhaps the only reminders that the waves of the North Sea are rolling outside are the blazing fire and the bevelled glass and hardwood screen to the right. The Society of Antiquaries, London

Opposite below:
The dining room at the Grand Hotel, Southwold *by T. Raffles Davison. Published in* The British Architect, *December 1903.*
This neo-classical interior of the luxurious hotel was designed by the architect Charles Mileham. The staff are waiting at tables with individual electric lamps and turned wood chairs in the fashionable Stuart style, supplied by the famous furnishers Messrs. Shoolbred of London. They could comfortably cater for 100 settings. The Society of Antiquaries, London

The Hall

The Dining Room

A Solitary Boot *by Eliot Hodgkin (1905-1987). Tempera. Signed and dated 1943-4.*
The artist and his wife Mimi discovered the boot in a sand dune when they spent a short holiday in Southwold during the war. Possibly the boot caught Hodgkin's fancy because it reminded him of William Nicholson's study of Gertrude Jekyll's gardening boots. Whatever the reason, he spent a happy time making a preliminary study for this painting. As they left the dunes to go home the Hodgkins ran into a young policeman who asked them if they had seen anything of the idiots who had spent the day sitting in a minefield. This remarkable painting was in the collection of Sir Gerald Kelly, and Sir Alfred and Lady Munnings.
                                                                                                    Mimi Hodgkin

the church as a landmark for the bombers. There were several highly destructive raids and a total of 13 people were killed and 49 injured. Despite the danger, people still ventured to the seaside for their holidays. The painter Eliot Hodgkin worked in London for the Ministry of Information and for Air Raid Precautions. Despite being all too familiar with the risks he came with his wife Mimi in 1940 and stayed at The Swan. Always hunting for unusual subjects the couple were delighted by the sight of an old boot lying far off in the dunes. Eliot Hodgkin spent the day making preparatory drawings of it without realising that he and his wife had strayed into a minefield.

After the war was over the town quickly regained its popularity with holiday-makers, though it managed to discourage most of the more garish modern popular entertainments that characterise so many English seaside towns. The few that are neatly contained at the front of the pier survived when the rest were washed away in the fierce storm of 1 October 1953. An anachronism by the early 1960s, these automata still boasted a 'British Execution', 'The Haunted Churchyard' and a challengingly old-fashioned 'What the Butler Saw'. Now all but the front of the old pier has been swept away and the focus of the holiday-makers is on its replacement, begun in 1998 and finished in 2001. Designed by the architect Brian Haward it is a perfect scale for Southwold. Here, for the first time in 48 years, it is possible to look back at the profile of the town, which continues to be dominated by its church and lighthouse. Tim Hunkin has filled the small rooms at the centre of the pier with a series of bizarre automata, which, in the spirit of post-modern irony, go under the title of 'Instant Weight Loss', 'Brain Washing', 'Eclipse' and, tellingly, 'Is it Art?'. Time passes slowly on the pier, particularly when measured by the slow tick of Hunkin's water clock. On the half hour the two boys who flank its sides drop their trousers and pee into a trough of plastic flowers.

Hundreds of brass plaques engraved with enigmatic and deeply personal messages surmount the railings of the new pier. Some are memorials to illicit loves and others to love that is lost. Reading them is compulsive and, little by little, it draws the holiday-maker further and further out over the sea to the end where it is customary to wish for a safe return by dropping a coin into the choppy waves below.

Arrival of the Ferry Boat at Southwold Harbour *by Frederick Baldwin (1899-1984). Pencil and watercolour on paper. 1961.*
Fishing boats are moored against makeshift wooden jetties on the Southwold side of the harbour. Fishermen's sheds line Ferry Road and in the distance is the profile of the Harbour Inn. Gulls await the return of the catch and the river is perfectly still. It is only the oars of the ferryman that generate the eddies on the mirror-like surface of the water.
Frederick Baldwin was a self-taught artist remembered for his immaculate draughtsmanship. His work was much admired and was used to illustrate greetings cards. He lived at Westhall, near Halesworth, and later at Stoven. Author's collection

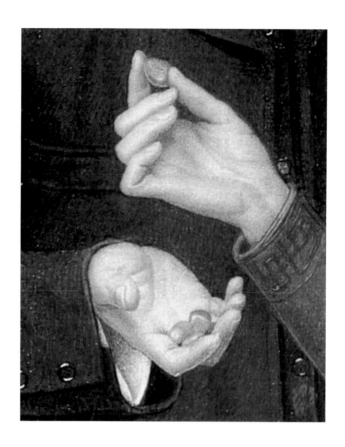

CARNELIAN BAY

The Romans arrived in Southwold in about 55BC and one can only guess the awe they inspired in the local inhabitants. Perhaps tribute was demanded but it is doubtful that the small fishing community had much to offer the invaders. The Roman historian Cornelius Tacitus maintained that the Romans came to Britain specifically to find gold and pearls[1], but in Southwold there were none and they had to make do with banded agates instead. Tradition has it that these were wanted as the raw material for engraved gems. The Romans had followed the Greeks in perfecting the technique of carving down one coloured striation in a stone to contrast it with the one below. This was the skill of the cameo carver and it was considered one of the noblest of art forms, often used in portraiture and in the endorsement of high status.

With the agates on Southwold's beach were found some of the finest carnelians and it was these semi-opaque stones, varying in colour from honey yellow to rust red, that were best used for cutting in intaglio. Just as the cameo relies for effect on its high relief the reverse is true of the intaglio. First the surface of the stone is highly polished and then its surface is deeply engraved like a die. This technique was also invented in antiquity and if the Romans coveted banded agates, then they would have admired the local carnelians for the same reasons. However, due to the difficulty of drilling and polishing these hard silica-based stones the ancient Britons did not wear them as often as they did the amber and jet, which were also found in abundance on the East Coast and which, because of their organic origins, were soft and easily worked into jewellery.

Right and opposite:

The Agate *by Joseph Southall (1861-1944). Dated 1911.*

Joseph Southall and his wife and first cousin Anna (née Baker) came to Southwold every year in July. They were Quakers and this may explain their cover-all beach clothes. In the painting Mrs. Southall has found a coloured stone on the beach and is adding it to the small collection that her husband holds in his right hand. Agates from Southwold beach have always been avidly collected. Until very recently Covehithe beach had the reputation for being the richest source of semi-precious material.

National Portrait Gallery

Below:

The polished slice of pebble (chalcedonic breccia) given by the Rev. Edward Morgan, Curate of South Cove, to John Ruskin as a complement to his extensive collection of native minerals. It is described in the Collected Works of John Ruskin *(Vol 26) as* "A slice of a pebble from the beach at Southwold, Suffolk, so far as my experience reaches, unique." *The stone was probably polished by one of the lapidaries working in Southwold (see p.177) before being presented to Ruskin. In March 1884 Ruskin began a revised catalogue of his collection and wrote that he hoped it would remain his as long as he could enjoy it* "and afterwards, somewhere and in some sort, serve as my monument."

The Natural History Museum, London

In this state they were valued as much for their magical and talismanic properties as for their beauty. When the Romans took them back to Italy they became some of the earliest souvenirs of Southwold.

Today all the jet has gone and the holiday-makers continue to mistake carnelians for the increasingly rare amber. When wet from the sea the carnelians gleam and are full of colour but as they dry they quickly lose their shine and their beauty is obscured; only careful polishing can revive the initial excitement of their discovery and make it permanent.

Mineral specimens have always been collected avidly even when there was little or no understanding of their origins. In the sixteenth century, agates, carnelians, quartz crystals and fossils were an important part of the contents of the Renaissance *wunderkammer*. What had started as collecting developed into an unprecedented enthusiasm for the natural sciences and during the reign of Queen Victoria had grown into little short of a mania. Indeed, in 1849 Prince Albert (1819-1861) himself was elected as a Fellow of The Geological Society, which had been founded only 42 years earlier. In Scotland he introduced Queen Victoria to his interest in geology and it was there that they collected mineral specimens together. Sometimes these were polished and made up into jewellery for the Queen to wear and some she gave away. The art critic and luminary John Ruskin was deeply fascinated by minerals and amassed an enormous collection, which was later divided amongst various museums, schools and colleges (see illustration on p.175).

In Southwold in the late eighteenth and early nineteenth centuries mineralogy and palaeontology were just some of the gentlemanly pursuits followed by those who had plenty of time on their hands. The sea was constantly eroding the cliffs and exposing a rich variety of fossils in the process; and there were also interesting discoveries to be made in nearby Wangford and Bulcamp. On 4 April 1786 the diarist and gourmand Parson James Woodforde (1740-1803) came to "*indifferent*" Southwold, to hunt for "*curious pebbles*" but after looking for more than five hours returned to The Old Swan empty handed. In the morning he continued his "*little tour towards the South East Coast of Norfolk*" by heading for Lowestoft where, according to Wake, ammonites and belemnites were sometimes to be had. A local stationer called Gowing offered them for sale amongst his stock of beautiful agates and carnelians. At Southwold and Pakefield the bones of elephant, rhinoceros, stag, horse, ox and pig appeared in the cliff in such profusion that a geologist called Charlesworth named the deposits the "mammiferous crag". Captain Henry Alexander, a Fellow of the Geological Society, monitored the most exciting discoveries. He cheerfully invited enthusiasts to see his collection at his house in Market Place and his proudest possession was said to be the jawbone of a bear, though he also had the molar of a narrow-toothed mastadon, weighing 3lbs, which had been dredged up off Southwold in 1839. Alexander had obtained some of his collection from a "*civil and obliging person*" called Davey, who lived in Kessingland where he sold all manner of curiosities excavated from beneath his house on the cliff, together with some that had been washed up from the sea.

At Southwold *by Helen Clarke. Watercolour on paper. c.1889.*
A view of Kill Cock Cliff with pebbles piled up against the primitive sea defences. It was amongst these stones that visitors to Southwold hunted for agates and carnelians. Amber, which is relatively light, was bouyed up by the sea to the high water mark.
Helen Clarke was a member of the Society of Woman Artists and came to Southwold from Derbyshire.

Heather C. Newman

There was no necessity for the visitor to Southwold to go as far north as Kessingland to find interesting geological deposits. Less than a mile or so beyond the bathing machines on the north beach was the cliff of Easton Bavents. There the pounding of the sea was constantly exposing strata and shells from a Pleistocene beach that was sandwiched between iron-rich beds of sand. Holiday-makers trudged there in cumbersome straw hats and long trailing skirts, armed with trowels and hammers in the hope of discovering Southwold's ante-diluvian past. For the less intrepid scholars of natural history there were two lapidaries: Benjamin Burwood on Gun Hill and Thomas Prestwidge in the High Street[2] who stocked all manner of curiosities including local agates, carnelians, jet and amber.

Overleaf:
The Beach, Aldeburgh *by James Sant (1820-1916). Oil on board. 1871.*
Here the artist has painted a group of people enjoying a sunny interlude on the beach entirely composed of silica-based stones, the family to which agates and carnelians belong. Sant was a painter of subject-pictures and portraits including that of Queen Victoria. It was during a visit to the East Coast that he perfected a technique for painting nocturnes in broad daylight by looking through a piece of clear blue glass so that he "could realise the same appearance of grass and foliage which they have under the lunar rays". The result was a sketch called Southwold by Moonlight.[3]

The Fine Art Society

Left:

An autographed photograph of Ellen Terry in the role of Imogen in Shakespeare's Cymbeline. *1896.*

She is wearing her necklace of amber from the East Coast. It may be that this striking Celtic style necklace was a gift inspired by Miss Terry's role in the play The Amber Heart *written by her friend Alfred C. Calmour. In 1888, in the character of Ellaline, she had worn a piece of heart-shaped amber round her neck that had proved an effective talisman against the pain of love. In reality Miss Terry was no stranger to it and would certainly have been grateful for the protection offered by a magical jewel of this sort.*

The Amber Shop, Southwold

Right:

A carnelian from Dunwich beach collected by Mrs. Cadbury c.1900. It was lapped into the form of a heart and mounted in silver by their friends and fellow Quakers, the artists and jewellers Arthur (1862-1928) and George Gaskin (1866-1934). The Gaskins were frequent visitors to Southwold and it was to Arthur that Joseph Southall wrote from Southwold in July 1905 (see p.160).

Birmingham City Museum and Art Gallery

However, Captain Alexander was disappointed in both of them because friends had come to Southwold specifically with the intention of acquiring local fossils and had left empty handed, vowing never to return. Robert Wake described this as an "*evil which ought to be remedied*" by the recruitment of professional fossil hunters whose duty should be to supply the local shops. At Aldeburgh things were better ordered and in Mr Smith's shop there was always a "*beautiful display of agates, recent shells, minerals and amber &c*". Back in Southwold there were simply never enough local hardstones to keep everyone happy; owing to the frenzied search for them, the surrounding coastline became known as 'Carnelian Bay'.

All this activity was in the name of science, but there was something else, something in the allure of these native minerals that was akin to the power of more valuable and exotic precious stones. Lapidaries targeted the fashionable visitors to Gun Hill not for their knowledge of geology, but for their willingness to spend their holiday money on a pretty souvenir. Wake observed:

"*...Passing promenaders... in fashionably dressed groupes, as if seemingly vieing with each other which shall most attract the admiration so readily rendered, where all appear equally determined to be pleased. There is the newly-married couple... as their bearing towards each other may truly indicate – are besieged by a number of young exhibitors of polished fossils, and pebbles, and native agates, and cornelians tastefully arranged upon trays, and plates and saucers; while the unbearded aspirants after profits of merchandize are anxious to undersell their less glamorous rivals.*"

By the end of the nineteenth century Southwold's list of attractions had expanded and the passion for local geology was on the wane. Nonetheless, it was still possible to take carnelians straight from the beach to the lapidaries in the high street where they could be polished into a brooch or bead necklace before the end of the holiday. This tradition was maintained by a couple called Craigie, lapidaries in Trinity Street until well in to the twentieth century.

Appetite for carnelians, and for amber in particular, was renewed by the taste of the ladies of the Aesthetic movement who preferred them to the artless and vulgar scintillation of precious stones. The same women affected a style of dress that anticipated the Hippy fashions of the late 1960s, incorporating ethnic textiles and long strings of beads. The look was especially popular with those who came to Southwold to paint and sketch, but it was the actress Ellen Terry (1847-1928) who took it to greater lengths when she wore a monumental collar of amber collected on the East Coast. It had been made up into a necklace by The Amber Shop where, in Southwold, a varied stock of jewellery is offered to this day.

Throughout the ages various stones and gems were believed to protect the wearer from harm, or to bring them luck. Even now fear of the evil eye persists and charms to counter it remain popular. On Southwold beach it is possible to find flints and pebbles run through with naturally occurring holes that allow them to be clustered together on wires and strings, traditionally these 'hagstones' are used as talismans against fascination by witches. Their power remains deep seated and inexplicable, but people still hang them above their beds to protect against nightmares; and in stables they are said to prevent horses from being hag-ridden at night. Some flints with three or more holes resemble a ghostly face and are treated with great reverence as they are believed to contain the spirits of those who have been lost at sea.

A Ghost Stone by Eyke Shannon. Pencil on paper. 2004.
Pebbles with natural configurations of this sort are said to
be the ghosts of those who have died at sea. In this
instance the stone appears to anticipate the face of the
subject in Edward Munch's The Scream. © Eyke Shannon

A colourful poster advertising Adnams Sole Bay Brewery, Southwold. The scene is a romantic one in which only the cart and dray horses are relevant to Southwold. They continue to be used by the Brewery to deliver casks of beer around the town.

Adnams and Co. PLC

INNS AND TIPPLING HOUSES

The well in Market Square was the centre of the community in Southwold. The water it provided was of enormous importance to life in the town and from it derived all manner of trades including the brewing of beer.

Until relatively recently ale was the preferred drink, particularly when the purity of water was under suspicion. Local beer always accompanied the meals of those who could afford it, and covered tankards would remain on the table from one sitting to another. Being mildly alcoholic it is a convivial drink sold in inns, hotels and alehouses. In competition with these regular suppliers were a variety of beer parlours known as 'tippling houses'.

Johanna de Corby was brewing in Southwold in the mid-fourteenth century, though she is remembered not for the goodness of her beer, but rather for her lack of honesty and inferior brew. In 1345 she appeared before the manorial court charged with breaking the Assize of Ale and was fined 3d. This was a large imposition, but it proved to be an insufficient deterrent and she was to appear before the same court many times in the following 20 years for overcharging her customers and selling unmarked measures. It seems more than likely that Johanna was not only in the habit of making beer but also drinking it to excess since she was frequently in trouble for breaching the peace. Johanna and her husband Robert, the baker, may well have owned an inn on the site of what is now The Swan. An ancient chimneystack bears witness to the fact that a building has been there since the early Tudor period and there was probably a brewery alongside it then. In the seventeenth century Goodman Wiggins ran both businesses, but they were

Detail from a poster printed in the early twentieth century to advertise Southwold Fine Ales & Stout, manufactured by Adnams and Co., owners of the Sole Bay Brewery. Carts drawn by dray horses are being loaded for distribution throughout the town. St. Edmund's Church can just be made out in the distance.

Adnams and Co. PLC

burnt to the ground in the great fire of 1659. It was only when prosperity returned to the town that a wealthy businessman, John Rous, rebuilt the inn and moved the brewery to its present position. During the eighteenth century it belonged to the Thompson family; in 1806 the Old Swan passed to its sitting tenant Henry Meadows who, in turn, passed it on to Thomas Bokenham in 1818. Included in the latter transaction were a "*stable, coach houses and brew houses*" and rights to the pasture on Southwold common. Bokenham decided to develop the building in the hope of accommodating the "*Nobility, gentry and commercial gentlemen frequenting the town*" who could expect comfortable beds, sitting rooms with sea views and the use of a bowling green and billiard table. The services of careful drivers and post chaises were available for those who wanted to explore the countryside and they returned to the "*unremitting attention*" of the staff and fine imported wines and liquors. Evidently these arrangements were a success as Bokenham was able to afford to build a grand house for himself next door, later to became the Town Hall.[1] On 21 July 1851, The Swan was the scene of a powerful *memento mori*: Francis Hallows, the Coast Guard Officer approached the bar as he filled his pipe with tobacco and ordered a pint of porter. No sooner had he taken his first sip of beer than he fell to the floor, dead.[2]

In 1756 the handsome building on the same side of the High Street, the Nag's Head, became The New Swan under which name it traded until 1829, when the owners decided to call it The Crown. It was a commercial hotel and the large stables that survive to this day are testimony to the fact that it was also an important posting house. It is characterised by its attractive bars and dining rooms and the scrolling wrought-iron sign that hangs out over the street.

The Lord Nelson, standing near the Sailor's Reading Room and within sight of the sea, has one of the most picturesque positions of any of Southwold's public houses. Inside, a sympathetic modernisation, a roaring fire and collection of Nelson memorabilia all contribute to a uniquely welcoming atmosphere. It was first converted into a pub in 1803 when two adjoining buildings were knocked into one for the use of the first landlord, Samuel le Strange. It was he who named it after Nelson who was to die just two years later, at the Battle of Trafalgar.

As Southwold gradually evolved from a rather diminished fishing port into a thriving watering place for the middle classes, so the demand for hospitality increased, and in 1872 George and Ernest Adnams acquired the Sole Bay Brewery. By the 1890s Adnams had taken over some 20 local public houses and wanted to expand their brewing interests to meet the new demand, however, the considerable expense of redesigning the Sole Bay brewery in 1896 was followed by a recession. To provide extra capital, Adnams took on a new partner, Pierse Loftus, in 1902. He transformed the business with a combination of new technology and further expansion and provided the foundations for the thriving business that Adnams is today.

As William Hogarth (1697-1794) made clear in his famous etching *Beer Lane* in 1751, the mood of the beer drinker is generally benign, especially compared to that of the

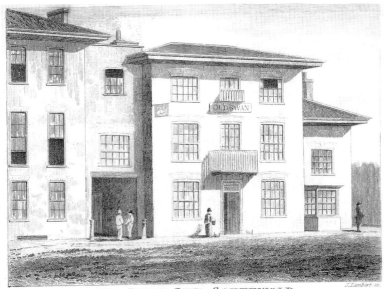

OLD SWAN INN, SOUTHWOLD.

T. BOKENHAM

RETURNS his most grateful acknowledgments to the NOBILITY, GENTRY, and COMMERCIAL GENTLEMEN frequenting the TOWN of SOUTHWOLD, and the Public in general, for the liberal encouragement he has received: and begs respectfully to inform them, that he has recently made such additions and improvements to the above old-established Inn, as enables him to accommodate Visitors for any period, with comfortable Beds, and Sitting-Rooms commanding extensive and pleasant views of the sea, and the adjacent country.

T. B. hopes, by an unremitting attention, and the select quality of his Wines and Liquors, all which he imports, to merit their future patronage.

An excellent Billiard Table and Bowling Green, commodious Stables and Coach Houses, neat Post Chaises and careful Drivers.

Lodgings engaged by applying at the above Inn, which is situated nearest the sea.

SLOMAN, Engraver and Printer, Yarmouth.

A printed advertisement for the Old Swan Inn issued by the owner Thomas Bokenham. c.1820.
The simple façade of the building is shown before various improvements were added, including bay windows and decorative ironwork. (See illustration on p.188-189)
Author's collection

drinker of the demon gin. Occasionally, though, greed and drunkenness, however induced, lead to social upheaval and this was the state of affairs in Southwold in the prosperous years of the early sixteenth century. Indeed local magistrates were forced to take action to prevent:

"...*tippling houses and drunkenness and the production of immorality and the impoverishment of whole families.*"

The number of public houses was limited to eight, a ruling that remained in force until 1833.[3] Quite how this was supposed to act as a deterrent to the serious drinker becoming "*cherry merry*" in a small town like Southwold remains unclear, and inebriation continued to be a fact in the town's night life. There are few details recorded until the nineteenth century, but it is safe to assume that drunks were confined in the town gaol, in the stocks, or tied to the whipping post that stood on Bartholomew Green next to the church gates. A list of crimes hanging from their necks, they were mocked and pelted with rotten food.

E. W. BALDWIN. 1933.

186

Southwold *by Frederick Baldwin. Watercolour on paper. 1933.*

The familiar profile of the church dominates this delicate drawing. To the left are the seventeenth century cottages on North Green and to the right Smith and Girling's grain storage and flour mill, which was founded in the 1890s. There they stored the hops and malt used by Adnams, the local brewery. These premises were purpose built by Whitmore and Binyon of Wickham Market and have now been converted into flats; in the process the distinctive cowl of the grain hoist has been removed. The artist has taken considerable artistic licence in moving the lighthouse into the composition where it is just visible behind the church. In 1933 this carefully detailed drawing was priced at 2 guineas. Private Collection

Market Place, Southwold *by Eric Scott (1904-1960). Ink on paper. c.1953.*
The Swan Hotel is on the left, with East Street leading to the sea. Originally a plain, two-storey building, it was raised to three storeys in 1826. The tall pedimented bays, and the attractive wrought-iron sign bracket were added in about 1907. The first extension eastwards is early Victorian; tall and towerlike it gives a glimpse of the sea. Another extension was built in 1938, neo-Georgian with a hint of Riviera elegance. The pump made in 1873 by the local iron founder George Edmund Child 'Pro Bono Publico' marks the centre of Market Place. To the east of this is a dress shop that survived from before the fire of Southwold in 1659. Between 1827 and 1841 it was a stationers shop run by Mrs. Bardwell, mother-in-law of the local painter Henry Davy.

This, a preliminary drawing for a watercolour, has been annotated with colour notes. Eric Scott was a professional painter and illustrator who lived in Walberswick. British Railways commissioned two paintings from him for reproduction as carriage panels.

© Richard Scott

One Robert Key spent six sobering hours in the stocks on 29 June 1850,[4] though it seems that his humiliation was no deterrent to others and attitudes continued to worsen until, in 1866, "*an inhabitant of Southwold*" felt compelled to write to the *Ipswich Journal* to outline a very sad state of affairs prevailing in the town:

"*In spite of all its amenities want and starvation stalk the streets of Southwold. These have become unfit for decent people after dark due to the language and fear of molestation from low profane youths. Drinking, gambling and the desecration of the Sabbath are the cause.*"[5]

Richard Sisley, writing in the *Pall Mall* magazine in May 1893 demonstrated that confinement in the town stocks was no impediment to the serious drinker:

"*I lately had the pleasure of meeting a man who was put in the stocks. He was sentenced to eight hours' punishment. He is proud to relate that he succeeded in liberating his arms and then his legs, and that he immediately adjourned to 'The Bear' – an extinct hostelry – where he passed his time in smoking and drinking a pot or two of stout. In the evening he walked back to the stocks, and arrived there just in time to meet the jailor who had come to liberate him – but who, on seeing him already free, was at first rather inclined to recapture him. However, he refrained, and the culprit, according to his own account, spent the night in his favourite pursuit of catching hares, and in the early morning evaded the officer by swimming the river.*"

Today, with binge drinking and street crime on the increase elsewhere, the peace and quiet of Southwold is at a premium, and it is difficult to imagine a time when it was any

other way. A change for the better probably came about when the town became the focus of family 'bucket and spade' holidays and local planners limited the expansion of the seaside amusements that spoil other seaside towns. Detractors say that Southwold has become beige and boring and the yet more cynical say that the weekenders have turned it into Hampstead-on-Sea. Certainly, they bring with them an appreciation of all good things and Adnams are now not only famous as brewers but as vintners too. From their shop at the back of The Crown yard they supply the finest wines. Of course, appreciation of the local beer is still keen and, despite competition on all fronts, Adnams continues to remain famous for it.

Sir Nikolaus Pevsner (1902-1983) described Southwold as one of the happiest and most picturesque towns in England, its mood enhanced not only by the smell of hops from the brewery but by the 100,000 pints of beer made there every day. As now, the ingredients were always the best, the flavour full and irresistible and, consequently, the temptation to overdo was always very real. A lesson in the danger of over indulgence can be taken from the story of a young man called Syer who had been visiting the beer houses of Southwold on the evening of 22 January 1865. On his way home in the dark he fell into a night soil vault and it was only his pitiful cries that saved him from an unimaginably awful death.[6]

191

THE SOUTHWOLD RAILWAY

The 1st Duke of Wellington was worried by the proliferation of the railways throughout the country as he believed that they provided the under classes with the means to travel about needlessly. The opening in 1825 of the first public railway in Britain was a service between Stockton and Darlington. By 1900 the Duke's fears were fully realised: there was scarcely a part of the United Kingdom that could not be reached by train and even "*far away Southwold*"[1] had a service all of its own since 1879.

Such a thing had seemed an impossible dream when first suggested at a meeting in the Town Hall on 3 October 1856, and again in 1860, despite the fact that Suffolk was connected to the growing national network and there were already services through Saxmundham, Woodbridge and Ipswich. By 1862 all the Suffolk services were amalgamated into The Great Eastern Railway.

Competition for business must have been keen. Londoners were already able to travel to Southwold by sea and it is likely that the railway companies were targeting travellers coming from across the country. In the early 1860s the closest one could get to Southwold by train was Darsham and from there visitors took horse-drawn buses through Blythburgh and Henham to The Swan's posting house in Southwold. This was an attractive journey of nine miles, though it may not have been a particularly comfortable one: road surfaces were very uneven and the carriages were crowded and lurched alarmingly; accidents were not uncommon. By comparison, travelling by train was fast, smooth, and direct and the wooden carriages spacious, light and airy.

Not only were the people of Southwold thinking of their own comfort and safety, they were also conscious of the economic benefits the train might bring to a town that was becoming increasingly popular as a watering place. Another attempt to push forward the idea was made when the Town Council met on 19 October 1871.[2] The Lowestoft, Yarmouth and Southwold Tramway Company asked the Corporation for permission to run a line from Lowestoft to Southwold. After a convincing presentation had been made, the council gave its permission, with various stipulations, for a tram to come from Halesworth.

Although this particular proposal came to nothing, plans put forward in Halesworth in 1875 were supported by various influential landowners, including Charles Easton of Easton Hall and the 2nd Earl of Stradbroke, Lord Lieutenant of Suffolk. The outcome of these discussions was that on 24 July an Act of Parliament was passed that incorporated the Southwold Railway and authorised the construction of a line between Halesworth and Southwold, 8 miles and 63 chains in length. There were to be two branches, one to the River Blyth Navigation Quay, the farthest navigable point for sea-going vessels; and the other to Blackshore Quay at Southwold Harbour, which was intended to serve the fishing industry.

The building of the railway required substantial capital investment, which was achieved in 1876 through the sale of shares valued at £67,990. Construction began on 3 May 1878; the gauge of the line was 3 ft. instead of the normal 2 ft 6 inches. Land had

The Southwold Railway *by Ernest H. Shepard (1879-1976).*

Wenhaston station is seen in the background and elderly villagers totter along on the platform. The carriages are painted with the initials 'SR' for Southwold Railway. Note how the bearded driver is looking out from the engine.

Shepard is best remembered for the drawings he made in 1926 to illustrate Winnie the Pooh *by A.A. Milne (see illustrations on pp.158 and 159) and in 1931 for* The Wind in the Willows *by Kenneth Grahame. He was probably aware of Southwold from Charles Keene's work for* Punch. *In 1904 he married Florence, the daughter of James Chaplin who was the son of one of the founders of the satirical magazine. Chaplin had a house at Hinton, near Southwold, and Shepard visited Florence there when they were engaged.*

Line drawing of "Southwold Railway" by E.H. Shepard from *The Work of E.H. Shepard* by Rawle Knox.

been acquired through compulsory purchase and substantial earthworks were necessary. Stations were built at Wenhaston, Blythburgh, Walberswick, and Southwold and the train travelled over thirteen bridges including a swing bridge over the River Blyth.

The first train ran on 24 September 1879 and the excitement it generated was tempered by just a little anxiety. A safety inspection had taken place the day before and the driver was made aware that breaking the speed limit of 16 miles an hour would result in two years' imprisonment.

All went well and the passengers were delighted, not only by the experience of the train itself, but also by the beauty of the landscape through which it passed. A *Railway Guide* directed the passengers to various points of historical interest including Wenhaston Church with its famous mediaeval rood loft called the 'Doom', the lost Abbey at Blythburgh, and the ruins of St. Andrew's Church in Walberswick. Passengers were told that this was a village popular with artists and indeed all who "*have eyes for quiet beauty*". This was to be found in abundance in the surrounding countryside and the same guide singled out the heather moors along the estuary flats that lead to Blythburgh. The train provided the first view of a line of pine trees called 'The Heronry' and it inspired artists to return on foot and paint it.

THE SOUTHWOLD EXPRESS. THE DRIVER DOES A ROARING TRADE OWING TO A DELAY CAUSED BY THE PORTER·OVERESTIMATING HIS STRENGTH – THE GUARD MAKES THE MOST OF THIS AND TRIES TO SPOT A WINNER – THE STATIONMASTER DOES ALL IN HIS POWER TO GET THE TRAIN AWAY.

The Southwold Express. *A postcard by Reg Carter.*
Holidaymakers are leaving Southwold by train. Their luggage has followed on Mr. Doy's cart. The porter has overestimated his strength and a trunk has fallen on him. The driver is selling potatoes baked on the engine and the guard is reading the racing results.
The Doy family is one of the oldest in Southwold.

Hilary Huckstep

With Wenhaston behind it, the train followed the banks of the River Blyth and, as it approached Blythburgh, it followed a sharp curve. For safety reasons the outer rail was raised and the carriages tilted at an angle that never failed to alarm those passengers who were unfamiliar with the track. The correspondent for *The Builder* magazine remembered it well when he wrote about Southwold on 24 January 1891:

"*The town is reached from Halesworth junction by a short three foot gauge line of railway of an agreeably primitive description, with carriages like tramcars, which wind up and down hill and jolt around corners as if one were driving through a country lane rather than a railway. This approach, in summer especially, through meadows rich in flowers, is attractive enough; but Southwold itself, excepting the air and the church, is rather a disillusion.*"

If the train was famous for its eccentricity then so too were the staff. Uniforms of blue serge with plain brass buttons and the letters SR on their lapels and caps gave them an air of military efficiency that was very far from the reality. The train driver and guard were scheduled to stop at every station, but they would also slow down to facilitate the deliveries to remote farms. Newspapers were thrown out of the moving train and sometimes a dog was waiting to fetch them for his master. The crew set snares for rabbits along the track and the driver would stop the train when he wanted to check his catch. As well as their eccentricities, the staff was known for the lassitude shown to late-comers who, on occasion, stood by the track, flagged down the train and were allowed to leap aboard. One bright, sunny Bank Holiday the train was so overloaded with holiday-makers that it was unable to mount the incline to Halesworth Station. The last three carriages were uncoupled and the brake applied but shortly afterwards it failed and the driverless carriages slid backwards, gathering momentum until they reached Blyford, much to the consternation of the travellers, but nobody was hurt. To avoid a recurrence it was sometimes necessary to hitch the station horses to the carriages before the train could complete its journey.

At the end of school term the girls of St. Felix would take the train to Halesworth on their way home, and on one occasion the driver even stopped the train on the middle of the swing bridge to give the pupils the chance to wave farewell to the headmistress as she stood, waving her handkerchief, in the school grounds.

Ellen Terry's young friend the musician Martin Shaw first came to Southwold as a baby, before the railway had been built; later journeys provided him with some of his warmest recollections of the town where he had once lived:

"*Southwold Railway is one of the smallest in England. Trippers make funny remarks about it; but the true Southwolder loves it. To me anyhow it is the most romantic railway in the world. It has a refreshing indifference to modern hustle, though it makes a fair amount of clatter as it jostles and sways... Sometimes the engine refuses to start. Nobody minds or gets excited. We all wait contentedly. In the end it is always persuaded. The locomotives (I think there are two), carriages and the rest of the plant were ordered by the Emperor of China in the 'seventies of last century. The story goes that he returned them all when he saw them.*"

Shaw knew that this was a colourful fiction but he repeated it in his memoirs, giving the truth in a footnote in the hope that his "*readers may miss it*".

The fact is that Ransome's, of Ipswich, supplied engines and irons for the Shanghai-Woosung Railway, which was of 2'6" gauge, and was built in 1878. They also sent one of the employees, W.G. Jackson, to drive the engines, which went under the exotic names of *The Flowery Land*, *The Exotic Land*, *The Celestial Land* and *The Pioneer*. Jackson had the distinction of being the driver of the very first train in China. The Southwold Railway engines and 3' gauge metals were also supplied by Ransomes. Striking a domestic note the carriages were called *Blyth*, *Halesworth* and *Wenhaston*, a fourth called *Southwold* came later. Jackson returned from the Orient to drive the new train. To commemorate his visit to China he named his bungalow in Station Road, Southwold 'Shanghai Cottage'.

The memory of the Southwold railway is kept alive and vivid in the photographs taken by Frederick Jenkins, but its true essence was captured by local artist Reg Carter (1886-1950), his series of drawings being issued as a highly amusing set of postcards. Like all caricatures their strength lies not in the exaggeration of the truth, but rather in the ability to identify it.

An active society that bears the name of the Southwold Railway has recently submitted several ambitious plans for a new train on a new track made in homage to the original. None of them have succeeded and never will until nostalgia is replaced by necessity.

A POINT OF VIEW.

Tomkins (he has heard his friend Stodge talk so much about that lovely spot Wobbleswick, whither he was going sketching, that he was induced to accompany him. A day has elapsed, and he is awaking to the horror of his situation!) "SEEMS TO ME AN INFERN——— I CALL IT RATHER A DULL PLACE!"

Stodge. "DULL, MY DEAR FELLOW! HOW CAN YOU SAY SO? LOOK AT THIS BEAUTIFUL, BREEZY COMMON! AND THE LINES OF THOSE OLD HOUSES ON THE BEACH, BREAKING THE HORIZON, AND THE COLOUR! AND THE JOLLY QUIET OF THE PLACE! NONE O' YOUR BEASTLY BARREL-ORGANS OR GAPING TOURISTS SWARMING ABOUT! I THOUGHT YOU'D LIKE IT!!"

ARTISTS AT THE SEASIDE

"*We are all artists at the seaside*" wrote the Birmingham painter Joseph Southall (1861-1944) in a letter from Southwold addressed to his friend the painter and goldsmith Arthur Gaskin. Quite how he found his way there is uncertain, but it may have been William Morris who recommended it as good place to paint; the fact is that by this time Southwold and Walberswick had a widespread reputation as a resort for artists. The pure sea air and open spaces must have been a refreshing change to Southall who came from the industrial Midlands. Being a man with fixed routines, Southall made the journey every July from 1904 until 1939. Precisely what he and his painter friends could expect to find when they came to the Blyth valley was eloquently described in 1897 in the magazine *Artist*:

Above:

A point of view. A cartoon by Charles Keene for Punch. *Published 14 December 1877.*

The painter Stodge has brought his urbane friend Tomkins to "Wobbleswick". On the first day Tomkins finds himself bored: "Seems to me an Infern– I call it rather a Dull Place!"   Punch archives

At Walberswick, an artist sketching *by Walter Osborne. c.1884.*
This is a portrait of Nathaniel Hill by his friend Walter Osborne, made when they visited Walberswick together in 1884 and 1885. Hill, an Irish artist, met Osborne when they were both students at the Royal Hibernian Academy. It is possible that the two young painters were at Walberswick because their teacher Augustus Burke was working there at the time. Wilson Steer remembered meeting Hill and Osborne in Walberswick in the 1880s. In this painting Hill is sketching under an umbrella. In the summer the open ground around Southwold was "dotted" with them.
Private Collection.
Photograph James Fennell

Southwold, Suffolk by Edwin Edwards. Oil on canvas. c.1875.
Two boys are enjoying the sunshine as they gaze out to a sea busy with traffic. The flagpole marks the
position of the Queen's Preventative Station. Just in front, a lady with a parasol enjoys the view. Note
that next to nothing but fields lay towards the north of the town; a memory of them lingers in the name
Fieldstile Road. The National Gallery of Victoria, Melbourne, Australia. (Given by Mrs Edwards in 1905)

"Here the professional artist may find as much to please him as the enthusiastic amateur, for one is truly 'out of town' ...looking either East or West, the horizon is scarcely broken, all is one dead level, yet such a lovely level, over which the setting sun streams the glories of his crimson, orange and purple rays, which are reflected a thousand times in its rivers, dykes and sea. As a sketching ground its popularity is constantly increasing, and during the season many artists occupy its clean little cottages."

Evidently Southwold and Walberswick were not only the perfect inspiration, but good accommodation was easily and cheaply found. Painters on unpredictable incomes found this an irresistible combination and arrived by sea and land to take advantage of the local amenities. In *The Etcher*, in 1881, it was predicted that the opening of the railway from Halesworth to Southwold in 1879 would eventually spoil the area as a *"sketching ground for artists"*, but this was proved wrong. In fact, the small trains brought ever more artists, armed with heavy easels, brushes and paints. *The Builder*, 24 January 1891, reported that the area *"is a well known haunt of artists, which in summer is dotted all over with the protecting umbrellas of sketchers"* (see illustrations on pp.196 and 197). There is a certain amount of evidence to suggest that art schools across the country had recommended Southwold and Walberswick to their students, though the close-knit society of the British art world was probably the driving force behind the annual summer influx. By 1880 the trend had been spotted by the satirical magazine *Punch:*

A Warble of Walberswick

O Walberswick's a village of very little tillage
In the northern part of Suffolk, and it's very picturesque;
And you fly from all the gritty, dirty bye-ways of the City,
To forget, in pleasant rambles, dreary duties of the desk.

There's a harbour old and rotten, planks and anchors long forgotten
'Mid the tangle of the cordage: boats whose sea career is o'er;
There's a ferry with scant traffic, which McCullum and the Graphic
Sketched long years ago, and the sea-gulls sweep along the lonesome shore.

There gathers many a sketcher, Dr Evershed the Etcher,
Stacey Marks and Haswell, Langton, Barnard and one Keene,
Who greatly love the queer place and declare it is a dear place,
And with skilful brush and pencil they've immortalised the scene.

There no horrible cheap tripper comes, a most persistent dipper
In the "briny", and Cook's tourist is unknown within these parts;
And the sunset waxing fainter o'er the church delights the painter,
No wonder then that Walberswick is dear to artists' hearts!

Mr and Mrs. Edwards sketching at Dunwich *by Charles Keene. c.1876*
Some of the drawings made by Edwin Edwards at Dunwich are preserved at Birmingham City Museum
and Art Gallery (see illustration on p.72). The Witt Library, Courtauld Institute of Art

The Southwold Ferry *by Frank Cox (1870-1894).*

A print after an oil painting now lost. This is a portrait of Old Todd gently helping his passenger into the ferry after parting with her daughter and before he rows her across the Blyth to Walberswick. At first sight the subject of this painting is social realism, however it may also be read as an allegory of death in which the blind ferryman Charon is paid to row departing souls across the poisonous river Styx into the Underworld.

The poet Saville Clarke, writing in the satyrical magazine Punch, *described the painters working in Walberswick:*

> *"They sketch the ferryman's old hut, the reeds that sway and nod,*
> *The early Christian countenance of Charon, Mr. Todd."*
> The Lord Nelson, Southwold

At the centre of this artistic community were Edwin (1823-1879) and Ruth Edwards. Edwin had been brought up in Framlingham and, after a broad education that included visits to Europe, he studied law, which he then abandoned in favour of a life devoted to literature and art. Edwards had made the acquaintance of Eduard Manet in France and his friendship with Henri Fantin-Latour grew to the extent that he became the artist's unofficial agent in England. It seemed that Edwards and his wife were at home to everybody in the art world. Friends were generally received at their house in Sunbury, but in the summer they were invited to a house called 'The Ferns' in Dunwich.

Perhaps the most famous, and certainly the most eccentric, of these guests was Charles Keene (1823-1891). He was working at time when black and white illustrative work was understood and appreciated in a way that is difficult to comprehend now. Keene was indisputably a brilliant draughtsman and in England his genius was mentioned in the same breath as Shakespeare; in France, Monet and Pissarro, admired him and Degas bought his work. However, Keene wanted none of this because he was acutely shy, hated handshakes and hated attention. He cannot have been an easy houseguest, living on his nerves, which were already inflamed by strong coffee and by dark tobacco, smoked in an antique clay pipe. The nerves of his host were also tried when Charles Keene brought his Northumbrian bagpipes with him to Dunwich. The noise they generated was too much even for the music-loving Mr and Mrs. Edwards. He and they were relegated to the exterior and it was on the beach in the morning that the mournful strains of the pipes could sometimes be heard above the pounding waves.

Although Keene was born and brought up in London he, like Edwards had family connections with Suffolk and he had briefly been a pupil at Ipswich School. Perhaps that is why he was drawn back to the East Coast, sometimes to stay with the Edwardses, sometimes on his own and, occasionally, arriving by boat in the company of his friend and fellow painter Henry Stacy Marks (1829-1898). One evening in Southwold harbour they had enjoyed a dinner of local eggs; Keene collected the shells and filled them with lighted candle stubs and, to the consternation of the coastguard, floated them out to sea. These pranks were never more than a temporary distraction as there was nothing more important to Keene than his work. The living he made as an artist was secured by his employment as an illustrator, first with the *Illustrated London News* and then, for the following 40 years, with *Punch*. The search for inspiration was always pressing, but in Southwold and "*Wobbleswick*" Keene found what he wanted in the absurdities of his fellow artists. Some exhibited a good deal more enthusiasm than talent and were ridiculed for it (see illustration on p.196).

Edwin Edwards's talent was cultivated by his devoted wife Ruth. She was a formidable woman who gave her life to the promotion of her husband's work, even after his premature death aged 56. An oil painting of the beach at Southwold (see illustration on p.198) shows him to be a perfectly competent painter, but it was only after he became inspired by the French artist and engraver, Alphonse Legros, that he found his real metier: etching. Ruth was always by his side as they toured the country in the search for inspiration. Edwards chose to start at first light when the weather allowed it. When it did not, he worked under a portable glass shelter and Ruth wiped away the condensation before it obscured his view. In a frenzy of activity he finished 370 etchings before he died, some of which were hand coloured by her.

Edwards was a regular contributor to the Royal Academy shows and it was widely known that he was an habitué of Suffolk, this and the publication of Keene's cartoons in *Punch*, must have made Southwold and its surroundings yet more famous in artistic circles. Although there was no formal art school established there, the most talented of the visitors who had flocked to Southwold and Walberswick were close friends. Some were also members of The New English Arts Club, founded in 1886 for the benefit of those who wanted to paint in the open air. A high percentage of the artists who made up the group had worked in the Blyth valley, and they included George Clausen (1852-1944), Maurice Greiffenhagen (1862-1931), Walter Osborne (1859-1903), Walter Sickert (1860-1942), and Philip Wilson Steer (1860-1942).

Southwold Harbour *by Walter Osborne (1859-1903). Oil on canvas. c.1884. A mother looks back to her son who has grown tired in the heat of the day. In this case the scene is a more informative view of the north side of Southwold Harbour.* Christie's Images

Opposite above:

On Suffolk Sands *by Walter Osborne (1859-1903). Oil on canvas. c.1884.*

This scene is clearly recognisable as the mouth of Southwold harbour. A small boy is offering donkey rides in the afternoon sun. This side of the river was associated with the fishing industry rather than the tourism that thrived on Southwold beach. It is likely that the artist has combined two of the scenes he encountered on the East Coast in this highly effective composition. In 1887 it was for sale at the Royal Hibernian Academy for £25 and a year later in Liverpool the price was reduced to £20.

Milmo-Penny Fine Art, Dublin

Below:

Children Paddling *by Philip Wilson Steer (1860 –1942). Oil on canvas. 1894.*

This dazzling evocation of sunny seaside holidays inspired the critic George Moore to write in The Speaker *of March 1894:*

"Around the long breakwater the sea winds, filling the estuary, or perchance recedes, for the oncoming tide is noisier ... a delicious, happy, opium blue, the blue of oblivion ... Paddling in the warm sea-water gives oblivion to those children. They forgot their little worries in the sensation of the sea and sand, as I forget mine in that dreamy blue that fades and deepens imperceptibly, like a flower from the intense heart to the delicate edge of the petals. The vague sea is drawn up behind the breakwater, and out of it the broad sky ascends solemnly in curves like palms. Happy sensation of daylight; a flower-like afternoon; little children paddling; the world is behind them too; they are the flowers, and are conscious only of the benedictive influences of sand and sea and sky." Fitzwilliam Museum, Cambridge

Above:

Southwold *by Philip Wilson Steer. Oil. c.1884.*

This spontaneous oil sketch may have been the preliminary for a painting intended to illustrate the duality of life in Southwold. Fishermen are at work maintaining their boat whilst a fashionable lady, seated in a long dress and a hat, gazes out to sea. A similar scene was photographed by P.H. Emerson c.1886 (see illustration on p.231).

York Art Gallery

Opposite:

Young Woman on the Pier *by Philip Wilson Steer. Oil on canvas. c.1887.*

This is a brilliant evocation of summer sunshine and sea. A young and fashionable girl is sitting at the end of Southwold Harbour adjusting her hat against the dazzling rays of the sun. The composition is made up of a high horizon and large flat shapes diversified by the human form.

Musée D'Orsay, Paris. Photograph: REM

Above:

Walberswick *by James Aumonier (1832-1911). Watercolour on paper. 1878.*

Although painted from the Southwold side of the River Blyth, this is a view of Walberswick. The windmill and tower of St. Andrew's Church dominate the profile of the village. The "Kissing Bridge" over the Went is on the right. In the foreground fishermen are loading wet nets on to a carrying frame to be taken to the drying sheds.

Aumonier was a painter of quiet pastoral landscapes and animals. He was a regular visitor to Southwold from 1877.   Stephen Wildman Esq.

Opposite:

The Tanning Sheds, Walberswick

by Myles Birket Foster (1825-1899). Watercolour on paper. c.1890.

Fishermen's children play with a toy boat in a pool as their fathers, in fishing boats, are braving the German Ocean in pursuit of herring. In order to preserve the nets and sails it was necessary to tan them. The crumbling chimney stands above a cauldron. Southwold's church and newly built lighthouse, finished in 1890, can be made out in the distance. To the left is the tributary of the Blyth, called Dunwich Cut. Behind the sheds to the right, obscured from view, is the famous Kissing Bridge (see pp.162 and 163). The view is recognisable, though today a visitors' car park occupies this site.

Myles Birket Foster may have been introduced to the East Coast by his friend Charles Keene. His visits there resulted in a number of attractive beach scenes and seascapes.   Sotheby's

On the East Coast *by Charles Robertson (1844-1891). Watercolour on paper. c.1883.*
This is a view of Southwold harbour with Walberswick and its windmill in the distance. The "Kissing Bridge" over the Went is to the left of the distinctive sheds at the ferry crossing (see illustration on p.223). The large boat to the right of the composition may be that which appears in Emerson's photograph illustrated on p.231.
Flocks of seagulls signal the arrival of the catch. The banks are strewn with disused anchors, the only reminders of a much larger fishing fleet. In 1880 an anonymous poet writing for Punch *noted that at Walberswick:*

"There's a harbour old and rotten, planks and anchors long forgotten..."

The smoking chimneys suggest that the weather has turned cold; the numbers painted on the anchor in the foreground (11:83) probably hint at the date on which this beautiful watercolour was made: November 1883.
Robertson was influenced by his friend Myles Birket Foster who was in Southwold at about the same time as this watercolour was made. Robertson died tragically young when he was at the height of his artistic powers.   Christie's, London

Opposite:
Summer's Day *by Francis Newbery (1859-1946). Oil on canvas. 1912.*
The artist's wife is sitting in the shade of one of the artist's studios on the side of the River Blyth at Walberswick.
Francis Newbery was director of the Glasgow School of Art in 1885. He had a summer residence and studio in Walberswick from about 1897 until 1915. There he entertained other Scottish-based artists, including Charles Rennie Mackintosh and Maurice Greiffenhagen.   Photograph: Peter Nahum

209

To take advantage of Walberswick's special light and uninterrupted views, a number of wooden studios were constructed along the south side of the river Blyth. Picturesque in their own right, they were further evidence that Walberswick was the perfect place to paint. However, it was two artists with divergent aims that have made the greatest contribution to its fame, Philip Wilson Steer (1860-1942) and Charles Rennie Mackintosh (1868-1928).

Wilson Steer came to Walberswick for the first time in 1884 and its wide beaches and piers inspired a flaring of genius of such intensity that can only be described as "*an effect outside the scale of paint*". However, it was Southwold that was the inspiration for *Children Paddling*, one of the most notable of this series of canvases. Steer made at least sixteen paintings in Walberswick and five in Southwold; in the majority, the observation of nature is secondary to the fleeting effects of brilliant sunshine.

When Mackintosh came to work in Walberswick in 1914 it was not only for sunshine, sea and sky. Although he made a number of detailed watercolours of the harbour, the artist's studios and local landmarks, it was the plant life that really inspired him. In a

Opposite:

Venetian Palace, Blackshore-on-the-Blyth *by Charles Rennie Mackintosh. Watercolour on paper. 1914.*

Mackintosh has highlighted the resemblance between the functional building on the north bank of the river Blyth, with its loft and hoist, and the architecture of Venice. The water in the foreground adds to the witty allusion. This interesting building has since been pulled down and replaced with a modern house. To the left is the beginning of Carnsey Road and on the right is the tiled roof and one of the window's of the ancient Fishing Buss Inn (now Harbour Inn). In the distance is the unmistakable tower of St. Edmund's Church.

Photo © Hunterian Museum and Art Gallery,
University of Glasgow, Mackintosh Collection

Right:

Gorse, Walberswick *drawn by Charles Rennie Mackintosh and coloured by his wife Margaret Macdonald Mackintosh. Pencil and watercolour on paper. 1915.*

This is not just a simple botanical study: Mackintosh and his wife accentuated the character of the gorse until it appeared angry and threatening. The drawing was made in 1915 when the Mackintoshes themselves were angry and threatened. That same year, just as the gorse began to bloom, they were falsely accused of spying and were forced to leave Walberswick forever. The British Museum

series of watercolours intended for publication, Mackintosh successfully identified the animus of his wildflower subjects by subtly accentuating their individual characteristics.

Mackintosh crossed to Southwold by the ferry from Walberswick armed with just a sketchbook. There he was obliged to turn from nature to art and architecture for his inspiration. The simple monumentality of the lighthouse caught his eye (see illustration on p.63) and, as Mackintosh walked up the High Street through Market Place into Queen Street, he noted the curvilinear qualities in the wrought-iron signs hanging outside *The Crown* and *The Red Lion* (see illustration on p.190). As an architect, it is not surprising that the grandeur and detailed decoration of the church was what Mackintosh admired most. In the same way that he imbued his flower studies with his own unmistakable style he made calligraphic studies of the gothic tracery of the church, the clock tower, the rood screen and even the linenfold decoration on the bleached oak door (see illustrations on pp.36 and 37).

Blythburgh *by Edward Seago (1910-1974). Oil on canvas.*
Seago was a pupil of Bertram Priestman and was taught by him in Walberswick between 1923 and 1927.
His connections with the area were strengthened by his friendships with John Masefield and Sir Henry
Rider Haggard (see p.129). His Grace the Duke of Westminster. Photograph: Richard Green

Mackintosh and his wife Margaret began their stay in Walberswick at the outbreak of the First World War and were to end it a year later, under a dark cloud of suspicion. The artist's unusual clothes, the very fact that he was an artist, and his habit of walking around after dark had aroused the suspicions of the locals, who already felt threatened by the risk of invasion. Soon the police exercised their new powers and searched Mackintosh's lodgings where they found correspondence, written in German, from the artist communities in Austria and Germany. Mackintosh was arrested on the suspicion of being a spy and, when he was finally released, was banished from East Anglia. Despite the fact that there had been no truth in the accusation, Mackintosh and his wife Margaret were obliged to leave immediately for London.

In his book *Artists at Walberswick* the author Richard Scott has made a painstaking survey of artists who worked in the village from 1880 until 2000. They flocked there from far and wide. Most had made the relatively short journey from London, some, like Walter

Southwold Harbour *by Bertram Priestman. Oil on canvas.*
The harbour mouth was extensively repaired and widened in the early 20th century in the hopes of reviving the dwindling fishing trade. In 1908 it was finished and 300 drifters landed herrings, which were prepared for export to Germany by the Scots girls lodging in town. Private collection

Langley, came from Newlyn; the Scottish contingent was headed by Francis Newbery (see p.209), that from Ireland by Walter Osborne and his friend Nathaniel Hill (1861-1934) (see p.197). It must be safe to assume that every one of them made the short boat trip over the river Blyth to Southwold. There the landscape painters often discovered that the complexity of the townscape, cliffs and beaches of the little town was more of a challenge than the open vistas of Walberswick. Edwin Edwards took it up (see illustration on p.198). Others who grappled with the challenge of the jumble of buildings close to the shore were Arthur Evershed (1836-1919), the designer and artist Walter Crane (1845-1915), the French trained Walter Osborne (1859-1903), the still life and landscape painter Alan Gwynne-Jones (1892-1982), and the painter and illustrator John Piper (1903-1992). Although all of them successfully conveyed Southwold's contradictory atmosphere of town and seascape, it was Stanley Spencer (1891-1959), undaunted by the difficulties of composition he faced in *Southwold Beach*, who painted arguably the most powerful evocation of the English seaside holiday ever.

The River Blyth Ferry *by Bertram Priestman. Oil on canvas. 1910.*
Both visiting artists and writers saw the crossing between Southwold and Walberswick as a metaphor or
the journey from one world to another (see illustration on p.200). The locals, however, saw it as a practical
alternative to the long route via Blythburgh. During the first nine months following its opening in 1885,
33,680 foot passengers made the crossing accompanied by 723 vehicles, 69 horses and 403 trucks.

Private Collection

However, as was so often the case, it was not the land and seascapes of the East Coast that attracted Stanley Spencer, rather the presence of his fellow painter Hilda Carline (1889-1950). They had become engaged in 1922 and Hilda was already keen to return to Suffolk. In 1924 the couple were at Wangford and it was there that work was to prove a powerful distraction from the deep flaws in the relationship. Nonetheless, they were married at the church of St. Peter and St. Paul, Wangford, on 23 February 1925. The following year the Spencers returned to Wangford, parents of a little girl called Shirin.

Then Stanley and Hilda were part of the artistic circle of friends that had been cultivated by the headmistress of the girls school in Reydon, founded in 1897, and named after St. Felix, Bishop of Dunwich. Lucy Silcox was softly spoken, but had a strong face that matched her quietly determined character. She began her career at St. Felix School in 1909 and from the start she had been determined to educate her pupils by example. She and her colleagues were responsible for the identification of beauty in both thought and nature; for the beauty in art she relied, to some extent, upon the help of her wide circle of friends. The school library was enriched with books auto-graphed and dedicated by John Masefield (1878-1967), Bertrand Russell (1872-1970)

The Ferry, Walberswick *by Maurice Greiffenhagen (1862-1931). Oil on canvas. c.1905.*
The artist has deliberately distorted the perspective for a better effect. In the foreground lovers are saying goodbye after a sunny day in Southwold; on the Walberswick side a group are waiting to make the return journey on the steam pontoon ferry.
The River Blyth Ferry Company was founded on 28 September 1885; though by 1931 it was making more than 26,800 journeys a year, it closed in 1942. In 1927 Martin Shaw remarked that Southwold "is getting very modern... tickets had been instituted for the ferry."

Southwold *by Stanley Spencer (1891-1959). Oil on canvas. 1937.* Although the scene is one of an idyllic seaside holiday, it was painted at a time of deep emotional upheaval for Spencer. He had abandoned his wife Hilda Carline for a turbulent relationship with Patricia Preece and was under some considerable financial hardship. In an attempt to resolve his problems he returned to East Anglia to paint. This powerful image of a sunny day at Southwold beach is the most famous result of his efforts.

City of Aberdeen Art Gallery and Museums Collection

J. Mac Neil Whistler

and Sir Henry Rider Haggard (1856-1925) and the corridors and chapel were hung with paintings and sculptures collected for the inspiration of the pupils. They included an altarpiece by Ranieri di Leonardo da Pisa, *The White Farm* by Christopher Wood, a bust of *Euphemia Lamb* by Jacob Epstein, and several portraits of Lucy herself. In 1925 she sat to Stanley Spencer, but the sessions were not a success; Spencer was so displeased with the first result that he wiped it away and started again.

Towards the end of her career Miss Silcox appointed Marjorie Lilly (1891-1980) to work as art teacher in the studio, the newest develop-ment at St. Felix. During her training at the Campden School of Art, Marjorie Lilly was inspired by Charles Ginner, Harold Gilman and, most significantly, Walter Sickert (1860-1942).

Sickert had been to Walberswick in the 1890s in the company of James Whistler (1843-1903), but they found it "*too cosy, picturesque and prosperous*". Neither did very much work and Whistler destroyed most of what he did do.[1] When Miss Lilly persuaded Sickert to return in 1927 it was to deliver a painting that had been intended to decorate the new art room at St. Felix. The visit was not a success because the school had wanted a vivid architectural landscape but, instead, was offered a tiny, gloomy portrait of the painter Therese Lessore. Masking her disappointment, Miss Lilly suggested to Sickert that they take a walk by the sea. He told her that he was delighted to find Southwold unchanged and she "*gave herself up to the charm of his company*". Dinner that night, hosted by Miss Silcox was difficult. When they eventually got up to leave the crowded table it was to head for the assembly room where Sickert gave his lecture. To the artist's eye the girls proved a distraction: "*Charming! Like a flight of little white doves!*". However Sickert's attentions were not returned and the "*pretty creatures"* found his talk obscure and dull. The entire visit was a disaster and Miss Lilly's humiliation was compounded by having to return the painting to Sickert. It was eventually exchanged for a more suitable portrait, wrongly identified as Virginia Woolf. Nonetheless, Sickert was unbowed by the rejection of his original choice:

"Ah well I am pleased the good lady is pleased. Probably it is another one of those forgeries and not by me at all."

In 1930 some of those artists who had been working on the East Coast formed an association called the Sole Bay Group with the intention of mounting summer exhibitions in both Southwold and Aldeburgh. Although its aims sounded serious these were in fact lighthearted events.[2] The founder of this society was William Crittal (1887-1956) and it was he who introduced a number of distinguished artists to the area including Sir George Clausen (1852-1944). Guest exhibitors were invited to send in to these shows; in 1933 Stanley Spencer and Sir William Russell Flint were amongst those who accepted. It was a turbulent time in the art world and shock waves of innovation were felt even in relatively remote Suffolk. The secretary of the Group, Tom van Oss (1901-1941) introduced the catalogue as follows:

"All is ferment and experiment... The turmoil must, at times, seem chaos, specially to the layman, and in this exhibition all sorts and kinds of work are brought together ... the only standard applicable is that of representativeness."

Although some were for the *avant garde* it was not to the taste of all the artists working in the region of Sole Bay and the majority adhered to traditional techniques and standards. In 1989, the

Stanley Spencer *by Sir William Rothenstein (1872-1945). Sanguine on paper. 1932.*   The National Portrait Gallery

Above:

The Blyth River (Walberswick) *by Katherine Hamilton.*
Oil on canvas. 2003.
This is the present prospect of Southwold's ancient harbour. Black fishermen's sheds and wooden jetties are a reference to a once thriving fishing industry now overtaken by tourism. A procession of holiday-makers is walking along the revetment on the right. At the centre of the composition a couple are waiting for the ancient ferry and its oarsman.
Photograph: Messum © Katherine Hamilton, 2003

Left:

Marmalade at Southwold *by Diana Howard (b.1947).*
Oil on board. 2000.
This painting was made at the beach huts south of Gun Hill. Its vibrant colour scheme is redolent of high summer. Diana Howard is a painter, writer and plantswoman who lives near Beccles. Marmalade was a painted dummy board cat who sat obligingly still for this portrait. © Diana Howard, 2006

writer Penelope Fitzgerald published her thinly disguised novel about Southwold life *The Bookshop*, in it she wrote:

"*Later middle age, for the upper middle-class in East Suffolk, marked a crisis, after which the majority became water-colourists, and painted landscapes. It would not have mattered if they had painted badly, but they all did it quite well. All their pictures looked much the same. Framed, they hung in sitting-rooms, while outside the windows the empty, washed-out, unarranged landscape stretched away to the transparent sky.*"

Amateur painters working in the town are just as prolific, informative, and reliable. They show their work at local art galleries and exhibitions, and please those who are looking for an uncomplicated souvenir of the town. However, there are just a few professional artists who, like their distinguished predecessors, have a vision that goes beyond simple representation, striving truly to identify the true essence of Southwold as it is now.[3]

A WIDE FOCUS:
P.H. EMERSON IN SOUTHWOLD

When the French artist Paul Delaroche saw a daguerreotype photograph for the first time in 1839 he declared *"From today painting is dead!"*. This was the starting gun for a debate that was to run and run: is photography truly art?

When Peter Henry Emerson (1856-1936) came to live in Southwold in 1884 the quietly sedate seaside town became the epicentre of this increasingly heated discussion. To clinch the argument in Emerson's favour all that was required was Southwold's inimitable light and landscapes, a camera and his own remarkable vision. The result was a personal triumph, but only a brief one: Emerson capitulated to his detractors in 1891 in a letter copied to the leading photographic magazines of the day.

Notwithstanding this very public, and needless, surrender, Emerson had already won his place in history, not only for the foundation of a new school of landscape photography, but also for changing the way that photography was perceived.

His father, Henry Emerson, was a coffee grower in Cuba (then a colony of Spain) with a plantation which, like the majority, was worked by slaves. It was into these surroundings that Pedro Enrique was born and baptised, and became accustomed to a life of comfort and privilege that may have spoiled him. In later life he is remembered as being cantankerous and confrontational, though fundamentally of good character. Although he maintained some

222

Walberswick. *Platinum print. c.1886.*

This a view of the net and tanning sheds beside The Went, a small tributary of the Blyth. Made of black painted wood these buildings had a striking presence and were a popular subject for the 'shoals' of painters who came to Walberswick in the summer. They figure in a painting by Charles Rennie Mackintosh (now lost), woodcuts by Frank Brangwyn and the watercolour drawing by Myles Birket Foster (see illustration on p.207). In the distance is the Kissing Bridge; another favourite of visiting artists. There has been some debate as to whether or not this view was the subject of Philip Wilson Steer's famous painting 'The Bridge' (see illustration on p.162). Emerson's unusual view clearly shows the platform levelling out on the Eastern side. It was there that Wilson Steer set the scene for the studio picture he finished shortly after this photograph was taken. It is tempting to suggest that the artist at his easel to the centre right of the photograph, is Steer himself working on the preliminaries for 'The Bridge'.

George Eastman House, New York

Opposite:

Southwold Fisherman. *Platinum print. c.1886.*

In this photograph, which is one of a small series, Emerson evidently intended to illustrate the dignity of the working man. Simple honesty and nobility of spirit were attributes that were highly valued in the cynical urban society of nineteenth century Britain. Queen Victoria's friendship with the gillie John Brown was one expression of it; the portraits of Walberswick fishermen made by Frank Brangwyn during Emerson's time in Southwold are another. The striking features of this young man are recognisable in Joseph Southall's painting Up from the Sea (see illustration on p.71). Although the painting was not finished until 1930 it is possible that Southall worked it up from drawings he had made many years earlier.

George Eastman House, New York

Walberswick in Winter. *Platinum print. c.1885*
This area was once known as Ferry Knoll; Bell Cottage is on the left. Emerson remembered the circumstances under which his photograph was taken:
"Fierce storms of snow and sleet swept across the common, and blow in straggly groups the home-returning crows and flighting ducks. On the ice-covered dikes the urchins skate, and the eel-pickers secure their slimy spoil. At eventide the village streets are empty, but from the cottage homes steal forth glowing lights and savoury smells of broiling fish and fragrant tobacco." George Eastman House, New York

of the least attractive attitudes of his time, the truth is that Emerson was a deeply religious man with a strong sense of duty and integrity. He was also handsome, persuasive, charming and compassionate; invaluable attributes when trying to entice the locals to pose for the camera (see illustrations on pp.222, 227 and 237). Recently local writers have, in the interests of sensationalism, exaggerated the flaws in Emerson's character. It is true his personality had been affected by serious bereavements: his only sister, Jane, died when she was six and this was a shattering blow to the nine-year-old boy. Shortly afterwards, in 1867, his father succumbed to dysentery and Emerson was sent to board at the newly established public school at Cranleigh in Surrey.

Baiting the line. *Platinum print. c.1886.*
Fishermen are gathered at the south end of Southwold beach and are baiting the long fishing lines. In the foreground floats are lying on the pebbles and to the right is a wooden bier used to carry both the nets and the catch, after it has been packed in wooden boxes for market.

George Eastman House, New York

After a reasonably happy education he enrolled as a medical student at Cambridge and from there he obtained the temporary post of Assistant House Physician at King's College. The date was 1881 and it was significant for two reasons. This was the year in which he married Edith Ainsworth, a nurse. Edith's compliant nature was a perfect foil to the strength of his own and Emerson acknowledged the fact when he described her as "*the best fellow I know*". It was also the year that he acquired his first camera.

Initially, photography was merely a pastime for Emerson, though a holiday in Southwold in August 1883 marked the beginning of a remarkable journey of discovery. Why exactly Emerson chose the East Coast we may never know, but Southwold's varied attractions persuaded him, not only to return, but also to make it his permanent home.

Packing the cod for the London Market – Southwold. *Platinum print. c.1886.*
Cod and herrings are being transferred from wicker baskets into shallow boxes for transport by sea or rail. The hut belongs to the owner of a fishing boat called 'Rosebud'. To the side of it a pair of leather thigh-length boots has been hung up to dry. These boots could be fatal encumbrances to the wearer during accidents at sea. (See illustration on p.71). George Eastman House, New York

Opposite:
East Coast fishermen. Platinum print. c.1886.
Three fishermen are resting outside their shed; leaning against it is a cork buoy. The men are sitting on the bier used to carry the nets and boxes, loaded with fish for the market. Emerson remembered them as follows:

"If you talk to them of their past voyages, their eyes will brighten, their faces flush with enthusiasm; and their whole being will alter and glow with excitement as they describe the wonders they have seen in the 'Chiney Sea' at 'Stockholom' or at 'Walperaiso'." George Eastman House, New York

Sea piece – Southwold. *Platinum print. c.1886.*
The waves are crashing against the north pier of the harbour, built in 1749. Emerson was clearly fascinated by the beauty and destructive energy of the sea when he wrote: "Then, too, does the angry North Sea beat this doomed shore with thundering waves, and year by year devours the land." (See illustration on pp.64/65)
George Eastman House, New York

As soon as his M.B. degree was finished, Emerson left Cambridge with his family and arrived in Southwold with his cumbersome camera and the processing equipment that were the essentials of his life's work. The residents of the little sea-side town were used to strangers but Emerson must have appeared an unusually exotic character.

It is likely that Edith stayed behind at their house on Southwold Common when Emerson set off with his brother on their first cruise of the Norfolk Broads. They had hired a yacht called *Emily* and the holiday was to prove the most momentous event in Emerson's artistic life. It was on this trip he made some of his most inspired and poetic photographs; and it was there that he made the acquaintance of the historical and

Wreck at Covehithe. Xmas 1884. *Platinum print. 1884.*
The tragic sight of the ships wrecked off the East Coast has been a constant source of inspiration to Southwold artists. In this photograph Emerson is following in the tradition of a number of distinguished predecessors, including Turner, Henry Davy and Henry Alexander (see illustrations on pp. 55, 56/57 and 58). The fact that this tragedy occurred at Christmas makes the scene all the more poignant.
George Eastman House, New York

landscape painter Thomas Goodall (1857-1944). Goodall was not only to become Emerson's intimate friend but also his artistic collaborator.

In 1886 they were back on the Norfolk Broads and the following year Goodall and Emerson took a beach yawl houseboat, the *Electra*, to Breydon skippered by William Rogers, a fisherman from Southwold. For six months Emerson and Goodall remained *"ever watchful for picturesque models"*,[1] Goodall spending some of the trip working on his big picture of Yarmouth; in 1887 he and Emerson published their work under the title *Life and Landscape on the Norfolk Broads*. The two books that quickly followed, *Pictures from Life in Field and Fen* and *Idylls of the Norfolk Broads*, were, however, published under Emerson's name alone.

Mending the sail. *Platinum print. c.1886.*

A group of local fishermen are repairing their sails on the sand beside the south pier of Southwold harbour. This complicated wooden structure, built in 1752 on the Walberswick side of the River Blyth, supported lookout huts and capstans. It figures in many paintings and drawings including those of Henry Davy, Charles Keene, and Walter Osborne. (See illustrations on pp.8, 9, 113 and 150).

George Eastman House, New York

Opposite, above:

Woman sitting by a large boat. *Platinum print. c.1886.*

The scene may be Walberswick. This large boat is similar to that in the painting by Charles Robertson called On The East Coast *(see illustration on p.208).*

Its scale and sweeping contours make an effective contrast with the figure of the woman sitting in the foreground of the composition. Her hat and clothes suggest that she lives a life far removed from the hardships of the local fishermen (see illustrations on p.157). George Eastman House, New York

Opposite, below:

Blackshore (River Blythe [sic], Suffolk). *Photogravure. c.1886.*

Emerson described this scene as follows:

"A few cottages clustering round a small tavern, 'The Fishing Buss' whose name bespeaks its history, a cow-house, a quay in places decayed, a couple of condemned smacks' hulls lying alongside the quay… some sheep are feeding along the Cansey, as is there wont in early spring, the shepherd following them. At the old decayed quay is moored the schooner 'Heart of Oak', well known to Southwold and Walberswick fishermen… some we know have nearly met their deaths in her… but now she floats at Blackshore quay as unseaworthy." George Eastman House, New York

Eel picking. *Platinum print. c.1886.*

Emerson noted that:

"After the fishing season is over, at the end of December, the Southwold fishermen, when not shrimping, fill up their time with eel picking, net-making and mending and other sundry jobs."

William Rogers, a fisherman from Southwold is teaching his boy how to catch eels. They are searching the bottom of the creek for telltale 'blows' from the fish hiding in the mud. Once located, the slippery fish is speared on the barbs of the iron pick "not unworthy of the sons of Neptune". Eels were once an important supplement to the diet of the working man in Southwold and part of the daily catch was sent to market in London. Today redundant spears known locally as 'gall-picks' are used to decorate the walls of Southwold's bars and restaurants.

George Eastman House, New York

Having availed himself of a substantial private income, Emerson was free to explore his metier; finally giving up medicine in favour of writing and photography. This was a career that was brilliant enough to eclipse that of his friend Thomas Goodall. Although Goodall had exhibited East Anglian landscapes and peasant studies at the Royal Academy, New Gallery and Grosvenor Gallery until 1901, little is known of him or his work thereafter.[2]

The three handsome books Emerson published in 1887 led to important commissions;

Furze Cutting on a Suffolk (Southwold) Common. *Photogravure print.*
The painful task of pruning back the prickly furze on Southwold Common was the responsibility of the
marsh and sluiceman of forty years, John Page known as 'Jocky'. Emerson described the furze as the
"denizen of bleak common and wind-cut field which blooms with all the luxuriance of torrid vegetation."
When cut it was used for fences and for building up the riverbanks. In Emerson's photograph John Page
wears thick leather leggings and gloves against the fierce thorns of the gorse. On the back of this print
it is recorded that Page considered himself the senior member of the corporation and that he died at
Andrew Mathews Home of Rest in Reydon.   George Eastman House, New York

in 1888 *The Compleat Angler*, written by Izaak Walton, was illustrated with Emerson's
photographs. In 1890 Emerson published both *Pictures of East Anglian Life* and *Wild Life
on a Tidal River*. This was the beginning of a life's work that resulted in at least 32 books
and 22 articles.

Emerson's guides quickly outshone every other, though, unaccountably, he published
only a small number of the spectacularly beautiful photographs taken in his hometown
and its environs. The titles of those Southwold pictures he did select for publication are

Cottage interior, fisherman's family. *Platinum print. c.1886.*

A slightly idealised view of life in a fisherman's cottage, probably in Southwold. A family of six are crowded in to a small room. They have interrupted their tea to watch the boy dance to the sound of the fiddle. The fireplace, wallpaper, pictures and ornaments and carefully laundered tablecloth contribute to a scene of domestic bliss that conflicts with Emerson's descriptions of the hardships of life on the East Coast (see opposite). The ropes and nets hanging on the walls and anchors in the foreground are reminders of a gruelling daily routine.   George Eastman House, New York

usually vague and not all of them have been properly identified until now. Perhaps the photographs he had taken in Southwold, Walberswick and Covehithe were considered too specific in their interest or too complex in their composition to appeal to the general public. Indeed, the sheer number of publications devoted to the Norfolk Broads during the nineteenth century demonstrates that the area had already become a popular holiday destination, probably superseding even Southwold as a fashionable watering place. Perhaps this is why Emerson decided not to include images of Southwold in his guides. Whatever the reason for their omission, the result is that Emerson's work is now more often associated with Norfolk than his home county of Suffolk. Nonetheless, a sufficient number of beautiful photographs of Southwold have survived to redress balance and to give a unique insight into the town's fast-fading past (see illustrations on pp.232, 233 and 234).

The collection at George Eastman House, Rochester, New York includes more than a dozen photographs of Southwold and its people at work. Several are captioned on the reverse and topographical details in others have made it possible to identify them as local views. Without doubt, the most affecting of them all are the portraits of the local people (see illustrations on pp.226, 227, 230 and 234). In common with writers and artists of his time, Emerson not only admired the simple, noble character of the working man, but also his resilience to the harsh realities of living.

"*The more we have studied the peasant life from our point of view the more fearful does it appear to us. A Terrible struggle for the bare necessities of life ... if his health fails his family starves.*"

The struggle that Emerson described is subtly reflected in the portraits he made of the Southwold fishermen (see illustration on p.237). At work they endured long hours of darkness, biting cold and wind, only to return home to overcrowding and squalor. Emerson described their pitiful circumstances in both his photographs and his prose:

"*The scanty cubic space filled with air poisoned by the organic exhalations of the eight human beings we saw sitting in the one room, where the hard-worked mother ... was preparing a coarse meal for the delicate children. Pure air and good food they needed and neither could they get. The day was biting cold and we were glad to get out once more into the air, and escape from that ill-smelling dwelling.*"

It was in the open air that Emerson took a happier view of country life: tending flocks of sheep, wildfowling with a punt gun, poaching hares with lurchers and picking eels on Southwold's Botany Marshes were all activities that Emerson managed to imbue with a special dignity and beauty. On the beach below Centre Cliff he made photographs of the fishermen baiting the lines, bringing home the catch and packing it for the London market (see illustration on p.225). As they rested in front of their sheds he enticed the Southwold salts to tell tales of the "furrin parts" they had visited in their sailing ships. These men led dangerous lives and Emerson was conscious of this when he fixed his lens on the angry waves smashing against the wooden piers of Southwold harbour (see illustration on p.228), the launch of the lifeboat from the beach, or on the ship wrecked at Covehithe during Christmas 1884 (see illustration on p.229).

In stark contrast the same lens was used in the summer to photograph the same sea on whose calm, reflective surface the sunrise was mirrored at dawn. It was the beauty of nature that had attracted painters to Southwold during Emerson's time and it is no coincidence that painterly influences are detectable in his photographs. Certainly Goodall's was the strongest; he had been a fellow pupil of Henry La Thangue, Samuel Melton Fisher and Alexander Stanhope Forbes when they attended the Royal Academy Schools and he was a good friend of George Clausen. Through Goodall, Emerson was first introduced to the work of Bastien-Lepage and at one time they both regarded him as the *"greatest painter who had ever lived as [he was] the greatest naturalist"*. Bastien-Lepage is best remembered for his peasant pictures and there are echoes of his compositions in Emerson's photographs of the working people of East Anglia. Emerson was happy to acknowledge a debt to Bastien-Lepage in *Pictures from Life in Field and Fen*, published in 1887, but his admiration was short-lived:

 "We had all along miss-judged him, thinking him a much greater painter than he really is … his sentiment is often false, untrue and brutal."

Emerson's allegiance quickly changed to Gustave Courbet and especially to his friends La Thangue and George Clausen. They showed him a new way of looking at peasant life and landscape. Emerson was in touch with all the Chelsea artists and, certainly, he was in correspondence with the luminaries of the Victorian art world: Frederick Lord Leighton, Walter Crane, John Collier, James McNeil Whistler and even John Ruskin. The majority had been sent complimentary copies of Emerson's publications; presumably in the hope that their comments would give weight to the contention that photography was indeed art. If so, then this was a tactic that was occasionally to rebound on Emerson. Although Leighton found his work *"very interesting and charming"* the famous art critic John Ruskin was full of scorn and told Emerson, in 1886, that photography was nothing more than one of the *"arts of idleness"*.

By 1891 Emerson had grown tired with his efforts to raise the status of photography to the level of art. Perhaps his detractors had briefly persuaded him to the contrary. Whatever Emerson's true thoughts, in a letter to the editors of all the photographic magazines he completely renounced his previous claims and apologised to his supporters for misleading them. Although Emerson's capitulation to his detractors was complete, the tone of it was bitter, petulant and fundamentally unconvincing. Had Emerson truly been persuaded that photography was *"the lowest of all art forms"* he would surely not have continued with it until he died.

Four years later, in 1895, Emerson moved to Lowestoft and the following year to The Nook in Oulton Broad, but it was in Southwold where he left a rich and lasting legacy.[3]

Opposite:
Southwold fisherman. *Platinum print. c.1886.*
This is a young man who has made fishing his business. Already his sun-tanned skin and contemplative expression hint at a hard life ahead. The oiled sou'wester hat, woollens and smock are a reminder of the harsh weather conditions in which he was obliged to work.   George Eastman House, New York

ENVOI

With the advent of the motorways and an improved train service it has been possible to arrive in Southwold from London quickly and efficiently. No matter how fleeting the visit, the memory of it is usually indelible. However, the rank of just a few visitors has been high enough to reverse the usual order by leaving their mark on the memory of Southwold. When the new King George VI arrived on August Bank Holiday 1938 it was not by train or car, but on the royal yacht, *Britannia*. As its founder-patron he wanted to visit the Duke of York's Boys' Camp, pitched on Southwold common. Queen Elizabeth and the two princesses, Elizabeth and Margaret remained on board *Britannia*, while their father was rowed ashore to an over-excited and crowded reception, not only from the boys, but also from the people of Southwold who had gathered to see him. Sadly, the burden of kingship meant that he was never to return, but many years later Princess Margaret did so when she became a regular visitor to Suffolk as the guests of her friends in Saxmundham, from where she made occasional visits to Southwold.

On 21 June 1940, soon after the King's visit, his Prime Minister, Winston Churchill, arrived. This was shortly after war had been declared with Germany and when the summit of Churchill's ambition was simply to survive the following few months. With a preoccupation of this magnitude it is doubtful that he remembered much about the town except perhaps the wines and famous hospitality of the Swan Hotel. His presence was a reminder that the East Coast was potentially the first stop for an enemy invasion force. By this time it is unlikely that Southwold's magical association with St. Edmund offered much comfort to the townspeople (see the chapter 'Holy Edmund Pray For Us'). However, the sight of the warrior leader Churchill, complete with cigar, waving from his car as it slowly progressed along North Parade imbued Southwold with the courage to face an uncertain and dangerous future.

Opposite:

Albert, Duke of York *[later King George VI; 1895-1952] by Simon Elwes. Oil on canvas. 1936.*
Southwold has been closely associated with three Dukes of York. Richard Plantagenet (1411-1460) held the manor of Southwold and its rights including tolls for anchorage and an annual payment of herrings. Soon after the restoration of Charles II in 1660, the King gave Long Island to his brother, James, Duke of York. There the new town of Southold (see page 16) was obliged to pay the Duke's agent "one fatt lamb", annually. The same Duke of York, later King James II, came to Southwold for the Battle of Sole Bay in 1672 and Albert, Duke of York and newly King George VI, visited the Duke of York's Camp in Southwold in 1937.
This formal portrait, in which His Royal Highness is wearing the uniform of Colonel-in-Chief of the 11th Hussars, was painted shortly before his visit to Southwold. It makes an interesting comparison with that of James, Duke of York painted in 1672 by Henri Gascars, the year he too was in Southwold (see illustration on p.85). Both are elaborate court portraits in which clothing, armour and uniform play an important part in the endorsement of rank.
In Southwold, the Dukes of York were dressed very differently. James, for sea battle and King George VI informally, in order to join the boys camped on the common. His Majesty had chosen to wear long trousers, but the outfitters Denny instantly made up a pair of shorts so that the King might take part in the field sports.

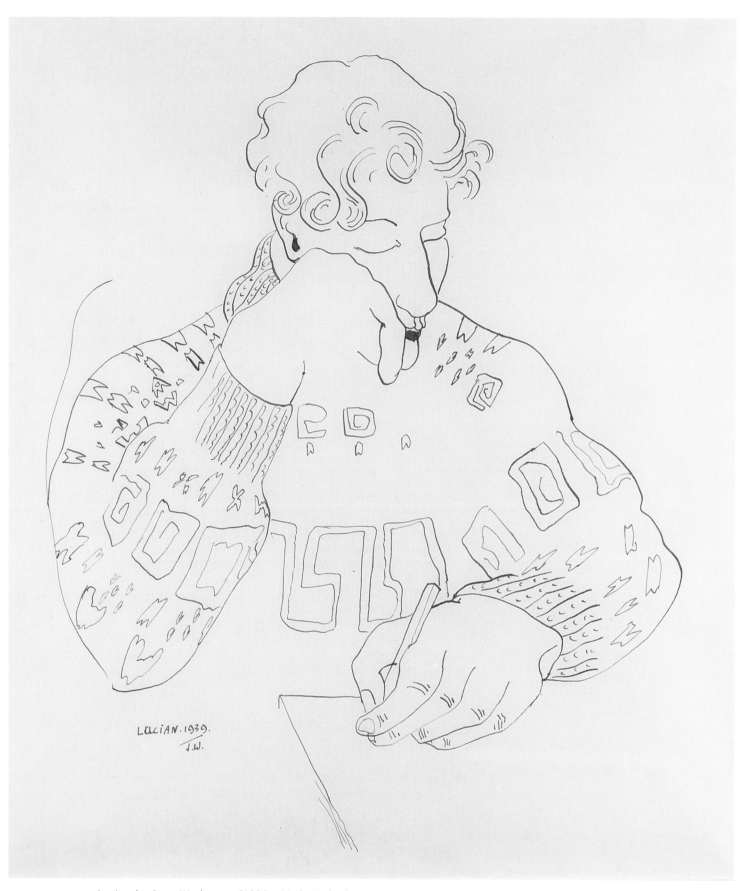

LUCIAN.1939.
J.W.

Lucian *by Joan Warburton (1920-1996). Red ink on paper. Dated 1939.*
A portrait of Lucian Freud aged seventeen, sketching with his left hand. This skilful and assured portrait was made when Freud was at The East Anglian School of Painting in Dedham, Essex. It was a time when Freud's connections with Walberswick were strongest. Though few works are known from his time on the East Coast, the pencil drawing of his mother is probably one of them. Mrs L. Wolfson

Mr. Churchill *by Max Beerbohm (1872-1956). Pencil and watercolour. 1943. The smoke from Churchill's distinctive cigar echoes his profile in this amusing caricature made shortly after his visit to Southwold.*   Bridgeman Art Library

However, that is enough of Southwold's past, it is time to consider its present and to foretell its future. Newcomers to the town invariably remark on how unspoilt it has remained; rich groups of Regency and Victorian buildings above a small cliff, the close proximity of the sea, the colourful beach huts and delightful pier – each contributes an atmosphere that has survived against all odds. Nonetheless, Southwold is not a place that is self-consciously twee or quaint. The novelist P.D. James, who has known it for nearly fifty years, noted that the town is progressive in the best sense of the word: honouring and valuing the past whilst looking confidently towards the future.

Southwold's modern identity was established in the last century. Now, as then, artists continue to be drawn by the sea, landscapes and the town's air of nostalgia though, paradoxically, their work is very much of our time. Lucian Freud lived in Walberswick during the mid to late 1930s, with his parents, Lucie and Ernst, the youngest son of the founder of psychoanalysis Sigmund Freud. The Freud family holidays were spent at Peggan Cottage, renamed Hidden House. It is likely that the young Lucian found the quiet atmosphere of the Blyth Valley stultifying; he once observed that there were far too many artistic ladies with amber necklaces in Southwold for his taste.[1] Despite the

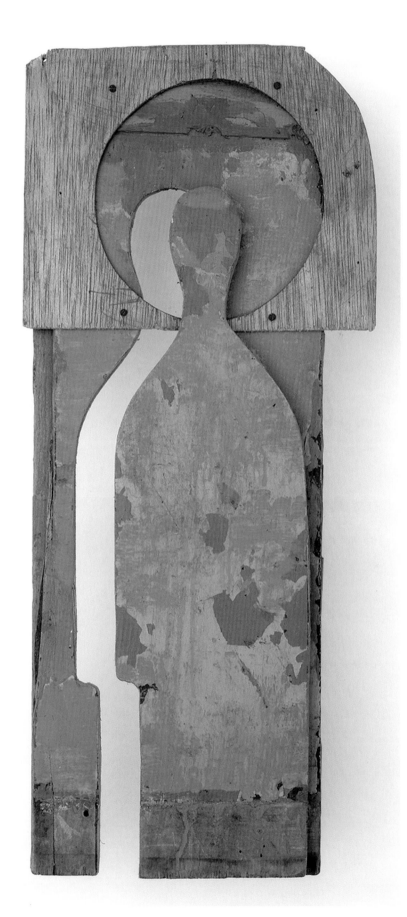

lack of grit that characterises his later work, it was there that Freud was developing a genius for portraiture. It was probably in Walberswick that he made a drawing of his mother; one of the earliest of a series of portraits, which climaxed in a poignant charcoal sketch made, *post mortem*, in 1989.[2] From Walberswick he went the East Anglian School of Painting in Dedham. From these quiet days Freud's horizons were to expand enormously, but the family connection with Southwold and its environs persists to this day. Lucian Freud's daughter, the novelist, Esther (b. 1963) maintains it in both her real life and in her novels and Jill, the wife of the politician and writer Sir Clement Freud, continues to run the Summer Theatre in Southwold. Even if the focus of Lucian Freud's creativity lies beyond the East Coast, then the presence of his family continues to endorse the area's established reputation for being the resort of artists, writers and thinkers.

By the 1960s the formal training that Freud received at Dedham was becoming rare. There it was believed that a facility and skill could only be earned by drawing, drawing and yet more drawing. This premise, held dear by artists since the Renaissance, was shortly to be called into question, sometimes as a result of a new ideology, and sometimes as a result of lack of sufficient funding to maintain it. At the East Anglian School of Painting the casts of antique sculptures were crushed and used as hard core for the car park[3] and a new kind of teaching took their place. If technique was to be demoted, then creativity was to be promoted. Experiment, form and colour filled the void left by the want of figure drawing and knowledge of perspective. Even in Southwold the effects of these fundamental changes was evident in the work of those

Untitled *by Margaret Mellis. Driftwood. c.1986.*
This sculpture and Saint, *shown opposite, were probably inspired by the famous rood screen of St. Edmund's Church (see pp.32,33,121,122 and 123).*
The Strand Gallery, Aldeburgh. Photograph: Nick Sinclair

who continued to be inspired by its light and landscape. The collage artist Francis Davison (1919-1984) and his wife Margaret Mellis (b. 1914) had come to Walberswick from France in the 1950s to take advantage of a fisherman's shed lent to them by a friend and they eventually settled in Suffolk. In 1976 they moved to Southwold and, shortly afterwards, Margaret began to make sculptures from the fragments of painted wood she found on the beach. She and Francis were welcomed into an already established artistic community that spent all or part of its time in Southwold; below are of just some of those who contributed to it.

Lionel Bulmer (1919-1982) brought a revival of pointillism to the holiday sands of the East Coast, and William Bowyer (b. 1926) continues to use a bold palette to define land, sky and sea and the scintillating light on the surface of the waves. The same effects inspired Mary Newcomb (b. 1922) to paint them from Southwold pier; in her work the laws of nature are sublimated to metaphor and lyricism (see illustration on p.244). Mary's daughter Tessa is a visionary; her fascinating paintings hover between reality and a very personal dream world. In contrast, Katherine Hamilton's paintings initially appear to be firmly grounded. However, a subtle spectrum of mood, ranging from sunshine and happiness to dark emotional disquiet, characterises her large canvasses. She lives close to Southwold and, of all the artists working there now, Hamilton has been the most successful at singling out its modern identity (see illustrations on pp.16 and 220).

Richard Scott (b. 1938) is not only an art historian and teacher but also a painter. His connection with

Saint *by Margaret Mellis. Driftwood. 1986.*
In these driftwood sculptures Margaret Mellis has made a link between Southwold's rich liturgical past and the source of its prosperity: the sea. Her "assemblages" are the product of "an immense desire to get the thing inside you transformed into something tangible."

The Strand Gallery, Aldeburgh. Photograph: Nick Sinclair

Skirts Blowing in the Wind *by Mary Newcomb. 2001.*
Three elderly ladies enjoy the sea breeze and the waves scintillating in the summer sunshine. They are standing on the new pier finished in 2001. The sailing ships were probably inspired by the sight of Girl Sybil *on which Marcus Gladwell conducted tours of the East Coast.*

© Mary Newcomb. Photograph: Prudence Cuming

Walberswick began in the 1950s and it is there, and in Southwold, that the evening light has continued to inspire him. In his pictures the shadows and silhouettes of sheds and houses are highlighted with lamp-lit windows or, perhaps, the red and green beacons on the harbour piers. Richard Scott's paintings have a jewel-like intensity; in some he has managed to catch that moment at dusk when purple and blue flowers appear to resonate in the afterglow.

There is no room to list all of the gifted artists who have come to Southwold to paint, nor even those who have stayed. However, a fleeting visit from a promising art student

Bunnies on Gun Hill *by Tessa Newcomb. Oil on board. Painted specially for this book in 2005.*
This is a personal vision of the 'Casino' and battery of guns that are one of the most memorable sights in Southwold. Rabbits are common there and the control of them has led to vigorous debate.

in the early 1980s has succeeded in pulling Southwold's identity right up to date. That year Damien Hirst (b.1965) wrote an admiring letter to Margaret Mellis and addressed it to her house on Constitution Hill. In her reply Margaret extended an invitation to visit Southwold. If her legendary hospitality was an inspiration, then Margaret's work was a revelation.[3] A small number of driftwood sculptures made in homage to it is all that remains of this formative experience except, of course, Damien Hirst's enduring admiration for his mentor.

In the footsteps of the painters and writers who have been drawn to the East Coast,

has come a new band of artists with an entirely new medium. Filmmakers have made several short and frenetic visits to Southwold, during which they have succeeded in making it more famous than ever before. In 1970 it was the responsibility of the ex-mayor Barrett Jenkins to remove all the television aerials from Market Place in anticipation of the making of Delbert Mann's adaptation of *David Copperfield*. A dazzling cast included Laurence Olivier, Richard Attenborough, Ralph Richardson, Wendy Hiller and Edith Evans. In 1988 Peter Greenaway chose Southwold for the making of his typically surreal and iconoclastic black comedy *Drowning by Numbers*; Joely Richardson, Juliet Stevenson, Joan Plowright and Bernard Hill had the starring roles. They were followed to Southwold by the film crew of *Iris*, a biographical film made in 2001, based on the tragic story of the mental decline of the novelist Iris Murdoch. In this instance the cast, headed by Judi Dench, included Jim Broadbent and Kate Winslet. In each of these films Southwold was chosen not for its own sake, but because it provided a colourful and nostalgic backdrop for a bigger picture. It was only the BBC drama, *East of Ipswich*, made in 1987 by Michael Palin, that successfully captured the reality of life in Southwold during the late 1950s. Opening with a brilliant evocation of the tedium of a family seaside holiday, the film develops into a rite of passage for a young man who eventually discovers the joys of lust, love and jazz cafés. More recently, Southwold's 'cream tea' coach party atmosphere has been savagely satirised in the comedy series *Little Britain*, made for BBC3 in 2005. Matt Lucas

---

April Moon *by Richard Scott. Oil. 2001.*
The distinctive sheds and concrete tank traps of Walberswick are silhouetted in the light of the full moon, which is reflected on the surface of the still water. In Southwold and Walberswick there is very little light pollution and the moon and stars are visible in all their splendour. This is a fine example of the very singular nocturnes painted by Richard Scott in Walberswick and the surrounding area. © Richard Scott

and David Walliams star in the role of transvestite men who cause havoc on a tandem and chaos in a tearoom in the High Street.

Southwold is rarely out of the news. It has been mentioned in *The Times* on 5,203 occasions since 1785; recently it has been the value of the colourful beach huts on the promenade that has attracted the attention of journalists. A renewed nostalgia for the traditional seaside holiday has created fierce competition for these simple wooden structures, and their value is rumoured to have escalated beyond all reason. This anomaly has provided the press with limitless copy and made Southwold more famous than, perhaps, it ought to be. In the summer season the High Street teems with holiday-makers who fill the car parks, crowd the pavements and bring enormous prosperity to the town. Residents who grumble about the holiday-makers, in my view, may have spent too long in Southwold and lost touch with modern life, where over-crowding, bad behaviour and aggression are commonplace. Visitors return because in Southwold these stresses and strains immediately give way to a deep sense of peace; but only a few are privileged enough to enjoy it permanently. This is especially obvious on Saturday mornings, when the short-term leases on holiday homes come to an end. The melancholy chore of loading up the family suitcases in preparation for departure is a ritual that has hardly changed since the end of the eighteenth century. Most of the holiday-makers are returning to school or work and, at this moment, there is a real sense of being turned out of paradise.

These emotions were vividly articulated in a letter from the artist Charles Keene to his hostess Mrs Edwin Edwards written on 12 September 1867.

"Dear Mrs. Edwards,

The face of Nature seemed to fall yesterday directly I had left Southwold; the horses toiled along as if they were dragging something very heavy, and the sky loured and the rain fell all in accord with my spirits as we crawled into Darsham. Here's an original distich to head a chapter of the Master's book on Suffolk: 'Lives there a man with heart so light, That Darsham couldn't daunt his sprite!'"

William Morris was writing his epic poem *The Earthly Paradise* when in Southwold in the summer of 1868 and, to the outsider, it must have appeared that he had already attained it. His wife was generally acknowledged as being one of the most beautiful women in the world and she was also the mother of two little girls. At home they lived

---

Opposite:

With Whites by Damien Hirst. Driftwood and flotsam. c.1986.
This subtle study of tone and texture in white was inspired by the driftwood sculptures made by Margaret Mellis at her house in Southwold. © Damien Hirst

together in a house that Morris had furnished and where everything was required to be either functional or beautiful. He was successful and prosperous and lacked for nothing, except love. For William Morris paradise was clearly not to be found on the East Coast nor, indeed, anywhere else on earth.

If the plaques on the pier are to be believed, some have been luckier in finding their version of paradise than others; when I am with my family in Southwold I am certainly one of them. In front of me, as I write, is Reydon Common Marsh where only the reeds and wild birds disturb my view to the edge of the North Sea, defined with brightly coloured beach huts, luminous in the setting sun. However, intrinsic to happiness is the certainty of its end and even Southwold cannot go on forever. Loss of community to part-time residents, sprawling development and an unbridled tourist trade are the focus of most people's fears for its future. Nonetheless, these are only a distraction from a single, absolute and terrible certainty.

In recent years the sea has persistently eroded the cliffs and is now threatening a handsome detached house situated at Southend Warren, just north of the town. There the owner, Peter Boggis, like a latter day Canute, is fighting a losing battle against nature. At his bidding a daily convoy of lorries brings hundreds of tons of topsoil and tips it over the cliff in attempt to halt its incessant erosion.

In turn, with Dunwich and Easton – and imminently Covehithe – Southwold will eventually be asked to repay a long-term loan. When the waves decide to call it in by turning their destructive attention to the town, nothing on earth will prevent it from plunging into oblivion. I sincerely hope that there is not a soul in search of paradise in Southwold when Gun Hill and Lady's Walk are finally gnawed away, when it's pretty greens and lighthouse are all gone, when the noble tower of St. Edmund's Church finally topples into the ruminating mouth of that insatiable and indefatigable beast: the sea.[4]

Southwold Beach Huts by Wladyslaw Mirecki (b.1956). Watercolour on paper. 2002.
This colourful picture evokes the sea and sunshine that characterize idyllic holidays in Southwold. On the small cliff above the beach huts wild flowers are in bloom and their scent is redolent of summer.
Wladyslaw Mirecki is a well-known landscape painter with a preference for watercolour. He was born and lives in Essex, where, in Chappel, he runs the Chappel Gallery with his wife Edna. © Wladyslaw Mirecki

BIBLIOGRAPHY

Bardwell, W., *Temples, Ancient and Modern*. London, 1837

Betjeman, J. (Ed.), *Collins Guide to English Parish Churches including the Isle of Man*. London, 1958

Blackburne, E.L., 'On the Remains of Painted Decoration in Southwold Church, Suffolk' in *The Civil Engineer and Architect's Journal,* Vols XXII-XXIII. December 1859, January 1860

Bottomley, A.F., *A Short History of The Borough of Southwold*. Southwold, 1972

Bottomley, A. and Hutchinson, J., *Discovering Southwold*. Southwold and Reydon Society, 1986

Bottomley, A., *The Church of St. Edmund, King and Martyr*. 1991

Browett, B., *Southwold in the Great Flood of 1953*. Southwold Museum, 2003

Carter, J.I. and Bacon, S.R., *Southwold, Suffolk.* 1976

Cawthorne, N., *A History of Pirates – Blood and Thunder on the High Seas*. London, 2003

Chitty, The Rev. C., 'Kessingland and Walberswick Church Towers' in *Proceedings of the Suffolk Institute of Archaeology*, Vol. XXV Part 2

Christie, C., *Walberswick Notes*. The St. Catherine Press, London, 1911

Clegg, R. and Clegg, S., *Southwold – Portraits of an English Seaside Town*. 1999

Collins, I., *A Broad Canvas*. 1990

Collins, I., *Making Waves – Painters at Southwold.* Norwich, 2005

Comfort, N., *The Lost City of Dunwich*. Lavenham, 1994

Cooper, E.R., *Mardles from Suffolk*. 1932

Cooper, E.R., *Storm Warriors of the Suffolk Coast*. London, 1937

Copinger, W.A. (Ed.), *County of Suffolk: Its History Disclosed by Existing Records and Other Documents, being Materials for the History of Suffolk*. 5 vols. 1904-5

Crabbe, *The Works of the Rev. Geo. Crabbe, with the life by his son*. London, 1834

Craig, E., *Gordon Craig – The Story of His Life*. London, 1968

Crick, B., *George Orwell – A Life*. London, 1980

Dutt, W., *Highways and Byways of East Anglia*. London, 1901

Dutt, W., *Some Literary Associations of East Anglia*. London, 1907

Fleming, G.K., *Southold* (Images of America: New York). Arcadia Publishing, 2004

Frost, R., *Southwold in Old Postcards*. 2002

Gardner, T., *An Historical Account of Dunwich, Blithburgh, and Southwold*. 1754

Gosse, E., *The Life of Algernon Charles Swinburne*. London, 1917

Griffin, F., *The Stricklands – Canadian Pioneers*. Southwold Archaeological and Natural History Society, 2002

Griggs., F.L.B., 'Churches by the Sea' in *Architectural Review*, No. XLV, Vol VIII. August 1900

Hake, T. and Compton-Rickett, A., *The Life and Letters of Theodore Watts-Dunton*. London, 1916

Hall, W.J., *Pagans, Puritans, and Patriots of Yesterday's Southold*. Cutchogue - New Suffolk Historical Council, 1975

Harris, F.R., *The Life of Edward Mountagu K.G. First Earl of Sandwich*. 2 vols. 1912

Haward, B. *Suffolk Mediaeval Church Arcades*. Suffolk Institute of Archaeology and History, 1993

Hayter, A. (Ed.), *Fitzgerald to His Friends – Selected Letters of Edward Fitzgerald*. London, 1979

Hemming, C., *British Painters of the Coast and Sea*. London, 1988

Howson, K. (Ed.), *Blyth Voices – Folk Songs Collected in Southwold by Ralph Vaughan Williams in 1910*. East Anglian Traditional Music Trust, 2003

Huckstep, H., *Reg Carter Remembered*. Southwold Historical Society, 2004

Hutton, J., *Glass Engravings of John Hutton*. Undated pamphlet. Printed by John B. Reed, Windsor

James, H., *English Hours*. London, 1905

Jarvis, S., *Smuggling in East Anglia 1700-1840*. Newbury, 1987

Jenkins, B., *Memories of the Southwold Railway*. 1983

Jenkins, B., *Remiscennces of Southwold During the Two World Wars*. 1984

Jenkins, B., *A Selection of Ghost Stories, Smuggling Stories and Poems Connected with Southwold*. 1986

Jenkins, B., *Southwold 1904-1992*. 1993

Jenkins, F., *The Story of Southwold*. 1948

Jones, E., *The Poppyland Poets*. Norfolk, 1984

Kirby, J., *The Traveller's Guide and Topographical Description of the County of Suffolk*. 1734

Knox, R. (Ed.), *The Work of E.H. Shepard*. London, 1979

Lambourne, L. and Hamilton, J., *British Watercolours in the Victoria and Albert Museum*. London, 1980

Layard, G.S., *The Life and Letters of Samuel Charles Keene*. London, 1892

Lee, D., *The Southwold Lighthouses*. 2004

Lilly, M., *Sickert – The Painter and his Circle*. 1971

Maclean, F., *Henry Moore R.A.* London, 1905

MacColl, D.S., *The Work and Setting of Philip Wilson Steer*. London, 1945

Mackinlay, Rev. J.B., *Saint Edmund King and Martyr*. 1839

Maggs, J., *The Southwold Diaries 1818-1876*. Edited by Alan Farquhar Bottomly. 1983

Miller, J., *Britain in Old Photographs – Southwold*. 1999

Moss, A., *Jerome K. Jerome. His Life and Work (From Poverty to a Knighthood of the People)*. London, 1929

Muir, D.E., *An Historical Guide to Southwold Parish Church*. 1980

Parker, R., *Men of Dunwich*. London, 1978

Phelpps, H., *Southwold to Aldeburgh in Old Photographs*. 1991

Pickford, O., *The Little Freeman of Dunwich – The Story of a Rotten Borough.* Dunwich, 1997

Powell, N., *George Crabbe*. London, 2004

Roskell, R.S., Clark, L. and Rawcliffe C., *The History of Parliament – The House of Commons 1386-1421*. 1992

Ruskin, J., *A Unique Catalogue of the Ruskin Mineral Collection, Written in John Ruskin's Own Hand*. 1884

Scarfe, N., *A Shell Guide to Suffolk*. Edited by John Betjeman. London, 1966

Scarfe, N., *Suffolk in the Middle Ages*. 1986

Scott, R., *Artists at Walberswick – East Anglian Interludes 1880-2000*. 2002

Sebold. W.G., *The Rings of Saturn*. London, 1998

Shaw, M., *Up to Now*. 1929

Shepard, E.H., *Drawn from Memory*. London, 1957

Shepard, E.H. *Drawn from Life*. London, 1961

Sisley, R., 'Southwold' in *Pall Mall* magazine, Vol I. 1893

Stansky, P. and Abrahams, W., *The Unknown Orwell*. London, 1972

Stirling, A.M.W., *The Richmond Papers from the Correspondence and Manuscripts of George Richmond R.A. and His Son Sir William Richmond, R.A., K.C.B.* London, 1926

Suckling, Rev. A., *The History and Antiquities of the Hundreds of Blything and Part of Lothingland in the County of Suffolk*. Lowestoft, 1847

Surtees, V. (Ed.), *The Diaries of George Price Boyce*. Norwich, 1980

Swinburne, A., *Studies in Song*. London, 1907

Talbot, M., *Medieval Flushwork of East Anglia and its Symbolism*. 2004

Tennyson, J., *Suffolk Scene*. Suffolk, 1939

Thomas, R.G. (Ed)., *Letters to Helen – the Letters of Edward Thomas*. London, 2000

Turner, P. and Wood, R., P.H. *Emerson – Photographer of Norfolk*. London, 1974

Vaughan Williams, U., *R.V.W. A Biography of Ralph Vaughan Williams*. Oxford, 1964

Wake, R., *Southwold and its Vicinity, Ancient and Modern*. 1839

Warner, P., *The Bloody Marsh*. 2000

Whistler, T., *Imagination of the Heart – The Life of Walter de la Mare*. London, 1993

White, W., *History and Gazetteer and Directory of Suffolk*. Sheffield, 1855

Williamson, R., *The Saga of the Southwold Salt Makers*. 1999

Wolfenden, S., *Portraits of Southwold*. Southwold, 2000

Wolfenden, S., *The Town Revisitied*. Southwold, 2004

Woodforde, Rev. J., *The Diary of a Country Parson*. Edited by John Beresford. Oxford, 1926

Exhibitions

"Joseph Southall 1861-1944 Artist Craftsman". Birmingham Museums and Art Galleries, Birmingham, 1980

"Arthur and Georgie Gaskin". Birmingham City Museum and Art Gallery, Birmingham, 1982

Puppet head by Edward Gordon Craig. Carved and painted wood. c.1900. Edward Gordon Craig, the artist, actor and stage designer, was the son of the actress Ellen Terry. He came to Southwold in 1898 and found it a powerful inspiration. The face of this amusing puppet head is made up from the wooden structure of the temporary lighthouse that stood to the south of the town on California Sands. The beard is suggested by waves, and the eyes, as binoculars, reveal swimmers out to sea.   *Tom Craig Esq.*

ENDNOTES

INTRODUCTION

1. Wake, Robert, *Southwold and its Vicinity*. 1839, p230.

2. Smith, A.R.L., *The Overton genealogy*. Centreach, N.Y. 1965

HOLY EDMUND PRAY FOR US

1. Whitelock, Dorothy, 'Fact and fiction in the legend of St. Edmund', *The Proceedings of the Suffolk Institute of Archaeology,* 31 (for 1969).

2. A cache of such coins was found at Blythburgh. See Clegg, R. and Clegg, S., *Southwold – Portraits of an English Seaside Town*, page 2.

3. Dr Richard Gem on behalf of the Arundel Scientific Committee made a full report of the examination entitled 'A Scientific Examination of the Relics of St. Edmund at Arundel Castle'.

4. Mackinlay, Rev. J.B., *St. Edmund King and Martyr*. London, 1893.

5. Gardner, Thomas, *An Historical Account of Dunwich, Blithburgh and Southwold*, 1754, p209.

6. This interesting suggestion comes from an undated cutting that hangs in a frame in *The Swan Hotel*. It is accompanied by another dated 1905.

PARADISE ON EARTH

1. Warner, Peter, *The Bloody Marsh*, p56.

2. Scarfe, Norman, *Suffolk in the Middle Ages*, p132.

3. For the fullest account of Russell see Rev. C. Chitty 'Kessingland and Walberswick Church Towers' in *The Proceedings of the Suffolk Institute of Archaeology,* Vol. XXV, p164. However, on the basis of circum-stantial evidence, Chitty suggests that Russell died in 1440-41, though at the House of Commons there is a record of him attesting the Dunwich elections to parliament several times from 1423 until 1450. He may be the same Richard Russell who died at Ubbeston, some 10 miles from Dunwich, in 1452. The similarities between the fabric and decoration of the tower of St. Andrew's, Walberswick, and St. Edmund's, Southwold, are striking and it is on them that an attribution to Russell has been made. They are particularly evident in the pattern of the flushwork at the feet of the towers, on the lines of napped flint facing of the buttresses and in the rectangular limestone quoins that bind them to the wall. In both churches the master mason has marked his work with a pair of 'R's. I believe the initials engraved at the foot of the great arch at Southwold puts the attribution to Russell beyond any reasonable doubt.

4. See *The Richmond Papers* by his kinswoman Mrs. A.M.W. Stirling, p79.

5. From a transcription reproduced in the *East Anglian* 1887-8, pp29 and 153. John Joy of Southwold left funds in his will for the supplying of a chrismatory for Southwold Church. However his executors Richard and Henry Joy breached this undertaking and the vicar of Southwold sued them for it. A record of the proceedings is kept in the National Archives under the shelf mark C1/98/17.

6. Thomas Gardner's *Historical Account of Dunwich, Blithburgh and Southwold*, published in 1754, is still the richest secondary source for details of local church expenditure.

7. Maggs, James, *Southwold Diary*, Vol. I, p61. 'Tom and Jerry' was a originally a pairing of names from Pierce Egan's *Life in London, or Days and Nights of Jerry Hawthorne and his elegant friend Corinthian Tom*. Egan was a noted chronicler of London low-life of the Regency period (1810-1820), when the rich young bucks like Tom and Jerry were notorious for roistering in the streets, breaking windows, and assaulting passers-by. Consequently "to Tom and Jerry" is a verb that means to engage in riotous behaviour. Tom and Jerry are better known today because they were adopted as names for the hapless cat and that clever mouse in the cartoon produced by MGM.

8 Stirling, A.M.W., *The Richmond Papers*. London, 1926

IN THE SHADOW OF THE CITY

1. Gardner, Thomas, *An Historical Account of Dunwich, Blithburgh and Southwold*, 1754, p40.

2. *ibid*, p4.

3. *ibid*, p93.

THE PHOENIX BOROUGH

1. Wake, Robert, *Southwold and its Vicinity*. 1839, p230.

2. *ibid*, p106.

3. According to Tanner's *Suffolk Manuscripts*, Southwold had been "pitifully defaced" by fire on a Friday in 1596. However, I have found no primary evidence of it and there is no reference to the fire in Gardner. It is difficult to believe that the historian could have overlooked a disaster of this magnitude that had

taken place in his hometown. Wake criticises him for what appears to be an oversight and it is likely that Tanner was in error and wrote 1596 when he meant 1659.

4. Gardner, Thomas, *An Historical Account of Dunwich, Blithburgh and Southwold*, 1754, p226.

5. Wake, p.256.

6. Maggs, James, *Southwold Diary*, Vol I, pp105 and 122.

AN ELEMENTAL STRUGGLE

1. Gardner, Thomas, *An Historical Account of Dunwich, Blithburgh and Southwold*, 1754, p128.

2 In the beginning of the fourteenth century Ralph de Monthermer, Earl of Gloucester, had the rights to wrecks from Easton Stone to Eye Cliff (Gun Hill), but in 1321 these were usurped by Richard de Boyland.

3 Maggs, James, *Southwold Diary*, Vol. I, p45.

4 *ibid*, Vol. I, p49. In the early nineteenth century at Southwold harbour there was a post office, which was probably set up as a facility for those who had come from the continent by sea.

5 *ibid*, Vol. I, p120.

6 *ibid*, Vol. II, p63.

7 *ibid*, Vol. II, p96.

8 Clegg, R. and Clegg S., (Eds.), *Southwold – Portraits of an English Seaside Town*. p35.

9 Maggs, James, *Southwold Diary*, Vol. II, pp75-76.

THE DARK SIDE

1. Maggs, James, *Southwold Diary*, Vol. I, p7.

2. Cooper, Ernest R., *Mardles from Suffolk*, p137.

3. *The Dictionary of National Biography*. See entry for Matthew Hopkins.

4. In 1732 there was a fight between customs men from Southwold and a gang of 40 smugglers. See Copinger, W.A., *County of Suffolk*.

5 Website of the "Foxearth and District Local History Society". See the article about the fate of Tobias Gill by Andrew Clarke.

6. *The Dictionary of National Biography*. See entry for Robert Rich.

BATTLE OF SOLE BAY

1. See Carter, J.I. and Bacon, S.R., *Southwold Suffolk*, p57.

2. Gardner, Thomas, *An Historical Account of Dunwich, Blithburgh and Southwold*, p217.

3. Wake, Robert, *Southwold and its Vicinity*, 1839, p202.

4. See Carter, J.I. and Bacon, S.R., *Southwold Suffolk*, p57.

5. Wake, p194.

6. Wake, p195.

7 Westfall, Richard, *Never at Rest. A biography of Isaac Newton*, p194.

8. Harris, F.R., *The Life of Edward Montagu, KG First Earl of Sandwich*, Vol. II, p274.

9. An example is in the National Maritime Museum.

PIRATES AND MARAUDERS

1. See Parker, Roland, *Men of Dunwich*, pp195-197.

2. *ibid*, p197.

3. Gardner, Thomas, *An Historical Account of Dunwich, Blithburgh and Southwold*, p178.

4. *ibid*, p188.

5. Cooper, Ernest R., *Mardles from Suffolk*, pp172-173.

6. See the frontispiece of *A History of Pirates* by Nigel Cawthorne.

HENRY DAVY

1. It was built by John Thompson at a cost of £300 as a reading room for subscribers.

2. For an account of Henry Davy's life and work see Denny, Rev. A.H., 'Henry Davy 1793-1865', in *The Proceedings of the Suffolk Institute of Archaeology*, 1962. See also the entry for Davy in *The Dictionary of National Biography* by John Blatchly FSA.

SOUTHWOLD AND THE ANTIQUARY

1. Sweet, R., *Antiquaries – The Discovery of the past in Eighteenth-Century Britain*. 2004, p310.

2. Maggs, James, *Southwold Diary*, Vol. I, p2.

3. See McHardy FSA, George, 'Joseph Sim Earle, FSA and his bequest to the Society', *The Antiquaries Journal 2004*, Vol. 84, pp399-410.

4. Wake, Robert, *Southwold and its Vicinity*, 1839, pp10 and 169.

5. *The Proceedings of The Society of Antiquaries*, 23 April 1909, p473.

PEN TO PAPER

1. "The Shakespearian Playing Companies" by Andrew Gurr. Page 391. Also "The Lost City of Dunwich" by Nicholas Comfort. p149.

2. For example: Kirby, John, *The Traveller's Guide and Topographical Description of the County of Suffolk*. Printed in Woodbridge, 1734.

3. Maggs, James, *Southwold Diary*, Vol. I, p142.

4. See Powell, Neil, *George Crabbe – An English Life 1754-1832*, pp82, 87 and 108.

5. Tehune, Alfred McKinley, *The Life of Edward Fitzgerald*, p337. See also Moss, Alfred, *Jerome K. Jerome – His Life and Work (from poverty to a knighthood of the people)*. 1929. On page 195 Moss says that Jerome visited Dunwich regularly in the summer staying in a house made famous by Edward Fitzgerald. Mrs Scarlett, the owner, kept a little shop there. Apparently Fitzgerald had worked on his famous translation of the *Rubaiyat of Omar Khayyam* in her house. Later, in that very same room, Jerome wrote *My life and Times*.

6. Letter to the poet Bernard Barton 11 April 1875.

7. Henderson, Philip, *Swinburne – The Portrait of a Poet*, p193.

8. An unpublished letter from Alice Swinburne to her brother Algernon. In the Brotherton Library, Leeds University

9. Gosse, Edmund, *The Life of Algernon Swinburne*, pp228 and 235.

10. Hake, Thomas and Compton-Rickett, Arthur, *The Life and Letters of Theodore Watts-Dunton*, p96.

11. Whistler, Theresa, *The Imagination of the Heart –The Life of Walter de la Mare*, p64.

PARADISE LOST

1. Rose, Andrea, *Pre-Raphaelite Portraits*. Oxford, 1981.

2. Kelvin, Norman (ed.), *Collected Letters of William Morris*, Vol. IV 1893-1896. Princetown, 1996.

3. Cline, C.L. (ed.), *The Owl and the Rossettis. Letters of Charles A. Howell and Dante Gabriel, Christina, and William Michael Rossetti*, Letter 80. Pennsyvania, 1978.

4. *The Letters of William Morris: A Life in Our Time*. 1994, p664. I am grateful to Ian Collins for drawing my attention to this reference. The "*others*" referred to by Rossetti may have included the architect and church furnisher Richard Norman Shaw (1831-1912). He was in Kelsale, near Saxmundham the same year that Morris was in Southwold. In the early 1870s he installed a reredos in the church of St. Mary and St. Peter, Kelsale. The stained glass in the nave includes windows designed by William Morris, Ford Maddox Brown and Edward Burne-Jones. Rossetti's friend George Boyce (1826-97) was in Southwold in 1870 and painted a watercolour called *Southwold – An Autumn Evening*, which he showed at the Old Watercolour Society in November that year. It was for sale for 8 guineas.

5. Rose, p108.

6. Mackail, J.W., *The Life of William Morris*, Vol. I, p201. London, 1899. I am extremely grateful to Peyton Skipwith for drawing my attention to this fact.

7. Society for the Protection of Ancient Buildings. *The Eighteenth Annual Report of the Committee*. November 1895.

HAPPY HOLIDAYS

1. Wake, Robert, *Southwold and its Vicinity*, 1839, p35.

2. Wake, p26.

3. These entertainments are listed in the index of *The Southwold diaries of James Maggs* edited by Alan Bottomly, 1984.

4. An undated advertising pamphlet of 64 pages issued by the East Coast Development Company c.1910 now in the author's collection.

5. For an account of the firm's history see a thesis entitled 'James Shoolbred and Co.' by Sophia de Falbe in the Department of Furniture and Woodwork, The Victoria and Albert Museum.

CARNELIAN BAY

1. Tacitus, Cornelius, *Agricola, AD98*.

2. White, William, *History, Gazetteer, and Directory of Suffolk*, 1855. Burwood and Prestwidge are both buried in St. Edmund's churchyard.

3. From an interview with the artist James Sant published in 1897 in a magazine called *Great Thoughts*. I am grateful to George Brown and Geoffrey Nunn for drawing my attention to this fascinating reference.

INNS AND TIPPLING HOUSES

1. Clegg, R. and Clegg, S., (Eds.) *Southwold – Portraits of an English Seaside Town*, p77.

2. Maggs, James, *Southwold Diary*, Vol. II, p49.

3. Gardner, Thomas, *An Historical Account of Dunwich, Blithburgh and Southwold*, p193.

4. Maggs, Vol. II, p36.

5. Maggs, Vol. II, p118.

6. Maggs, Vol. II, p115.

THE SOUTHWOLD RAILWAY

1. Craig, Edward, *Gordon Craig – the Story of his Life*. London, 1968.

2. Maggs, James, *Southwold Diary*, Vol. II, p87.

ARTISTS BY THE SEASIDE

1. Lilly, Marjorie, *Sickert – The painter and his Circle*. 1971.

2. Scott, Richard, *Artists at Walberswick*. 2002, p86.

3. In 1990 a number of these artists founded an association called The Suffolk Group. They have organised a number of exhibitions at Buckenham House in Southwold and have also shown in the Peter Pears Gallery in Aldeburgh.

A WIDE FOCUS: P.H. EMERSON

1 This information comes from a hand-written note on the back of a photograph called *Eel Picking in Southwold Waters* taken by Emerson in 1888. Rogers and his boy were the models. It is in the collection of George Eastman House, Rochester, New York. No 77:0550:0017

2 There is a picture by Goodall in the Walker Art gallery at Liverpool.

3. Whilst Emerson was living in Southwold, J. Godfrey Martyn opened a photographic business at 92 and 95 High Street selling all manner of photographs and photographic supplies. Some of the larger prints were inspired by Emerson's work and there can be little doubt that the two men were close acquaintances. Martyn eventually sold his thriving concern to the photographer and local historian Frederick Jenkins in 1901, though it seems that Jenkins continued to sell Martyn's work next to his own informative views of the town and countryside. Half the premises was devoted to "artistic views of the district", which were priced from 6d upwards and were "pleasant and lasting souvenirs of a stay in the neighbourhood". Jenkins also offered a selection of Kodak cameras, together with a range of chemicals and films for the convenience of the "numberless amateurs who are more or less proficient in the art".

Even today numberless amateurs in the art of photography flock to Southwold; amongst the most notable of the professionals is Stephen Wolfenden. Like Emerson before him, Wolfenden has published his photographs in the form of a series of fascinating books that are a unique document of Southwold's recent social history. Whatever the status of the photographer visiting Southwold, John Wells and his son Richard cater for every need; professional photographers, they run the wonderful photographic shop in Queen Street. Like their famous predecessor Peter Emerson, John and Richard have brought their beautiful landscape photographs up to the highest level of art, and about that there can be no debate.

Before the dive *by Joseph Southall. Crayon on paper. 1912.*
A young swimmer regains her balance before diving from
one of the pontoons anchored off the beach at Southwold.

Author's collection

INDEX

I don't want to leave Southwold. A postcard illustrated by Fred G.H. Sadler. c.1914.

A small boy, having seen the train leaving for Halesworth, anticipates the end of a lovely holiday. This emotion is shared by everyone lucky enough to visit Southwold. This example was sent by Jack to his mother in Eye, saying "Just a note to say I am getting on fine and shall not be home till Tuesday." It was sent in August 1914, the eve of the First World War, and we can only hope that Jack returned home from that as well.   Private collection